THE SUDDEN DISAPPEARANCE OF JAPAN

A hut in spring:
  There is nothing in it—
  There is everything.

Sodo (1641-1716)

THE SUDDEN DISAPPEARANCE OF JAPAN

JOURNEYS THROUGH A HIDDEN LAND

J.D. BROWN
WITH A FOREWORD BY PICO IYER

CAPRA PRESS
SANTA BARBARA

To Margaret and the memory of a black cat.

❋

Typesetting by Jimmy O'Shea.
Cover design by Frank Goad.

Portions of this work in earlier versions have
appeared in *Winds Magazine,* also in *Islands Magazine.*

Library of Congress Cataloging-in-Publication Data
Brown, J.D. (James Dale), 1948-
The Sudden Disappearance of Japan: Journeys through a Hidden Land / J.D. Brown;
with a foreword by Pico Iyer
p. cm.
ISBN 0-88496-381-0: $14.95
1. Japan—Description and travel. I. Title.
DS812.B76 1994
952.04—dc20
93-4237
CIP

CAPRA ♈ PRESS
P.O. Box 2068, Santa Barbara, CA 93120

CONTENTS

FOREWORD
Pico Iyer

We've grown accustomed, in recent years, to seeing Japan from a variety of strange angles—through the keyholes of baseball and pottery, sumo and geisha, elementary schools and companies, and every other gimmick the human mind can devise. What we haven't seen so often is how Japan appears to a fresh and observant newcomer, traveling around without expense-accounts or contacts or higher agendas, but simply following whim, with an eye that's open and a history book in hand. Enter J.D. Brown, an "ordinary traveler," in his own typically modest estimation, pursuing "ordinary routes in ordinary ways," and armed only with a trusty partner, a quiet sense of humor and a prose of graceful restraint. Instead of the usual agonized accounts, by longtime residents, of their torturous love-hate affairs with the country, Brown gives us a sane and unintrusive depiction of an ancient modern enigma seen with the clarity of first impressions. From his first mysterious entrance into a lantern-lit temple, to his final glimpse of a two-story Santa, he shows us a Japan so instantly recognizable that it makes me homesick.

Through the two trips recorded here, in fact, Brown and his companion, Margaret, travel as lightly as cats, free of preconceptions or axes to grind. They go to places that everyone cherishes (Nara and Takayama), and places that almost nobody knows. They trace the gold and silver "seams" of Kyoto, and find the smiling grandmothers of Wajima, but they also see hotels that look "like Gumby in bell-bottom trousers," an "Institute for Research in Human Happiness" (in Nagasaki, no less), and police cars that say "I KISS YOU." They follow the classic itineraries of such nineteenth-century forebears as Percival Lowell and Isabella Bird, but they also follow the inimitable Dino as he fast-talks them through the karaoke bars of Toyama. They are even alert enough to locate my old school-friend Ivo Hesmondhalgh (a London hotelier), ensconced in a Buddhist monastery! Brown searches for an old Japan, often finds a new one, and is wise enough to accept that the country cannot be wished back into a state of medieval purity: Japan today is cherry-flavored rice balls and McDonald's.

Perhaps the most valuable thing that Brown brings to the journey, for me, is his deep and informed knowledge of ancient China and Buddhism. And his very openness to Japan prompts him to read up on its past in a way that many a jaded Japanologist would never dream of doing. Thus he not only compares it with his two other homelands, China and America, but also fills out for us all kinds of aromatic history, excavating eighteenth-century samurai codes that give women permission to "go mushroom hunting," or retelling the arrival of Captain Jukichi, in a storm-tossed boat in 1815, in what he regarded as "animals' hell" (it was, in fact, Santa Barbara, California).

Best of all, in a sense, moving "close to the earth," and seeing Japan with their feet, Brown and his companion realize that the truest trips always arise when you lose yourself—and so find yourself amidst the unexpected. J.D. and Margaret miss the bus, are out of season, are shut out of hotels—and, in the process, they show us what it is really like to be adrift on this strange island where everything is backwards and the signs are hard to read and the best, the only epiphanies are unlooked-for. Whatever else it may be, Japan, the land of so-called conformity, is a province of surprise. And surprises light up every chapter, from ten-story hand-painted kimonos to the Pension Lambchop.

What the reader may take away from this, then, are spirits such as the wildly gesticulating matron met on a train who, in between offering to trade earrings with Margaret and spitting out bits of salmon, exclaims, "Whoosh, darling, whoosh! Dinner party! America is wonderful!" And, beneath that, something else, more plangent, and enticing, that always remains a little out of reach. Listening for the laughter of ghosts, looking for the vanishing points of light, Brown manages to catch something haunting, and fleeting, in a land that calls to many of us like a temple bell, a sense of "a familiar place we can't name where we walk like ghosts through a stranger's dream." Unlike almost any writer on Japan I know, Brown is not afraid to admit that much of the country eludes him, and so, instead of struggling for conclusions or analyses, he is content to let it remain itself, and half-unseen, like the tail of a cat disappearing around a corner.

Indeed, the reader is hereby advised to keep a sharp eye out for cats. They glint in and out of this narrative like—well, like the fugitive soul of a hidden Japan.

PRELUDE
The Vanishing Point of Light

We traveled twice around Japan: once clockwise around the main island of Honshu, once counterclockwise around the southern island of Kyushu.

We traveled in an ordinary way, at ground zero.

We traveled, too, with a double vision, that of Wallace Stevens's snow man who "nothing himself, beholds / nothing that is not there and the nothing that is."

In what follows, therefore, we want to appear as little as possible, hoping to clear the way, to see nothing that is not Japan—and the nothing that is.

We enter Japan from space. The door slides open. We are inside a cyclotron, a thousand-year-old cyclotron that's brand-new. Each panel is fitted to the next with extreme precision, producing a seamless tolerance approaching zero. The surface is as polished as a mirror, reflecting not so much Japan as the distant nations it has chosen to copy.

Inside, every particle is accelerated toward the speed of light and the curving surface is ablaze, but nothing appears in the depths. The center is dark, dark as liquid gravity.

Japan, meanwhile, has disappeared somewhere between ancient East and modern West. There are no instructions for finding it. Except, perhaps, those a Japanese-American poet hands us as we board the plane, bound for the dateline.

He knows we will be looking for things Chinese and for things American, and he knows we'll have no trouble finding either in Japan. But locating Japan itself requires unusual procedures.

He hands us a three-legged poem as a guide. It reads:

> Go far from Tokyo
> Listen for the laughter of ghosts
> Locate the vanishing point of light.

Who knows? With such obscure directions and a little blind luck, we might pinpoint an original Japan between the cracks, a Japan that copies only itself.

There's nothing to lose; we're lost from the first step.

We start with the first line.

I.

Koyasan:
Mountain of the Dead

"Go far from Tokyo." And we do. Landing in Tokyo, we arrive to depart. Tokyo offers no change of worlds at the end of a long flight. Everything is too familiar. The Ginza looks like a VCR, shop and office architecture out of a box, Modular Monumental; and the modern capital is like a fun house where all the mirrors are straight up and down, shaved of distortion, true as telescope glass. Tokyo we recognize: it's an American remake.

Like the great poet Basho, we are driven "by the cloud-moving wind, filled with a strong desire to wander." We immediately make our first destination Koyasan, the peak sacred to Shingon Buddhism, west of new Tokyo, south of old Kyoto.

In 818 AD the monk later known as Kobo Daishi—called by some the greatest single figure in the history of Japanese religion—established a monastic center on Koyasan. Today there are over 120 monasteries on the peak, half of them open to overnight guests. The cemetery is said to be one of the largest and oddest in this graveyard-struck nation. So many have been interred there over the centuries that Koyasan is called "the burial place of all Japan." Kobo Daishi's own tomb still attracts the dead; they hope to be resurrected when, in a sort of Buddhist Second Coming, he ends his deep meditation.

What better place to wake up—if not in eternity, then at least on a morning different from the rest. Or as the great essayist of idleness, Kenko, writes: "It wakes you up to take a journey for a while, wherever it may be."

Hightailing it out of Tokyo, we stop at Nagoya to visit Yumi, a friend from earlier years in Shanghai. But Nagoya is a disappointment, too, hollow as its Castle, even more strictly modern than Tokyo.

Yumi takes us in hand and makes our arrangements: she plots our changes of train and phones in our reservations to the cheapest monastery on Koyasan. Not many inns are open in March, she reports. She warns us that there can still be snow on the ground. As we depart Nagoya, Yumi presents us with a sketch map of our journey. Folded inside are numbered sheaves with distress messages in two languages, addressed to successive stations should we become lost or delayed.

We leave on the bullet train at noon, change lines at Kyoto for Nara and at Nara for Oji and at Oji for Hashimoto. At each transfer, the trains grow shorter and smaller. The final tiny train, leaving from Gokurakubashi at twilight, hauls us up the lush arc of a ridge into a fortress of remote peaks. The final ascent requires a cable car.

Koyasan is packed in half a foot of fresh snow. The bus to town slides down a winding road in complete darkness. Baffled as to where to get off, I have forgotten the name of our monastery, and in the dark it is impossible to read Yumi's last slip of paper. But something—no outward sign—suddenly orders us to disembark. We find ourselves standing on a long stretch of unlighted road, our soft shoes lace-deep in snow.

I don't know which way to turn, but Margaret does: she backtracks uphill to a gate where a lighted lamp hangs. We stoop down and go under. A short path of laurel and rhododendrons ends at the porch of a monastery. Some skateboards are parked on the step.

A twelve-year-old boy parts the shoji screen. Removing our shoes, we place them on an outdoor shelf. Inside, to the right of a shrine, three more boys sit reading graphically violent comic books. We sign the guest register. Then by grunts and gestures, we are ushered out onto another porch, through sliding doors, and down a corridor of glass and paper panes. Dinner is waiting in a matted room. We set down our packs and fall on the soup, too numb to taste it.

There is not the slightest bit of heat anywhere. Though the doors are closed at the end of every corridor, the temperature is indifferent—always freezing, inside or out. But I like our inn, truly: it has the look and scratch of an authentic Buddhist monastery, the odor of dark wood going to rot. No pretensions, either; tea is served in an airpot.

After a single cup, the boy, always in a grimace, shoves us toward the bath. We counter that we will bathe at 9 p.m., not a minute earlier. The boy scowls, looks to heaven, and marches us upstairs to our room.

The well of the stairs is of poured concrete. A latter-day addition to the original wooden structure, it gathers the chill of the night like a hollow steel rod. At the top of the stairs is an ugly aluminum sliding door with opaque glass, difficult to part, reluctant to slide. On the other side is a landing with sinks, all the taps shut off at the main for winter, and toothbrushes neatly spaced along countertops—whose toothbrushes remains a mystery. Down the hallway are the winter guest rooms, but there aren't many guests; and not much heat, either, save that of the *kotatsu*.

The *kotatsu*, descendant of the coal hearth, is a standard fixture in most Japanese homes. The one in our room is a low square table with a weak electric heat lamp attached underneath. We plug ours in, drape a quilt over the top to trap the heat, and slide our legs under. Presto! we are each half a baked potato. From the waist up, however, we can never get warm. The room is simply too cold for the cozy table ever to thaw us out—the place possesses an entire winter. With a *tokonoma* alcove and a closet, futons, and thick *tanzen* robes, it's the room we expected, except for no heat and, nailed to the wall, a mirror painted with the face of a clown.

Three other rooms are occupied tonight: one by an Englishman, one by a Thai Buddhist monk, and one by a Japanese banker.

The banker lives at the foot of Koyasan but rents a room here for those late nights when he misses the last cable car. The monastery serves him as a Buddhist capsule hotel, albeit without the refinements of Tokyo: no running water or sheets, no TV or towels.

The Englishman turns out to be, like us, an ordinary traveler. He is also managing director of two fine Victorian hotels in London. We come upon him in the hall, where he is walking up and down to keep warm. "Call me Ivo," he says, short for I.L.G. Hesmondhalgh. He has spent the whole of this spring day tramping through temple, town, and cemetery, but now he is unable to warm up with a bath; he's brought no towel and none will be provided. Fortunately Ivo has a sweater, although it is not nearly enough; he is flapping his arms like a woolly crow. Still, he is remarkably chipper and cheery. "You can reach the cemetery on foot," he says. "No need to take a bus. Just walk. You won't be disappointed. The worst part is keeping your feet from freezing off."

After we unpack, the third guest comes in to introduce himself. "I am a Thai Buddhist man," he says, tapping his chest with a long finger. This Thai Buddhist man is rooming in the monastery while attending classes in the village. He has been on Koyasan all winter. He is one of the loneliest figures we have ever met; no doubt as a result, he is also something of a pest. He displays a snapshot of his monastery in Bangkok, where it is some ninety-five degrees. Wrapped in many layers of orange, he also wears striped athletic socks and a green and yellow stocking cap. We are obliged to sign his guest book and exchange addresses. He gives us printed address labels so we can write to him. He is eager to come to America. A friend of his from Bangkok has already made it there—or to Venice, California, at any rate.

He explains to Margaret that he can not so much as touch a woman's hand. She passes him a cup of tea by setting it on the table. As for the monks of Japan . . . well, they are too worldly. Even permitted to marry. The Abbot of this monastery has a wife. There is an Assistant Abbot as well. (The Thai monk whispers an aside: the Assistant Abbot is the Abbot's son!) Then there are the four "errand boys," as the Thai monk calls them, paid room and board only, including the one trying to bully us into an early bath. These "errand boys" are entirely incorrigible: cheap and obstinate labor. As for the Japanese banker, the nights he stays are horrible; he snores so loudly a Thai Buddhist man can't get a wink of sleep.

"By the way, about tomorrow," he says, "I would be humble to act as your guide." He knows the temples of Koyasan and the graveyard. He yanks a brochure from his robe. I explain that we have pledged to make our tour of Koyasan alone; it is a private pilgrimage. The Thai monk nods solemnly; he understands. The problem with our bath, he adds, is that the boys always take theirs at 9 p.m., after the last guest, at the very hour we have chosen.

At 9 p.m., we strip down, don robes, and dash for the stairwell. The bathhouse is at the end of the farthest corridor. The monastery is a shambles: dark slats, floorboards sprung, panes frayed and splintered—the whole rattling house an exquisite deconstruction in paper and glass. Lanterns are silhouetted on the screens. We pass an old inner garden—a garden for ghosts: moonlight, snow, and bush. The water in the bath turns out to be so very hot that we can not immerse ourselves—the errand boys' revenge. We fill buckets and splash ourselves. But the heat of the bath perishes before we can reach the stairs. All that keeps us moving is a faint desire to see Koyasan in the light. I can barely haul the aluminum doors down their tracks; it is like parting two blocks of marble.

This is springtime in the mountains, but I have never felt so cold. We put our clothes back on and wrap ourselves tight in the curtain folds of our *tanzens*; strip the cozy table of its quilt; prepare the futon and climb in; but it's just no good. No good. Our faces freeze to air like snowballs.

In the end, we tip the table on its side and drape the quilt over the tips of its two raised legs, trapping the frail warmth of the lamp at our heads. Much later I drift off, in search of the Western Paradise, of Nirvana, of the future Buddha, of the wisdom of Kobo Daishi, of a room with central heat.

✳　✳　✳

Koyasan keeps the old connections with China, but the links are difficult to trace from one end to the other; difficult even to uncover. I happened to find a few strands when I lived, some years ago, in the interior of the People's Republic—lived, in fact, in the same Chinese city where Kobo Daishi was trained in Esoteric Buddhism. In Kobo Daishi's time, under the Tang Dynasty, the city was called Changan; it was capital of China and model for Japan's two ancient capitals, Nara and Kyoto. When Kobo Daishi arrived in 804 AD, Changan was the eastern center of Buddhism, too, not to mention the largest city in the world, and the grandest.

When I arrived eleven centuries later, the gilded edges of that ancient capital had crinkled into the modern city of Xi'an. Reduced to provincial status, Xi'an was composed almost entirely of dust—the dust of the land and of its coal. Dust penetrated the thickest enclosures, settled everywhere, coated everything—the wide avenues, the monotonous low apartment complexes that looked thirty-years-worn the moment they went up, the donkey carts, the manure wagons filled by hand from the city outhouses. At first glance, Xi'an had no color at all, excepting gray—gray on its new offices, on its slate-roofed houses, on its repaved avenues—nothing of the glitter of an ancient capital. Yet it still contained two tall pagodas which Kobo Daishi had seen in the ninth century, as well as the temple site where he discovered a new form of Buddhism for Japan. I had visited the very place, in fact, where Kobo Daishi was received with open arms by the Seventh Patriarch of Esoteric Buddhism in China. A few months later, at age thirty-two, he was to succeed his Chinese master and, although a foreigner, became head of the Qing Long Monastery.

When he returned to Japan in 806 AD, Kobo Daishi established the Shingon sect of Buddhism. He petitioned the Emperor of Japan, writing: "There is a quiet, open place called Koya located two days walk to the west. . . . High peaks surround Koya is all four directions; no human tracks or trails are to be seen there. I should like to clear the wilderness in order to build a monastery there." In November 818 AD, he broke ground on the peak; in April 835 AD, he died there; and in 855 AD, he was moved to his present tomb—more way station than tomb, according to his followers, who believe that Kobo Daishi has entered into a state of perfect suspension. In the first 1,135 years of Kobo Daishi's meditation, a cemetery has grown around him like a city, monasteries like a forest.

As for the Qing Long Monastery, it was hammered hard during China's Cultural Revolution, then completely rebuilt in 1982 with materials donated by four counties in Japan. The restoration was in the Tang style. The main courtyard contains an elaborate white marble *bei*, a monument to Kobo Daishi. I visited it after a heavy summer rain, long before I ever heard of Koyasan. No monks were in residence there; no tourists about, either. The groundskeeper reported that the tourists always came on big buses, that they were always Japanese. I'd come on my bike, leaving the highway for a trail of mud, slick as fish scales.

The monastery was a disappointment. The Meditation Hall, the largest structure at Qing Long, was more museum than shrine. Walls decorated in scrolls, poems, and paintings depicted the great monastery as it appeared in the year of Kobo Daishi's residence. Otherwise, it felt empty: a collection of pretty pavilions waiting for the next group of Buddhist tourists. Nothing but dust resided within. Even the spirit of the place, if it survived at all, must have fled China long ago, forever to the east.

Years later I wake up on Koyasan, in the cold room of a monastery.

*   *   *

Roused by the soft peal of a gong at 6 a.m., I begin the long march down: down the hall and through the sliding doors; down the stairwell as into a catacomb; down the corridors of frost; down to the bathroom.

There I ladle standing water from a tiled trough, fill a plastic basin, and splash my face. The banker has filled a basin with cold water, too; he eyes me hopelessly, attempting to work up lather for a shave. I slide open the inner door and step into toilet shoes, selecting a urinal; no running water or flush here either. Upstairs, Margaret discovers that the sliding door to our balcony does not fit its frame; there's a spray of ice in our room, like a flower blown in from an arctic sea.

We're late for breakfast. It's nearly 7 a.m. The morning's fare is colorless, mushy, soft as a bog. Followers of Kobo Daishi have been vegetarians for centuries, and the Koyasan cuisine, *shojin-ryori*, is reputedly a meatless gourmet's delight: tempura and tofu, seaweed and sweet potatoes. Each dish is cooked without flesh or fish, of course, but curiously enough without garlic or onions either—just the underpinnings of vinegar, sesame seed, and starch. Some of the recipes of Koyasan are a thousand years old, passed from monk to monk in high secrecy. Here the Abbot's wife does the cooking; she mashes everything to a pulp. Her meals befit the place. You'd not expect to find some frilly Shingon chef in here, not where *fusuma* doors are fashioned like shower-stalls.

The Thai Buddhist man picks us up right after breakfast; in another incarnation, he'd have make a smooth streetwalker. He insists we snap his picture. He removes his wool stocking cap, his head shaved bare; he winds himself into his best saffron robe. He ascends to a meditation hall on the third floor, a matted expanse where he knows how to pose, kneeling, eyes closed, serene as a macrobiotic cherub. When he embraces me in a final pose, I can feel his bones through his unfattened skin. From his wrists to his fingertips, he's unnaturally long, like the stem of a tea rose.

The morning is sweet, the sky sharp blue, the snow fresh, the air scented with cedar. We step out on the porch, stretch our arms, breathe deeply, and then pry our shoes out of the ice box where we left them overnight. With the aid of a shoehorn a yard long, we slip on both blocks of ice; the laces relax in the warmth of our hands; our socks are quickly steeped in ice water.

Out in the street, we wave farewell to Ivo. He's at the top of the hill, striding for the cable car station, heading back to toasty Kyoto. He's already removed his sweater.

We head downhill for the village. The road is lined with magnificent monasteries, temples, gates, and pagodas; stone lanterns mark the roads; there is snow on the bushes and trees and tile roofs of the temples; it's an astonishing collection, half for profit, but half for real. A taxi fishtails by, heading uphill; we look back a second time. The cab pulls up to our monastery gate, and the Abbot, dressed in red robes and a blue down vest, pops out, shopping bag in hand; he settles into the back seat like an industrialist.

We turn away. At a monastery grand as an Italian villa under a Mediterranean sky, we examine a car emblazoned with six tall white letters on its door: POLICE, it declares. We don't believe it: this tiny two-door candy-apple red Suzuki automatic, plastered with bumper stickers in English like a steamer trunk, looks more like a squad car for circus clowns. White letters are taped across its back window, too; they read I KISS YOU. That's an unlikely constabulary message. All the same, perhaps this really is the car of the Koyasan cop; there's no other about.

We ignore the treasures of the village proper. Neither the Kongobu Temple nor the Dai-to Pagoda interest us. The Reihokan Treasure House: ditto. Even the Fudo-do Shrine, oldest of the buildings and the blackest, cannot waylay us. We walk straight through this Buddhist alpine village, more interested in seeing what treasures the vending machines dispense: cigarettes, soda pop and beer, whiskey by the quart, coffee hot and cold. On the sidewalk in front of a convenience store, leashed dogs lie obediently on cardboard mats while their owners shop.

The path through the Okuno-in Cemetery is not cleared of snow, but the way is evident, flanked by a thousand—indeed, several hundred thousand—monuments and markers. Cedars, some said to have stood since Kobo Daishi's day, umbrella over an assortment of armchair graves, bronze statues, wooden posts, marble headstones, and terraces fenced in stone, large as house lots. It's an eclectic patchwork: every conceivable token of termination from headstone to pavilion, from Western mausoleum to Shinto torii gate.

For centuries the *Koya-hijiri*, the wandering priests dispatched from this mountain, combed Japan for the offerings and physical remains of those who wished to rest with Kobo Daishi. Since 1019 AD, the practice of burial in the Okuno-in Cemetery had been followed by emperors and shoguns, samurai and bureaucrats, farmers and business tycoons. As often as not they have deposited only a proxy on the peak—a flake of ash, a sliver of bone, a lock of hair, a paring of nails (just enough to garner a ringside seat at the Resurrection).

Across two bridges draped in quilts of snow, past the Basho Haiku monument, under a dark embankment of pines and cedars, is the Nestorian Stele—or rather, a copy of the original stone tablet in China. I pick it out instantly in this haystack of steles. The original was carved in 781 AD near Xi'an by a monk named Ching-Ching, Pope of Zhinastan. Ching-Ching was a Christian, but by no means was he the first Christian in China. In fact, the Nestorian Stele tells the story of the arrival of Christianity in China in 635 AD and how it flourished there for two centuries. Kobo Daishi may have seen this stele, maybe even met a few Christians in China; no one knows.

The Nestorian Stele disappeared after the great religious persecutions of 845 AD; was unearthed eight centuries later; and in 1907 was shifted within the city walls of Xi'an, to the Forest of Steles in the Provincial Museum, a vast repository of ancient tablets. As for the Japanese copy: on September 21, 1911, the Honorable Mrs. Gordon of Ireland commissioned a replica to be carved in Xi'an and transported to Koyasan. Its connection to the mountain Buddhism of Japan is obscure, but it is a superb copy: nine feet tall, a yard wide, a foot thick. Weight: probably two tons. A cross floats in a cloud of lotus leaves above its long columns, which are inscribed in a polyglot of Chinese, Syriac, and Estrangelo—another dim passage in the running text of ruins linking China to Japan, recast here by an Irish Lady for a Buddhist saint.

✳   ✳   ✳

It's half a mile more to the apex of Okuno-in, the Matrix Realm, where eight peaks enfold Kobo Daishi's meditation crypt like lotus petals. Our legs are cramping.

At the top is Toro-do, the highest temple of Shingon Buddhism, a wide pavilion of lamps, some said to have been burning continuously for nine hundred years. The interior is a sea of pinholes in the darkness, and for a moment, perhaps owing to the abrupt shutting out of sunlight and snow, I undergo a profound disorientation; I feel a rush of sublime exhilaration, then the chill of catastrophe, as if in a euphoric moment I have stepped out onto a dark cloud and am about to tumble into the mouth of the earth. I'm unnerved for a second; but the sense of some other geography in the shrine quickly shrivels up. I toss some go-en coins into a grated box at the altar.

In this palace of light, all is in order; each lantern has a number. In the Toro-do's basement, stuffed with four-inch-tall figures of the Buddha, each devotion is numbered, too—each tiny figurine with a nameplate and a slot in the great grid of vaulted shelves. The lower level resembles a mammoth switchboard of the underworld.

When we emerge again, on the north porch of the Toro-do Shrine, we are face-to-face with the Gobyo Grave where Kobo Daishi lies. He's not due to wake, by some calculations, for five billion years. He's long since passed into the realm of legend. He sleeps in a night as long as a nebula.

In life Kobo Daishi was a great calligrapher, priest, and builder of lakes. He founded the first college in Japan to admit the poor. He also authored a prohibition against women visiting Koyasan, which was not lifted until 1872. What lasted longest, however, was something very simple: Kobo Daishi established a Buddhist place of worship on a mountain peak. He brought Buddhism out of the low cities, stripped it from the hands of State and priestcraft, and delivered it to the summits of nature. There the new religion he helped import from China was swiftly integrated with the indigenous religion of Japan, Shinto, the magic that ruled the natural realm. Another piece of China was cemented into place.

As we descend from Kobo Daishi's grave, we pass all the strange monuments erected in recent times: the conical pyramids of doll-like *jizos*, dressed in red bibs and stacked like unborn embryos for the cleansing tears of the Buddha; whole fiefdoms of families with their mausoleums and markers set on marble slabs like patio furniture; three life-sized ivory-black bodhisattvas, each holding a golden infant Buddha; wooden grave sticks like organ pipes; and a stadium for *jizos* with plenty of seating left in the bleachers.

Farther down are stationed a husband and wife in bronze. He wears a lapelled vest, necktie, suit, and high-laced shoes; she wears a long dress, possibly Korean, sash over her breast. She stands on his right, while he sits erect in a plush armchair. It must be his favorite old armchair, because it's bronzed too. They're lifelike; they could be posing in their parlor for a family portrait, drawing up familiar terms with eternity.

In the distance is a monument of another order: a silver rocketship positioned for lift-off. It looks like the refill for a giant ballpoint pen.

I've had enough walking in this cemetery. My shoes are soaked through, my feet are numb. There's a bus stop ahead, a souvenir store. I laugh off the moment of uneasiness I felt in Kobo Daishi's temple of light. A brochure prepared by Kobo Daishi's followers states that Kobo Daishi "entered the dhyana on 21 March 855 at Koyasan. 49 days afterward his disciples moved him to Okunoin. It is generally believed that he is in meditation until today waiting for Maitreya to appear to the world. At that time he is expected to deliver the people who are in distress."

Deliver the people who are in distress. . . . He'd have to deliver the whole world. But we're too distant from the ancient capitals to believe in sleeping Buddhas or second comings. Not that it matters, but don't get your hopes up for a resurrection of hair locks and toenails—not on Koyasan, not anywhere.

Then we hear the clang of a bell. Walking directly toward us from the lower entrance is a Buddhist pilgrim. He wears the white waistcoat and purple stole, the white pants and shoulder bag, the rosary of prayer beads (108, to represent the 108 illusions of the soul) and the traditional sedge hat like a nose cone. He appears to be stalking us, measuring out his pace with a long pine staff, the kind Kobo Daishi was supposed to have used to bring forth new springs in times of drought; but he does not see us. We separate; he passes between us. He's a man my age, eyes cast straight ahead. He seems to be straining, as if hauling a painful weight—but nothing is visible except the brass bell tied to his belt.

Eleven centuries ago, Kobo Daishi wrote: "The mountain is high, the snow is deep, and the walking is painful." He did not mention the cold; and the pilgrim we happen to pass in the cemetery—the only one—probably never complains either. After all, he's found the supreme solution to the cold: he wears no shoes.

We watch him disappear, bare feet in snow, taking the true temperature of the earth. Suddenly Tokyo is more than five train lines and a cable car east; it is centuries apart; and we've woken up in deep space.

It's the sound of the pilgrim's bell that's changed the moment. We hear it long after we leave the cemetery—perhaps that's how pure and still the air is. All day long the cold clang of the bell echoes against marble slab and cedar, temple gate and lantern—making a kind of ancient music.

Later someone says this is the music for counting graves, particularly the graves of Koyasan, believed by many to be without end.

II.

Kyoto, Nara:
A Cat in the Streets

We come down into Kyoto looking for a bridge to the past—a long, elegant bridge that extends to China's ancient capital, the original model for Kyoto. We half-expect to find a Kyoto unchanged after twelve-hundred years, rich as a silver-threaded kimono, stately as an Emperor's robe inlaid with gold. What we find, of course, is modern Kyoto, plump and sprawling, dressed in polyester and steel, up-to-date and Westernized; but we are not disappointed. The seams of Kyoto are silver and gold still, and the precincts of the past are spacious, preserved here on an unequaled scale.

Turning off a modern avenue—the kind we are at home with in the West—we enter the Higashiyama District, where we plan to stroll for hours among Buddhist temples. The temples are in such superb condition that they seem impervious to change, as if the centuries decelerated here and stopped. Inside, priests move like shadows. But the two Kyotos turn up together even here, like incense sticks and cans of spray deodorant on a single altar. The courtyard of Kiyomizu Temple fills with visitors dipping ladles in a basin of purifying water where a copper green dragon is coiled. They sip playfully, these tourists—forty million a year in Kyoto, only one in forty a foreigner. They wear Western jackets, blue jeans and T-shirts, parking their high heels and white Reeboks at temples like tiny tour buses.

Power-wound cameras rise and flash. We retreat to a quiet temple garden, transplanted from China by seafaring monks clutching the first sutras to their hearts; but taking one more step, a wide stairway opens at our feet, lined with twenty tiers of schoolchildren posing for a group portrait. The girls wear dark navy blue sailor uniforms with red scarves and pleated skirts; the boys, high-collared black uniforms with brass buttons and matching military caps. In the background the

Kiyomizu temples and shrines, laid into the foothills of Mount Otowa by a shogun, are trimmed in rock walls, pine trees, and stone lanterns. In the foreground, the schoolchildren fan themselves with comic books.

We tumble down Sannenzaka Slope, a mishmash of power poles and tiled awnings where the crafts and curios of old Kyoto are hawked by ceramic cats in shop windows, one paw raised to yank in customers. Over the next rise, Kannon, Goddess of Mercy, drifts above the trees like a colossal bubble. Sitting snugly atop the Ryozen relics museum, she measures twenty-four meters from waist to topknot, and she is a modern creation—fashioned from concrete in 1955.

This Kannon's whiteness is stark and uncanny, a whiteness that might have shaken Emperor Ichijo. White was his color. In 999 AD Emperor Ichijo witnessed the birth of five white kittens in his Palace at Kyoto and decreed that they should be raised as if princesses. For the next six centuries, felines were members of the court, until rats attacked the silkworm harvest. Cats were sent into the streets to practice their trade and forbidden to be owned. Today, cats are again kept as objects of beauty in some classy households, but we saw many still earning their living in the streets, cemeteries, and temples.

It is said that the first Japanese cats were pure white and came from China, as did silk and tea, Buddhism and this city. The Japanese completed construction of Kyoto in 794 AD, replicating in minute detail Changan, the capital of Tang Dynasty China. We had been told many times that while the old capital of China, now called Xi'an, had withered beyond recognition, Kyoto had not. Kyoto would look more like the capital of China in its Golden Age than anything left in modern China.

That is not entirely so. Kyoto has little or nothing Chinese in it. While the links between the two ancient capitals have been severed, or at least obscured, today it is Xi'an that feels like an antique city, even if most of its temples, palaces, and pagodas have been erased. Walls of pounded earth and a moat encircle Xi'an—a modern city, to be sure, but one that many still enter on donkey carts, passing under the archers' tower at the southern gate. Fearful of losing itself—of losing all of China—should it wear the mask of the West into its dreams, Xi'an has not made the great leap from its ruins; but Kyoto has. Kyoto has a subway and a rush hour; its treasures are consigned to well-groomed tourist strips; its past is an amusement park. Kyoto has remade itself as a capital for a new world, more Southern Californian than Northern Chinese.

✳   ✳   ✳

Sometimes the master copyists of old Kyoto were overruled. The Temple of the Golden Pavilion in the Kinkaku-ji gardens, for example, served as a Zen Buddhist temple for six centuries, but it was never a Chinese clone. The Japanese imported Zen from China, but altered it, producing a strong secular component that many artists, samurai, and business people adapted as a way of life. The Golden Pavilion illustrates this transformation: it was built as a private villa, and its screen walls and geometric lines set it well apart from the temple in Changan where Zen first took up residence.

The Zen temple at Xi'an today is indistinguishable from the other Buddhist temples of its time. It resembles certain temples in Kyoto, but not the Golden Pavilion. In China, shrine and villa were kept separate; in Japan, they can be one and the same.

The Japanese difference is even more pronounced at Ryoan-ji, where the fifteenth-century Zen garden—the most celebrated in the world—escapes not only the magnetism of the early imitators, but the bonds of all logic. The temple gardens of old Kyoto were derived from Chinese models; their heritage is obvious. In the classic Chinese gardens, as in the Japanese versions, nature is supreme; the designer mimics natural forms, reducing them to a frame for human contemplation and pleasure. But the Zen garden at Ryoan-ji, while it employs basic Chinese elements, carries this reduction to its outer limits. The representational becomes the abstract.

To Western eyes, the result is not a garden at all, but a landscape: a field of raked white sands punctuated by fifteen boulders, enclosed on three sides by burnt-red walls and, on the fourth, a raised platform under a temple roof where visitors dangle their unshod feet over the edge.

This garden invites decoding. It is a tantalizing cryptogram. If one retreats to its Chinese origins, Ryoan-ji unravels effortlessly: rocks represent sacred peaks or animals; sands represent the flow of water. Before us, then, are islands in a white sea mist or tigers fording a river. But this Zen garden is simpler and more abstract than any I have seen in China. It has no satisfactory representational or historical solution. Instead, it suggests something familiar, something we should know but don't—the title page of a subtext we cannot read; a rubbing lifted off the back of a parallel world underlying our own. As we leave, we ask a monk. The garden is a joke, he laughs: rocks and sand thrown like dice.

Beyond the gates of Ryoan-ji, the other Kyoto resumes, the one that the modern copyists are importing from the West. If the Japanese broke down China a thousand years ago and elevated each piece to a state of extreme perfection, so altering the original as to create Ryoan-ji, what will they do with America? Already the automobiles and electronics that clot Kyoto's new arteries and internal organs equal their Western cousins. Mass consumerism is not far behind. Shopping malls hawk knockoff crafts. Revolving restaurants serve French cuisine. At Gion Corner it is always show time, with programs in flower arrangement, dance, puppet theater, koto music. Tokyo has a Disneyland, but Kyoto has a version of Universal City—Toei studios—to dazzle moviegoing tourists. Then there are the samurai and geisha houses, the traditional schools for artists and artisans, the two thousand Buddhist temples and Shinto shrines. Old and new Kyoto both need all these outlets. By summer, the heat of the throngs reaches critical mass, and nothing escapes the auto-focus, the zoom lens, the unshuttered mind of forty million Minoltas; even a garden of rock and gravel might melt under the assault.

※　※　※

After circling Kyoto, we are accustomed to the abrupt appearance of past and present in the same space; but the closer we look, the fewer connections we make with ancient China. Turning to Nara, thirty minutes south by train, we find ourselves on firmer ground. Nara preceded Kyoto as Japan's capital. The Emperors resided here from 710 to 794 AD; they instituted Buddhism and practiced Chinese ways before their successors did the same in Kyoto; and at Nara they built the first great city in the image of the Chinese capital. Whole temples have disappeared in Nara, reduced to particles of dust and iron, but one architectural wonder that did survive is grander than anything left from old Xi'an or even from old Kyoto: Todai-ji Temple. Completed in 752 AD to house Daibutsu, the world's biggest bronze Buddha, Todai-ji is the largest wooden structure on earth—unmistakably so. Its size cannot be exaggerated easily; no photograph I have seen fully expresses its scale. Of all the temples in China or Japan, only Todai-ji approaches the vastness of Mont-Saint-Michel. Unlike the great cathedrals of Europe, Toda-ji is not a celebration of the spirit ascending heavenwards; rather, it directs us earthward, with the fury of a vortex. Its wooden walls and timbers—black with age and exposure—drive downward like pistons, while its rooflines stretch out and clutch the horizon. At the entrance a massive dormer bulges into the shape of a warrior's helmet. Inside this holy samurai sits Buddha, fifty feet tall. The statue has been repaired many times, its most recent reincarnation in 1692. The temple has been rebuilt too, always subject to fire. Many of the great wooden temples of Nara were never rebuilt, but the sacred shed at Toda-ji was carefully reconstructed in 1709 as it neared its one thousandth birthday. It is said to be an exact replica of the original temple, but lacking giant timbers, the engineers reduced Toda-ji to two-thirds its original size. Even so, Todai-ji places everyone who comes before it in proper perspective.

✳   ✳   ✳

There is a second mission we want to complete in Kyoto, unrelated to looking for China. It is to find the cat who did not weep at Buddha's funeral.

This event is depicted in a painting at Tofuku-ji Temple that is unveiled once a year on Nehane, on the Ides of March. According to tradition, the cat, alone of all living creatures in attendance, arrived late, then disrupted the solemn rites by pouncing on a snake; even worse, the cat never shed a tear at the departure of Buddha Sakyamuni. As a consequence, the feline was banned from the zodiac of animals, and nowhere in the Orient is there a Year of the Cat.

We arrive at Tofuku-ji early on Nehane, but it turns out to be a confusing complex of temples and halls, and we try a number of doors looking for the painting without success. Our inquiries are not understood, or are ignored, but eventually we stumble into the correct temple. It must be correct, because here the monks have lined two walls with tables selling souvenirs. A painting, presumably the fabled Nehanzu—largest such in Japan—hangs from the rafters above the altar. We toss coins into the box and zero in.

The painting is stiffly executed, flat and two-dimensional; its colors are faded, its outlines blurred. The Buddha lies on his death pallet, surrounded by thin bare trunks of trees rising like columns. The mourners, dressed in a variety of costumes, stand nearby in the background or lie prostrate in front. The animals peer in from the edges. We scan the four corners, but the cat eludes detection. In the temple shadows, the finer details, if they exist, are obscured. There are candidates here and there, but the most likely one proves, on close analysis, to be a fox.

Unable to locate the cat, we are relieved to escape from Tofuku-ji, which failed to welcome us—cold as a cloud of comets halfway on its journey to the nearest star. Perhaps it is time to give Kyoto its full due.

We head downtown, passing a forest of steel girders, the American copy under construction. Perched on the tips of the highest posts are two steeplejacks, working without safety harnesses or net. Dressed in black shirts and ballooning pants, they strut like acrobats and, when a crane drops a crossbeam into place, fasten either end to their posts. They cross and sit together. Spotting us fifty feet below, they stand and pull off their hard hats, flashing the Victory sign.

We walk faster. The traffic thickens as the avenue widens, accelerating. We pass a Love Hotel, its rates posted outside in English. Ahead, the center of modern shopping begins under a streamlined awning, shading the sidewalk for blocks. Our pace picks up; everything around us speeds up. We're almost running as we lurch past a package in the gutter. Margaret goes back first. Between parked cars she finds a cat, turned on its back and sheathed in a slick plastic envelope. The sack is ripped open; the cat is soaking wet, as though someone unable to drown it flung it from a getaway car. The cat shivers. When we lift it onto the sidewalk and kneel down, stroking its moist fur, it begins to emit small cries. This gives us hope. We keep staring up, hoping to arrest some passerby, but they stream past until a young couple stops. They squat to appraise the situation. We dig the word for veterinarian out of our dictionary, but they shake their heads as if there are no veterinarians in Kyoto.

That's impossible. An American businessman stops. He asks what is wrong. Speaking Japanese with the couple, he confirms that there are no vets in Kyoto. Can that be true? The American shrugs. He eyes the cat sympathetically and walks on. We warm the cat with our hands, but it seems in so much pain that we're afraid to touch it. Margaret removes the plastic wrapping and folds the cat in her scarf. It continues to shiver. The sun bores down; cars blast up and down the street. Margaret leaves to buy a carton of milk. She places droplets on the cat's chin and nose, but it does not respond with its tongue. We decide to ferry it uptown to our hotel room. Margaret asks a grocer if she can use a cardboard box; he refuses. The couple who stopped do not intervene. As soon as the grocer goes inside, Margaret snatches the box.

We lay the cat inside. It is silent. The couple put their hands on the box and make it clear that they have decided to take the cat home themselves. They carry the box into the crowd and disappear.

Walking on, looking for a subway entrance, we stop at a pachinko parlor. At lunchtime the place is in full mindless swing. We wait our turn at the sink on the wall, wash our hands and dry them as our ears are pelted with the plink-plink-plink of pachinko balls colliding like hail blown from compartment to compartment in a metallic sky.

✳ ✳ ✳

We begin our final day in Kyoto with a tea ceremony at the Prince Hotel. The Prince is a white circle, the shape of a high-tech donut, and across the way is the Kyoto International Conference Hall, a series of interlocking triangles and trapezoids. These two buildings border Lake Takaragaike, beneath the green wooded hills of northern Kyoto. Together, they look like a space center for the Garden of Eden.

The Prince's teahouse is a separate structure. With a thatched straw roof and matted rooms, it is new but traditional. We have a view of a small garden and pond through a parted screen, and as the resident tea master performs the rites, he makes it all so simple. For a moment, two Kyotos converge, generation bonded to generation.

Tea drinking is another custom imported from China, elevated to ceremony there, but in Japan each detail has been aesthetically refined, including utensils—cups, whisk, long-handled wooden ladle. The Way of Tea penetrates the Oriental culture of Japan today; in China, it is seldom practiced. Visitors from afar, we cannot give it a close reading, but the ceremony calms us and we change our bearings: no more bridges to the past to cross. Instead, we will attend fully to what's present.

If Kyoto fails to obey the laws of organic growth that other cities follow (ordinarily requiring progressive excavations to retrace), then perhaps it follows those of nuclear physics. After countless collisions, new permutations leap forward from the old: a Kyoto/anti-Kyoto, parallel and simultaneous, like a discontinuous world held in orbit by the discarded nucleus.

After tea, we set out for the Fushimi Inari Shrine, just south of Kyoto on the line to Nara. Disembarking at Inari Station and washing up in the sink on the platform, we set out in search of lunch. We contemplate the plastic foods in the restaurant windows like irresolute robots. Suddenly, a passing housewife snatches us up. We can't understand a word she's saying. She leads us away from the station, across the tracks, up a blind alley, and into a small noodle shop on the first floor of her neighbor's house for some home cooking, Inari style. We plunk ourselves down at the counter. The proprietress addresses us just as rapidly as her friend did, breaking into laughter, shaking her head. All we can say is "soba," and she begins lunch from scratch under our gaze, raiding the bins and the fridge, pulling down a cast iron pan, igniting the burners on the stove. She switches on an overhead TV, and her friend sits down where the counter takes a bend, chatting up a storm.

The noodles require twenty minutes to prepare in a ceremony that might not be as flawless as a flower arrangement, but does not lack warmth. This is like sitting in your mother's kitchen, watching her whip up grilled cheese sandwiches and tomato soup, the next door neighbor in for gossip and midday soaps—except that here you are a stranger and your mom doesn't speak a word of your language. She laughs. We laugh, too. The noodles must be the best we will ever eat in Japan.

By the time we walk out, the fine mist thickens into a drizzle, and we must unspring our umbrellas. The grounds of the Fushimi Inari Shrine are emblazoned with statues of the fox, the messenger of the gods that is able to transform itself into scores of seductive forms. A black fox of polished granite rises from its haunches atop a high pedestal, its long thick tail erect, an old lock and key clamped between its teeth. Visitors have tied red and white bibs around its neck. Just ahead is the first of the ten thousand torii gates. Each time one passes through such a gate a bit of good luck is thought to rub off. Someone has told us of a particularly clever soul who installed a swing on his backyard torii, creating a sort of playground prayer wheel.

We step through the first massive gate, where two black foxes with yellow bibs stand watch. The path splits. Smaller gates, all painted the same bright orange-red, form two tunnels that run side by side up the mossy hillside, ending at a shrine more than a mile away. Back of that shrine is a final reduction: a jumble of miniature torii gates, copies small enough to fit in a shopping bag.

We take the tunnel on the left. The ten thousand gates are so close to each other that they almost touch; there is scarcely a gap. Only a fine mist squeezes through, and we collapse our umbrellas. The rain has discouraged tourists. We are alone.

We recall the dictum that Kenko composed in Kyoto, six centuries earlier: "Visits to shrines and temples are best made on days when others do not go, and by night."

It is dark in this maze the color of the sun, but we can see a temple cat ahead, meandering side to side. With the introduction of Buddhism from China came the custom of keeping cats to protect the sutras from rats. In modern Japanese cities, there are always plenty of cats for temples; it's where people dump them when they cannot drown them.

We keep the cat in our sights. It does not acknowledge us; we do not ask it to. It crisscrosses left and right, receding as we advance, then leaps through a gap between two columns and vanishes.

We examine the gap. Through it we see the green blotches of the hillside, the trees of the forest. Before us and behind us the curving walls seem infinite, a cyclotron of torii gates, bending light. In the center of this double parallel passageway, in a torrent of mist, there are only these gateless gates between worlds, screens opening and closing silently in translucent cat's paws streaking across a damp field, leaving no print.

III.

Kanazawa:
Out the Other Side

We want to come into Kanazawa, on the far west storm-raked Sea of Japan, without fanfare, on little cat's feet, if possible, and soak it up gradually, like trout in sake, because we have heard that this is the other side of Japan, partitioned off by alpine peaks, unbombed by the Americans during World War Two, uncrushed by the vortex of twentieth-century change. In the end, this is not to be, of course; few true wishes are ever granted.

From the train station, Kanazawa looks exactly as we expect a city of a half million in Japan to look: chaotic, modern, uninviting. Yet in minutes we can walk through the present into the precincts of the nineteenth century and all the way back to the feudal era of shoguns and sixteenth-century lords. Our feet itch to settle into the narrow lanes of two-story wooden houses and shops, their bamboo-slatted panels peeking shyly out from under black-tiled roofs that serve as massive skids for coastal snows. Yet before we can walk away even from the front desk of our hotel, we are grabbed, arrested, and assaulted in English by an employee of no discernible function except importance. He wishes to be called Dino, after his favorite American singer, and he will show us Kanazawa. He insists on this, and to make his point he nudges us forward like a snowplow to the stairs and down into the guts of the wedding and reception halls in the basement. Ripping open a door, he flicks us into the midst of a private celebration.

It's not a wedding that we've been forced to intrude upon, but a reception staged for those about to graduate from a local girls' college. Seven of the girls are under colored lights on stage, attired in kimonos and Western cocktail dresses, reciting speeches and singing songs to honor their teachers and administrators, men in suits who look no fun at all. The graduates couldn't be happier, and they seem happy to see us, coming down and speaking a few words of English, posing with us for snapshots, offering us snacks from the long tables.

Dino provides no explanation for bringing us in unannounced. Later, we realize it is probably his way of swaggering. His English is superb, highly idiomatic, and he is facile in other languages as well; lacking the polish of higher education, Dino fits his slick employers to a tee, and they keep him as a retainer for those awkward events when foreigners visit or the bosses themselves go abroad. As for us, since we are of absolutely no importance, perhaps Dino is just using us to sharpen his nails.

Finally breaking away to our room, we plot how to escape our host. It isn't easy in polite Japan, even for frank, rude Americans, and besides, Dino is onto our sort and will not only see a brush off coming but probably bat it aside, shovel us into a hotel car, and scoop us from sight to sight like a business delegation on tour.

Sure enough, as evening falls, he's at our door. We start with a meal we could never afford, sequestered in a private tatami-matted room, sampling specialties of the Kaga region: *iibu* (wild duck stew), *gori* (river fish in miso soup), quail eggs, lotus root, cherry-flavored rice balls, and cuttle fish, ink-black and raw from the sea. Dino even takes us on an inspection of the kitchen, perhaps to show it off: long stainless steel tables, the menus posted in French, and the raw meat laid out lovingly in orderly rows on trays, awaiting the chopper. Then it's fourteen floors straight up, to the sky lounge and the bar, Dino's constant haunt. We sit at the bar and cleanse our hands and face with hot steaming towels. Here Dino drinks endless rounds of sake night after night, assuring us it has no bad effect the next morning. This is a piano lounge, and as our eyes shift toward the baby grand, we are surprised to find an American at the keyboard, a bejeweled woman in low-cut gown, her throat curdled with sentimental pop ditties and her own compositions.

She is Beverly, and, as she tells us herself, she is dedicated to making a career as the singer of her own songs. The reason she joins us is Dino; he has brought us to the lounge in the sky to impress her, and now he has hauled her over to be impressed. At this time of year almost no one is in attendance and the applause is faint, except from Dino. He is a relentless Lothario, one whom Beverly must somehow keep at bay for the length of her three-month contract. Beverly sighs, she sighs often. When Dino disappears for a moment, she assures us she can handle this pest. Nor does she try to set up a day with us, as many foreigners do in Japan, where loneliness is an affliction. She talks about her previous contracts in Asia, and the trunks of costumes and makeup and sheet music she carries, and the lack of sightseeing she has done in Kanazawa. She returns to the piano when she sees Dino approach.

Dino sits down, ignores her song, and tells us about his wife and children and his fabulous house in Toyama, which he insists we visit. Then he pumps us for details about California, Beverly's home. The bartender keeps his sake cup topped off with warm rice wine. The lounge is empty when we leave at midnight, save Dino at the bar and brave Beverly at the keyboard. She sallies forth into "My Way," and in ways too sad to admit, she reminds me of myself: If she is a rotten singer and a piss-poor composer of songs written in a second-rate genre, the same could be said of me as a writer.

Approaching middle age, she too is unrecognized in her own land. She has wandered here, and she will continue to wander so long as her dreams persist. She will also continue to sing off-key into rooms of drunks, the smoke pouring back into her eyes. I am put in mind of Muro Saisei, the Japanese poet who spent his youth here orphaned in a temple, whose poem about home ends with "the world gone wrong" and a yearning for the "heart's true capital," never to be found. Weeping thus in my sake, I fall asleep under a sky of darkened stars, and in the morning, as a dusting of snow swiftly melts, I hear lightning, then wake to Dino banging on our door.

❋   ❋   ❋

Kenroku-en is a garden of ten thousand trees, many of them ancient, supported from fall to spring with elaborate *yuki-tsuri*, skeletons of bamboo and straw erected and tied as protection against heavy seaside snows. Exposed, they resemble the frames of monumental teepees. We come for a stroll, in need of a few slow hours. Our journey from Tokyo to Nagoya to Koyasan to Kyoto and Nara has left us whirling; now we take our time in Kanazawa, and time almost stops. We pass women gardeners in wide-brimmed white bonnets kneeling in the flower beds. They are weeding by hand, slowly filling wicker baskets with trimmings. Kenroku-en is like a well-groomed old gentleman, the cherries and pines pruned faithfully twice each year, the sands reraked every day. We come to a wooden teahouse standing on weathered stilts in a lake, standing like a birdhouse, waiting for wooden cranes. We go up and down the garden hills, pausing over a pond that marks the *himuro* icehouse, where great chunks of winter ice were once stored to chill the summer drinks of the Maeda lords. Every year in the heart of July, four men were chosen to deliver slabs of Kanazawa's precious ice to Edo, now Tokyo, as a gift to the Tokugawa shogun, a journey that required five days on foot, the ice insulated by packed straw and fine silk.

Finally we come upon an old man by the lake shore, his canvas propped up on an easel. He is painting the portrait of a stone lantern, *kotoji-no-toro*, whose unequal arching legs connect pond water with the rocky shore. This lantern has become a symbol of Kanazawa, and we have seen no more graceful lantern in Japan. The old artist has opened two cases of brushes and paints, and we would like to talk to him, but Dino pays him scant attention. He is impatient. He has his eyes on the groups of schoolgirls touring the garden, and he engages them in leering conversation, possibly about us. He has seen the garden too many times, and as he guides us all over Kanazawa, his boredom accumulates until we can feel it like a stone in his throat. His eyes will only light up later, when he is elevated to his sake cup and his heart will sing only in time to the piano in the lounge.

We exit Kenroku-en at Kanazawa Castle. Nothing remains of Kanazawa Castle now, save a gate with a roof of lead tiles. On this site in 1471, the radical priest Saint Rennyo established a Buddhist republic that would stand unchallenged and independent for a hundred years. His peasant followers belonged to the *Ikko-ikki* ("Single-minded") sect, and their domain was renowned for its low taxes. In 1580, they were crushed by a warrior family and the Maeda lords began their three hundred year rule over Kaga.

They constructed Kanazawa Castle in 1592. It was designed by Takayama Ukon, a Christian warrior who fled the Tokyo region when Christians fell from official favor. As measured by rice, Kaga became the wealthiest fiefdom of Japan. When the end came for the Kaga lords and their samurai retainers with the restoration of the Meiji Emperor in 1868, Kanazawa declined. Even rice was hard to find. The castle burned in 1881 and was never rebuilt. Behind the surviving wall, last rebuilt in 1788, is a modern college. Before the wall is Kenroku-en Garden. We depart it before we can know it, tugged by Dino's remorseless thrust into the vacant future.

One of the three supreme landscape gardens of Japan, Kenroku-en began as a stroll garden for the castle in 1624, reaching completion almost exactly two hundred years later. Commoners were forbidden entrance until 1875; in 1975, admission was first charged, and is now paid by a million visitors a year. Kenroku means "six combined," the six being the classical virtues of landscape design: vastness—its rolling twenty-five acres; solemnity—its lack of gaudy color and sculpture; antiquity—its venerable trees and shrubs; scenic charm—its many artificial hills and overlooks; harmony—the graceful interlacing of its elements; and above all coolness—imparted by its rivulets and streams. The streams of this garden are the exposed veins of a seventeenth-century engineering marvel that tunneled mountain spring water and runoff to the Maeda Castle. The underground channels (*yosui*) resurfaced in the garden and in the town, east and west, to irrigate fields and clean the streets of snow, although today metal sprinklers installed in the main avenues automatically blast away the slush.

We, too, are carried down. The coolness of the streams gives way to the Higashi District's rows of geisha houses. The Eastern Pleasure Quarter, in turn, is balanced by the samurai district to the west, where a few authentic houses, enclosed in tile-topped mud walls and moats, still stand. Leaving Dino in the hotel car, we explore the winding alleys, where children play baseball, and we settle like good tourists into the Saihitsuan Yuzen Silk-Dyeing Center. Hand-painted silk kimonos are produced here in the seventeenth-century manner that's made a Yuzen kimono worth a million yen, famous for its bold floral designs outlined in white. The process is tedious, requiring several months, and is nothing if not Japanese . . . that is, meticulous: The drawing, the inking, the tracing of the design onto silk with rice paste, the soaking in soybean water, the drying over a charcoal fire, the steaming to make fast the dyes, and the washing. Yuzen silks were always washed in the rivers, but as the tour brochure explains, "The rivers are not as clean as they used to be, so in a factory we have a basin with underground water powered electrically" to do the job. Miyazaki Yuzensai, inventor of the process, might creak and crack in his nearby temple tomb at this technological incursion, but there is hope. "Now the anti-pollution movement has made rivers cleaner," the brochure explains, "so sometimes early in the morning you may be able to see it. Quite a picturesque scene." Later we hear that river washing is usually done only on demand of film crews. However it is washed, the silk is steamed a third time, the panels sewn together, gold and silver embroidery added, family crests dyed on scraps, and the kimono is complete.

Dino snorts. His daughter was given the choice of a wedding kimono or a new car when she graduated and chose the gown. He is showing us through the hotel, now that it is after dark, and it is apparent that like so many other Western-style hotels, this one depends as much on weddings as guest rooms. Cost of a catered wedding here is 20,000 yen per person attending, and everyone you've ever known seems to attend. There are hotel shops that do nothing but rent bridal gowns. The beauty salons contain dressing rooms for brides and grooms, who often change from Japanese to Western attire in the middle of the wedding, where two services are as common as one.

Dino's palms itch for the skytop lounge, but we feign fatigue. He has tired of us for sport; he's giving us tomorrow off. He has to tend to business at another hotel in Toyama, miles away, near his home. He hasn't seen his wife for a week.

We sink into easy sleep, as into the well in the center of Kenroku-en garden that five centuries ago gave Kanazawa its name, meaning Marsh of Gold. It is a well that when stirred yielded flecks of gold which floated to the surface like lotus petals. Even today, Kanazawa is the capital of gold leaf production, accounting it is said for ninety percent of the world's supply. Gold leaf has been pounded into thin sheets by mallet for century after century here and transferred to exquisite works of lacquer and paper. Flecks are added to tea sometimes or powder to honey, for gold can be safely consumed—good for rheumatism, they say. In our time, however, much of Kanazawa's gold leaf has found a new application: as decorative trim for plastic goods.

❋   ❋   ❋

With Dino in remission, we head for the hills, upriver, out of Kanazawa, taking a local bus. The trip is a meander, the sun is steady for March, there's no snow or lightning today. At the top, there's a deep blue reservoir in the belly of Mount Io. We pass through the village at Yuwaku Spa, and the bus drops us off, turning back at the Hakuunro Hotel. Hakuunro is a first-class mountain resort, but with a distinct queerness: its formidable facade is not merely half Chinese; it is also half Spanish.

We have come up here to look around Edo-Mura, a collection of some twenty feudal houses and shops, something like a theme park for history enthusiasts, but the hotel pulls us in. The interior is Japanese. We strike up a conversation with an assistant manager who spent a year in Oregon, at Tektronix; he's now married into the resort business. He takes us on a tour: four immense, fanciful baths, seventy-five Japanese-style rooms.

This was one of four hotels the American Occupation Forces requisitioned after World War Two, and for almost four years it was our General Headquarters and, we assume, an R and R outpost. Our guide points out some of the old signs the Americans put up on the doors. The officers never quite took to the indoor baths, it seems, and built a large outdoor swimming pool, still used in the summer; we saw it as we came up in the bus.

We look inside some of the vacant rooms. They are exquisite. A few combine Japanese and Western features. Our guide confesses that many Japanese prefer the modern arrangement. Matted floor and futon are falling from favor. We nod. For us, their charm is already fading; they can be painful to use.

The last room he shows us, at the end of a dim corridor, is permanently locked. It has been locked since the day Emperor Hirohito stayed in it a single night; it will stay sealed off from the world outside (so far as anyone can judge) forever, the invisible bed in the heart of Japan.

✳   ✳   ✳

When Dino catches up with us the next morning, he points the driver to the local sake factory. It's one tour he takes with us. The owner is the sixth-generation boss. He assigns one of his neatly uniformed underlings to do the showing. The building reminds us of a beer brewery, with its vats and rice mash. Although the floors are cement, we must remove our shoes and wear plastic bags over our socks.

At the end of the tour, the boss draws us into an impersonal back room for sake samples. It is fine sake, sweet in the tradition of the region, and we are served sake and tea and treats by all the young women from the office. It is invariably the women who serve us, wherever we go as honored guests.

Sake takes fifty days to create here; only water free of iron is used. As we leave, we are each handed a massive plastic shopping bag filled to the top with liter bottles, miniatures, and tiny straw-covered casks of sake. The bags outweigh our complete luggage, which we haul on our backs, and we haven't a clue of how to rid ourselves of such problematic gifts. Instead, we bow and re-bow, murmuring the words of thanks that are forever on our lips.

Dino is sorry to see the outside of the factory again, a cement box in a field of rice, because he must now take us into the Higashiyama hillside, where scores of temples dating from the 1600s—when everything seemed to start in Kanazawa—make for steep wanderings. We climb the stairs to a few, but they are silent and a bit ragged today.

Even Sanbo-ji Temple is closed up, the shrine dedicated to the cure of hemorrhoids, where twice a year, in late May and September, the piles-curing Buddha is put on display. The priest is said to hold the cure: a special sutra, a sacred salve, an envelope of red paper pills. The altar is festooned with the photographs of those who found relief. The depths of superstition here are of considerable length. Just a few years ago an old woman at this temple routinely took on the ills of worshippers like a medium, and many swore by her powers. We see nothing of this, and turn back with nothing to report from the Preparation-H Temple.

In fact, we miss all the festivals and annual rites of Kanazawa, and so much of its essence, for otherwise even Kanazawa resembles a modern city of the West. But in no city of the West is there such a calendar. On January 6, firemen in loincloths scale the icy ladders to demonstrate traditional fire-fighting skills. On February 8, a needle mass is held at a sewing school—a ceremony for disposing of tired and broken needles. On the vernal equinox, at Zengyo-ji Temple, the hairy head of a mummy with three faces is displayed—the three faces being male, female, and demonic. At the end of March, the Kanazawa University Medical School holds a memorial service at the grave sites for those who donated their bodies and organs to the school for research. Broken dolls are burned at a temple on April 29. In late July, the *mushi-okuri* is performed, a ritual to rid villages of mosquitoes. This festival dates from a curse laid on when the Buddhist peasants ousted the local pack of lords in the fifteenth century. "Bugs will torment you forever," the dethroned leader swore. In the middle of August, researchers at the University Hospital pray for the souls of lab mice, rabbits, and dogs. On December 5, farmers invite the gods in for dinner and a hot bath, thanks for the harvest.

We witness none of these rituals. We feel distant from Japan and hounded by Dino. Only when we go shopping on our own the next morning in the Yoko-Yasue-cho Arcade, snaking through the center of downtown, do we stray from guide, taxi, Mr. Donuts, and the Yellow USA coffeeshops. At the center of the shopping arcade—a typical one in Japan, restricted to pedestrians and bikes, capped over with translucent plastic roofs, lined with a mix of small specialty stores and restaurants, like an artery in the body of a steel and concrete giant—we come to a large rupture. What spills in is not only a flood of natural sunlight, so white it seems to come from the center of another solar system, but a temple as well, the spacious Higashi Betsuin Temple, a

Buddhist shrine where grandmothers with baby buggies and shopping carts pause on park benches to snack and chat, where children swing baseball bats and locate home plate on the steps to the altar, first base at a stone lantern, and the outfield on the sidewalk inside the arcade. It is a quick view—a rip in the wall—and a view of what we aren't quite certain, except that it is warm, idyllic, and protected from ruin and desire.

✳   ✳   ✳

Dino excuses himself the next day, so we set out early on the city bus. A block away the high hotel opposite has caught fire. Two ladder trucks pull up and extend their firefighters to the twelfth story, where we see smoke pouring out, and as our bus pulls around the corner, a single figure in a yellow rubber coat rappels down the glass cliffside like a spider.

Fire is the great fear of wooden Japan. Kanazawa was in its infancy when the city fires struck. In 1631, several neighborhoods caught fire and the winds whipped the flames through a thousand dwellings, destroying large portions of the castle as well. An even more extensive fire wasted the city four years later. The earliest municipal codes addressed this plague: "Each house and each ward shall maintain rain barrels." "Each Household Group shall maintain two ladders, a water barrel, sickles, and rakes." And even this: "When the wind is blowing, the Ward Representatives . . . should go throughout the city and warn households to exercise caution about fire."

When we ask at our hotel that evening about the nature of the fire, no one admits to its existence. There's not a word or picture of it on the TV news, either. The Japanese are quiet, reserved—or at least it seems that way so far. In China, we were constantly approached, pried at, sometimes abused, but seldom kept at a distance. Here there is a coldness, and it complements an ordinariness, a familiarity, imparted no doubt by the sheer Americanness of the landscape, the fashions, the technologies, the smallest items, even though our eyes constantly seize on the Oriental differences, and sometimes even the peculiar differences that might be especially Japanese. But there's little time and often no possibility of opening the more revealing doors to tradition, for example, the one to a ryokan run by a former geisha, said to be a great beauty who selects her clientele carefully, usually the best-to-do of Tokyo's businessmen. A high-level introduction is always required, and so the door to Japan's supreme courtesies remains closed to ordinary outsiders such as us—to ordinary Japanese as well, who congregate in the very places we find ourselves.

We leave the bus at Ninja-Dera, the Temple of the Secret Agents, inspiration for myriad B-movies, of flying fists and sweeping swords and secret passages leading to the moonlit river. The ticket booth turns out to be a window in a wall, where we overhear the attendant inquiring if two *gaijin* (foreigners) can tour the temple. We laugh and everyone inside the ticket booth laughs. We seem to be acceptable. It is so crowded outside that tourists are admitted inside only every twenty minutes, in large groups, and seated on the wooden floor before the temple altar, where a long lecture ensues. We understand nothing. Then the big group is divided into manageable subgroups of twenty or so that are lined up to wait for their tour of the labyrinth: the hidden stairways, the escape passages leading underground, the false walls from which the Ninja agents—or perhaps it is now the Ninja-turtles themselves—will spring. The whole trek through the maze is conducted strictly in Japanese; although a few Japanese tourists try to translate, they fail to unbaffle us.

Ninja-Dera is four stories high on the outside, but seven levels within. Completed in 1643 by a Maeda lord for his wife, it is certainly a baroque fortress, but its purpose is no longer known. I suspect a love of the strange and cute is at the root of it. Outside, at the bottom of the steps, we retrieve our running shoes from among hundreds of pairs lodged in a honeycomb of open wooden racks. Ours are always the biggest shoes on the shelves. There's a lot of shoes here; it's a good way to rate at a glance the popularity of a tourist trap in Japan. Ninja-Dera has even installed a wall of green metal shoe lockers, coin-operated with keys.

Shoes tied, we study the regulations printed on the back of our elegant ticket of admission, and realize we must be somewhere like nowhere else on earth: (1) Keep yourselves neatly dressed and walk gently while in the precincts. (2) Keep hands off the mirrors, drums, and other articles. (3) Refrain from smoking in the precincts. (4) No photographing is allowed. (5) Any visitors, if drunken or otherwise unable to behave themselves, are not allowed in the precincts. (6) Take off your sunglasses and hats when entering the buildings.

We walk gently away, and from a distance, through our sunglasses, the temple of the Ninja looks like a massive video game.

❋　❋　❋

Kanazawa was born in the sixteenth century and grew up in the seventeenth, the very period in which Westerners first saw Japan and Japan in turn was urbanized and centralized under the Tokugawa shogunate. In 1700, when barely two percent of Europeans lived in large cities, three times that proportion moved into large urban centers in Japan. Tokyo became the largest city on earth, Kyoto was as big as London or Paris, and Kanazawa ballooned into one of Japan's five super cities.

This sudden growth of Japan is linked to the triumph of a single shogun who compelled allegiance from some 250 regional lords, the daimyos. The daimyos and their feudal warriors, the samurai, constructed castle towns from which they ruled their domains. In the 1600s, the Maeda clan was second in wealth only to the shogunate; Kanazawa became their well-ordered castle town.

Underlying the government of Kanazawa and the polity of a new Japan was a Confucian doctrine borrowed from China. The lords of Kanazawa, some of whom had tutors from China, applied the Confucian principles of moral suasion, reason, harmony, and civil order to their burgeoning city; and they went further, transmuting the Confucian virtues and social hierarchy into precise, unambiguous legal codes.

Working from the Confucian blueprint, they built a society that depended on maintaining orderly behavior as defined for each class. Samurai, for example, could not loiter, sing in public, insult passersby, play the flute, cavort with streetwalkers, or dance in the streets. The legal menu for a samurai dinner party was spelled out: two soups, five vegetables, pickled vegetables, a fish, cakes, and two rounds of sake. Wives of samurai, like women everywhere in Japan, were placed on short leashes. In 1729, a member of Kanazawa's Council of Advisors wrote:

> Recently the wives, mothers, and daughters of samurai have been seen taking walks and strolls to temples and shrines for the purpose of amusement. In old times no woman behaved like this, but recently such behavior has become common. . . . Women should not be doing this; fathers, husbands, and sons will be held responsible. . . .

The code did admit of exceptions: "A woman who is married shall on occasion be permitted to visit the home of her parents. . . .

Women are also permitted to go mushroom hunting . . . but they should not wear heavy makeup or take extravagant picnic lunches."

Merchants were even more restricted. They could not possess "a large number of luxurious clothes," could not "keep dogs as pets," could not "walk along the street next to samurai." As the 1624 city code of Kanazawa put it: "Behavior inappropriate to one's status as a merchant is forbidden. Do your jobs well." This meant monitoring the way one sat: "Merchants are not to gather in shops and gossip loudly about others, nor are merchants in shops to sit around in rude positions."

On a rainy day, the merry merchants of Kanazawa could not wear tall clogs to avoid the puddles because, according to the law, the "height of clogs and the quality of materials shall be in accordance with one's status." In 1660, merchants were also forbidden from throwing snow on passersby.

As for the hapless traveler arriving in Kanazawa in 1642, there was this dainty code to observe:

> Persons who urinate from the second floor of houses in the city, regardless of whether it is night or day, shall certainly be punished. If a traveler at an inn commits such an act, the innkeeper shall be held responsible. This is to be explained to all children, travelers, and persons of low status.

Travelers situated on the second floor were also unable to spit, throw water, stare, or shower rude comments upon those in the streets below.

The conversion of etiquette into law made the Confucian hierarchy visible to all. Each class was defined by privilege, by personal behavior, by banquet dishes, by the shoes its members were allowed to wear. Each class was also defined by its place of residence in Kanazawa. In this Confucian microcosm, the castle keep was at the center, royalty in the first circle, the samurai in the second, and the artisans and merchants in the third. Outside the city limits were neighborhoods devoted to common laborers, to licensed beggars, and to untouchable groups who hauled garbage, cleaned corpses, dug graves, stripped carcasses, and tanned hides.

The infusion of Western ways, culminating in the imposition of an American constitution, remixed the layers of this stratified world. Merchants moved up; the literati fell into a lower orbit. Business came first. A new generation of daimyos ran for office on the Shogunate ticket, the Liberal Democratic Party that has controlled Japanese politics since the war. A new generation of generals ran the corporations like armies. The samurai workers kept the nation marching straight ahead. The city lost its visible and encoded social order, but every Japanese still knew to whom to bow and precisely how deep. The new Japan runs like America, but under the hood there's a vertical engine from a Confucian machine shop, with a carburetor like a chambered pyramid; and no one pisses from the second floor.

IV.

Noto:
The Discovery
of Peninsula X

When the day comes to leave Kanazawa, we find ourselves in lock-step with a compatriot from a previous century. "The fancy took me to go to Noto," wrote Percival Lowell, the American astronomer who first worked out the position of the ninth planet, Pluto. He had arrived in Japan in 1883, a full seven years ahead of his more celebrated countryman and fellow Japanophile, Lafcadio Hearn, and in 1889, he struck out for Japan's remote Noto Peninsula on a whim. "Scanning, one evening, in Tokyo, the map of Japan, in a vague, itinerary way, with the look one first gives to the crowd of faces in a ballroom," Lowell explained in his now forgotten narrative, "my eye was caught by the pose of a province that stood out in graphic mystery from the western coast. It made a striking figure there, with its deep-bosomed bays and its bold headlands. Its name, it appeared, was Noto; and the name too pleased me. . . . The more I looked the more I longed, until the desire carried me not simply off my feet, but on to them."

Finding ourselves entertaining a nearly identical fancy a hundred years later, we set out from Kanazawa for land's end. Booking a rattling train north, we settle back into our bench seats for the five-hour milk-run past deserted seascape and villages. We are not following precisely in Lowell's footsteps, however. For one thing, Lowell started in Tokyo, and in those days his journey to Noto required five days. "To reach this topographically charming province," he wrote, "the main island had to be crossed at its widest, and, owing to lofty mountain chains, much tacking to be done to boot."

For another thing, Lowell did not travel light. Accompanied by his cook, Yejiro, Lowell packed enough to feed a small tour group: pots and pans, homemade bread, beer, a bottle of whiskey, and a "large and motley stock of canned food." Without such a larder, Lowell explained, "my digestion would have played the devil with me," feeling as he did that foreigners were "not inwardly contrived to thrive solely on rice and pickles."

Lowell also took his own sheets and blankets for use in the Japanese inns of the time, but he refused to sleep at ground level. "The bed itself Yejiro easily improvised out of innumerable futons, as the quilts used at night by the Japanese are called," Lowell explained. "A single one is enough for a native, but Yejiro, with praiseworthy zeal, made a practice of asking for half-a-dozen, which he piled one upon the other in the middle of the room." It reminded Lowell of sleeping atop a Greek funeral pyre.

"When to the above indispensables were added clothes, camera, dry plates, books, and sundries, it made a collection of household gods [sic] quite appalling to consider on the march," Lowell admitted. "As my property lay spread out for packing, I stared at it aghast." Stuffing his belongings in interlocking wicker baskets, Lowell caught the new train that ran north from Ueno Station. By 1889 the train had already compressed days of arduous travel into a matter of hours, leading Lowell to observe that "one of the things which imitation of Western ways is annihilating is distance."

Nevertheless, much of the distance remained uncompressed. The tracks then ended at the Sea of Japan, and Lowell was forced to hire three rickshaws, at about a penny a mile, for a three-day journey west along the mountainous coast. And at times, even rickshaws proved inadequate. Lowell resorted to walking, relying on porters to haul his effects across sand dunes and over mountain passes.

Finally reaching the faraway Noto Peninsula, Lowell hurriedly passed through the "very fair-sized town" of Nanao, still Noto's capital, and pressed on for Wakura-Onsen—which happens to be our destination as well. Even then Wakura had acquired a reputation in Japan for its baths, but Lowell did not partake of them. In fact, he found precious little to admire. Wakura-Onsen was dismissed as a "collection of barnlike buildings," and at the inn where he spent his first night on Noto, he became an unwilling curiosity. Everyone from fellow guests to servants made an excuse to inspect this strange foreign specimen. Since he was apparently but the third Westerner ever to check into an inn at Wakura, the stir he created is understandable. The previous summer, two European chemistry teachers living in Kanazawa had arrived to try the spa waters. Miffed at being scooped, Lowell dismissed Wakura-Onsen as among those destinations "which have already been seen" and "were not worth seeing" in the first place.

He was wrong.

※　※　※

We detrain at Wakura-Onsen with an overnight reservation for Port Inn, but lacking a map we are lost. We ask directions from two women on the main street. They know the way to "Porto Inn," but unable to describe the route, the daughter-in-law leaves her elderly mother-in-law to wait on the corner while she, ignoring our objections, leads us the whole way herself, five blocks on foot. Port Inn is an uninviting four-story edifice of cement poured with geometric precision in the form of a massive A-frame, set on the shore of Nanao Bay, but its proprietor welcomes us warmly. Speaking a machine-gun English acquired, he says, from watching American action movies, he insists we refresh ourselves in the dining room with a cup of coffee "on the house." We join three young British women at a long common table. It is nearly noon, but they look sleepy, as though they've just gotten out of bed and have nowhere to go. They are wearing thick terry robes, the sort you don't often see in *yukata*-clad Japan, but despite appearances we assume that like us they are ordinary travelers who have somehow found their way to Noto.

Our room, on the third floor, is Westernized, meaning it contains two tiny beds, higher than any pyre of futons. Heavy glass patio doors open onto a stand-up balcony facing the bay. The bathroom is among the tiniest we've seen in Japan, but it is ingeniously outfitted with a white plastic module in which the sink nozzle swivels to fill both basin and tub. The Toto toilet handle has two flush positions, half and full. Gray water from the sink is routed to help refill the toilet tank. We unpack our luggage—just one-and-a-half pieces each, devoid of pots and pans and canned foods, and string up a short laundry line like a tightrope, then fill the tub where we soak, wring, and hang a few days' laundry. We decide to take a look at the town. As we leave, we hear the rat-a-tat bark of a tiny lap dog emanating from a locked room down the hall.

Wakura-Onsen is deserted and, like sea resorts everywhere in the down season, looks forlorn. Volcanic spa water was discovered here in 1048 AD, bubbling up from the sea, and was once barreled and shipped all over Japan. Departing from Lowell's itinerary, we promise ourselves a hot soak tonight. Wakura-Onsen contains at least one sight we've missed in other towns: a coin-operated sneaker washer. The Japanese fetish for clean feet has reached even unto Nikes and Reeboks. A special soap is dispensed by the packet.

Near a thicket of vending machines, we board the local bus for Notojima, an island in the bay where Lowell, who had hired a rowboat in order to explore Noto's inland sea, reported that "Schools of porpoises turned cart-wheels for our amusement, and in spots the water was fairly alive with baby jelly-fish." But we fail to observe a single porpoise, not even a jellyfish. Notojima is joined to the peninsula by Japan's second-longest suspension bridge, a mile across. On the other side is what has become a popular summer resort, teeming with aquariums and souvenir stands, alongside excavations dating to the Stone Age. We disembark and decide to cross the bridge on foot. Halfway across, we are confronted by a bob-tailed black cat, who eyes us and flees. Then the wind picks up. Chilled, I stop to snap a picture from the bridge, and the shutter freezes shut. I almost beat my camera to death on the railing. Lowell came to Noto with a camera, too, but there are no photographs in his book. I imagine his camera freezing up, too, and can almost see it now at the bottom of this bay.

Back on the bus, we notice a lurid poster pasted above the driver announcing the appearance of a Las Vegas-style group named "The Pride of London." The act appears to consist of six women and a black man, and the dancers displayed on the bus poster are topless. Three of their faces are quite familiar: those of the three women staying at our inn. The Port Inn is located next door to the classy Kagaya Hotel where the "Pride" performs nightly; by day, the group is put up in our cheaper digs next door. The poster also lists another headliner, "Shinko and Miki." Pictured are a perch of trained birds and a little dog—surely the same canine star who spent her daylight hours confined to the room down the hall, barking her heart out.

The Port Inn's set dinner turns out to be superb, consisting of corn soup, local fish with butter and lemon (lemon squeezer provided), two white bread rolls, a hot vegetable, a breaded roast with carrots and snow peas, ice cream, coffee, beer, whiskey, wine, and toothpicks probably honed from old-growth logs. From room to cuisine, even this minor seaside inn on a peninsula, seldom visited by foreigners, has copied with admirable skill the ways of the West.

Luckily, the Port Inn is affiliated with its rich uncle, the Kagaya Hotel next door, which extends use of its famous hot pools to guests of our humbler establishment. Fortified, we gather up our room towels and *yukatas* in plastic bags and strike out for the great baths of Kagaya, where rooms run about $500 a night—per person.

Kagaya was rebuilt in the fifty-sixth year of the Showa Emperor. In fact, Hirohito spent a night at Kagaya, in 1983; as at Hakuunro, his room is sealed off. There are many such sanctified rooms across Japan, and their locations would make for a map as interesting as the one that drew Percival Lowell to Noto. Kagaya's interior is sleekly modern—again, strictly Western on the surface—with padded furniture, marble floors, and earth-toned walls. The vast lobby contains an Oriental carpet, and in keeping with the foreign ways it emulates, guests are permitted to cross it with their shoes on. In the center of the hotel is a glass elevator that we take up and down not for a view of the Bay or the village lights, but for what is nailed to the opposite atrium wall, a touch of the Orient: a hand-painted silk kimono ten stories tall.

The great baths, one for men, one for women, lie on the other side of the shops, and are busy. Plenty of guests come and go, and I try my best to imitate them. In the lavish locker room I strip down and place a diaper of a towel on my head. The bath is Olympic-size with a waterfall at one end. I squat on a six-inch bench before one of the dozens of hand showers along the wall and soap every inch, rinsing myself from a plastic basin, scrubbing the skin hard with my towel. Clean enough to bathe, I ease myself into the pool. No one pays me the least attention there. I drift into the heat as somewhere high above, the "Pride of London" dances onto stage in silver costumes, the tiny dog in the spotlight yaps on cue, and the little birds begin to tweet.

✳   ✳   ✳

Waiting in the hotel lobby for Margaret to emerge from the women's bath, I watch others going in and out of the shops in their robes, filling their shopping bags. Most of Kagaya's guests are groups of Japanese women, middle-aged housewives who have left their salarymen husbands home. When the tour buses pull up and the groups of these ladies are marched into the lobby, they are met by a special staff of ladies in kimonos who serve as individual companions for guests during their stay. Later, when a group checks out, these smiling personal attendants line up in the lobby like a chorus, bow, and follow the guests outside. As the big buses pull away in clouds of exhaust, they wave forlornly.

Lowell departed Noto with considerably less fanfare. He spent just two nights here altogether, the first in Wakura-Onsen, the second in Nanao. In between, he spent an hour at Anamizu, where a monument to Percival Lowell stands today—although, in truth, Lowell was quite disappointed with Noto. Departing the peninsula by rickshaw, he covered forty-three miles in a flash, remarking that the "day grew more beautiful with every hour of its age." Of Noto, he would remember only "how I had pictured it to myself before starting, and then how little the facts had fitted the fancy." He did not look back.

Had Lowell lingered a few more days, perhaps he would have been less disgruntled; perhaps he would have found someone to match his general description of the Japanese people "who are among the very happiest on the face of the globe, which makes them among the most charming to meet." At any rate, we are luckier, perhaps because the train today goes as far north as the fishing village of Wajima, to its street market. It's a street market even Emperor Hirohito had to place on his itinerary in 1965.

From Wajima station, we follow two women shoppers, obviously tourists, to Asaichi-dori avenue, where the vendors have pitched their sidewalk stalls, fashioned of wooden posts and translucent plastic awnings. Rain is threatening. Among the vendors are the village grandmothers who dived for shellfish and seaweed in their youth. Now they arrange their handicrafts on straw mats spread out on the street, and begin to smile.

They smile, these grandmothers, because they know something everyone else has forgotten. Scarved, their backs bent nearly horizontal so that they can not be more than three feet tall, they smile up at the parade of shoppers with unrelenting freshness; they smile out of a mold now broken elsewhere in a Japan of downcast eyes and pressure-sealed lips. When the grandmothers of Wajima smile, their mouths blaze with golden caps from ear to ear, and one lady, who springs up like a jack-in-the-box every time I pass, begins to dance when the rain picks up. She wants me to dance with her, but I am too shy.

Just before noon, the stalls are collapsed, the vendors pack up their fresh fish and vegetables, and the old ladies roll up their mats, their lacquerware, their rope sandals, folding up their entire stores in a single cloth which they tie to their backs like rucksacks or else lash to wooden baby strollers. Stooped, they walk home. As they disappear, the avenue returns to the age of neon signs and vending machines, as if some invisible Japan of wood and straw has been spirited away.

✻   ✻   ✻

Our last night on Noto, the shore is deserted, the wind down, the sky open to the stars. It seems impossible that Lowell came away disappointed, but then the secret of his journey is that he was in love with the idea of Noto, with the abstract Noto he plotted out before he ever left his study. No Noto could ever equal what he had imagined. He was enchanted with the very name: "I liked its vowel color," he wrote. "I liked its consonant form, the liquid *n* and the decisive *t*." He was in love with its topographical form, its "coquettishly irregular" coastline, and imagined that there could be "no happier linking of land to water." Most of all he was in love with its position on the map, "standing alone in peninsular isolation," and its obscurity, "almost unvisited by Europeans,—an out-of-the-world state." He ended up enjoying the journey far more than the destination, the reckoning far more than the actual place.

So it would be with Pluto, too, the last world discovered in our solar system. Lowell dubbed it "Planet X" and located it numerically in a far corner where he would never see it, even through the lens of a telescope. Two years after predicting the location of Planet X, Lowell died, and fourteen years later, in 1930, another astronomer discovered the elusive last planet, just where it was predicted to be, while working at the Lowell Observatory in Flagstaff, Arizona. Percival had founded that observatory in 1894, a year after his return from Japan.

Noto was Lowell's Peninsula X on earth, just as Pluto became his Planet X in the heavens. He relished those remote worlds that he could project from his charts and color with his own imaginings. Had he lived to see Pluto, as he had Noto, he would have been disappointed again: just a point of light, reflected by the coldest of the planets, with not even the hint of an *onsen*.

Our last night on Noto we locate the handle of the Great Dipper, but not Pluto. Pluto has never been seen by the naked eye, of course— a perfect world for a mathematical dreamer like Lowell. But we can see and feel Noto. Like much of Japan, it has its own complicated weave of realities, ancient and modern, East and West. Imitation of Western ways has indeed annihilated distance, as Lowell pointed out, for on any given day Noto can now receive emissaries from the far corners of the world—a couple from Oregon, a troupe from Piccadilly Circus.

We depart Noto in the morning. The train clanks to its first stop, Tatsuruhama, where a dozen school children catch sight of us. They coalesce, clamber up the wooden fence along the track, shout and grin. I jump up and walk to the opening between cars, raise my camera. They go wild, shout the sound so silly to their ears ("Hello, hello"), and laugh. I pretend to snap frame after frame with my empty camera, their red school jackets loud against the black tile of the village roofs. They flash the V-sign and the train jerks away.

My camera shutter is still shut, black as a hole in space. It records nothing of Noto, but the eye engraves its own negative, boring deeper than any instrument or chart, an image of the new Noto superimposed on the old—a perfect fit, standing out, as Percival puts it, "in graphic mystery from the western coast."

V.

Toyama:
Singing in the Suburbs

A t Tsubata, north of Kanazawa, we change for Toyama, heading east for the first time. We board a less interesting, faster, smoother train, its interior as fastidious as white linen, the woman pushing the concession cart down the aisle bowing as she enters each car.

Dino lies in wait for us at Toyama. His wife is fixing dinner in the suburbs. Dino tells us he has lived in Toyama since he was six. He remembers the American bombings; we leveled plenty of towns then. His two children are teenagers. His daughter he hardly mentions; she will marry next year. His son plays in the youth orchestra and dad wants to find him a college in America. Dino has visited forty-nine countries, he says. When he retires, he wants to open his house to visiting students from around the world. His house cost some fifty million yen. He has a new car, with a few features unavailable in the American models; tiny wipers sweep rain drops off the wing windows, creating a clean path to the rear view mirrors. When we ask him what happens to used cars in Japan—we have hardly seen one— he's irritated and puzzled. "Ship them to the Third World," he supposes.

Driving into the suburbs, for the first time on our journey we experience a remarkable sense of familiarity. The six-lane highway, the clusters of shops and malls, the road signs and neon advertisements, the open terrain: we could be in Kansas or California. Indeed, we have sunk into just that familiar a world, at the edge of home. I remember that during the time I lived in China, I experienced an even higher degree of absorption when I attended a performance of Tang Dynasty dancers put on for tourists in downtown Xi'an. Suspended in a sea of large Americans, I felt a complete alienation from my countrymen; I had become as a Chinese. Now, in the suburbs of Toyama, surrounded by Japanese, I had become like them, an imitation American—yet at heart, invisibly, something far apart.

Dino's house is spacious in every way, something the apartment dwellers of Greater Tokyo can live in only in their dreams or in the American cinema. He gives us the grand tour. There are rooms he doesn't even use. Tony's den includes a wall of swiveling bookcases. His is the big house you'd find in any upper middle-class suburb in the States. I count five color televisions and three VCRs. Still, there are Japanese touches. We park our shoes and walk through in plush slippers; while there's an electric dryer, it isn't used much; and, despite the lavish wealth of the place, there's no central heat—just space heaters in every room. The bathroom embodies this divided world. There's an Eastern-style toilet on one side and American toilet on the other, rigged with a heated thermostatically-controlled seat that contains a built-in bidet. The bidet is operated from a high-tech control panel and consists of a jet nozzle tucked under the rim that shoots a spray of water and dries you with warm air. Better than toilet paper, says Dino, and gentle on hemorrhoids. The heated toilet seat-cum-bidet comes in ten designer colors—yours for about a thousand dollars.

Dino's wife is lovely. She's fixed us an elaborate meal of meat and vegetables, simmering at the table on an electric griddle. I notice a microwave in the kitchen. After dinner we retire to the unheated living room. Dino's son has his books spread out on the *kotatsu*. Dino's daughter shows us an album of her engagement party. We admire her kimono in the pictures. Dino's wife brings out a picture from her mother's wedding, and later, her mother's hand-painted kimono, the one she was married in, too. We are all kneeling on the carpet, except Dino's wife, who is clearing the table and cleaning up. We think of Beverly, back in the sky lounge over Kanazawa.

Then it's time to visit Dino's favorite Toyama bar. We'd rather stay with his wife and children, but they don't speak English. Dino's son comes along as driver. He drops us off downtown, in a sleazy back alley section of countless bars, where men, just off work at eight, are cruising for a home away from home. Dino's bar is one of the small ones where each customer lodges his own bottle behind the counter. The middle-aged ladies behind the bar know him and the other customers and do their best to keep up a conversation with their customers, all men of course. It's a dreadful place if you're not a salaryman; Dino and a pal he meets love it. They drop in most evenings, it seems, and take a turn at karaoke, the "empty orchestra" of high technology, in which a laser disk broadcasts music and video, complete with the bouncing ball. The amplifier is equipped with echo enhancement, and the customers take turns at singing ballads in English. The laser disks are double-formatted, meaning that much to our chagrin they broadcast the songs on the color monitor in the format of your choice, one with dreamy landscape scenes, the other soft pornography. The porno wins out most of the time, and the customers sing like Frank Sinatra as young ladies, Japanese or American, bare their bodies to their lovers. We're not sure what the vivacious middle-age ladies behind the bar will do as the evening lengthens. Mostly they just chat in the gentlemen's ears, try to induce us to sing into the microphones, or dance quite innocently when asked by a partner. Dino's voice, of course, is smooth and deep. Everyone loves him here. As we leave, he tells us that he brought his wife here once and for reasons that completely mystify him she didn't like it at all.

It seems to us a sort of samurai existence in modern dress. Dino's a top retainer of the new order of daimyos—the business owners with dark political connections. He's a master of the foreigner's lingo and comfortable with Americans and Europeans, but here's where he checks his sword, with the modern geishas who fawn and pet the grown-up, prurient little boys who serve the latest shogunate.

Dino puts us in a cab for the hotel, then recedes into the center of Toyama. The men in suits and ties are still weaving like sharks in a cage of streets. Before departing, we ask Dino about the future: will Japan become the wealthiest nation of the twenty-first century? He thinks not. He says it is all a bubble, soon to burst, no one knows precisely when, but soon. Wealth is always a temporary condition. Then he says, out of nowhere, that if he were to be reborn, he'd want to be born a singer in America, free to make his own way. "Which," he adds, "is the single most terrifying thought I have ever had."

VI.

Takayama:
Mirror of the Gods

The guidebooks give Toyama the shortest shrift of any city its size in Japan, ostensibly because there's so little to see there: two sentences of text, an hour's worth of touring. Toyama's sole fault is that it was leveled by American bombing raids, then rebuilt from scratch in the high-tech era. The past is barely visible. A century ago, when Percival Lowell passed through Toyama on his return from Noto, he described "the old feudal capital" as "still a bustling town" doing "a brisk business . . . in patent medicine," but even he concluded that "the former splendor of the place has left it forever." Today as yesterday, Toyama serves the traveler merely as a gate to the Japanese Alps, and we dutifully board the train for the interior, for Takayama, which means High Mountain. When we pull in, the village reminds us of a Swiss ski town, quaint as an Old World postcard.

We walk a solid fifteen minutes to our inn, a family-run *minshuku*, away from town and across a bridge into the less-than-quaint sprawl, along a busy thoroughfare lined with 7-Elevens, Nissan showrooms, and a Shell gas station with digital pumps and young uniformed attendants at the ready to clean not just your windows but your floor mats and to step out into traffic and clear the way for your exit. Our inn, however, is in keeping with Takayama's historical image, the building 150 years old, its entry like that of an Edo era farmhouse. We are shown a matted room on the second floor. The place is old and dark and actually rather dusty, even grimy. The toilets and sinks are down the hall; so's the bath.

We've so little time and the sun is so glorious we head back to town as soon as we check in. The inn is empty anyway, dozing in the quiet of noon. Takayama was born in the sixteenth century and during the Edo period supported a score of wealthy merchants, who routinely bribed the shogunate inspectors so that they could build and maintain showy, solid houses. Many of these houses still stand and now line three narrow lanes in the San-machi-suji district, where the tourists—entirely Japanese this afternoon—always take a stroll. The custom house of the shogunate's official also stands, the oldest of its kind in Japan, kept clean and showy, but still with its eathern floors, open beams, the rice granary for payment of the village tax, and even the torture chambers of the district jail.

Yet Takayama was not a rice capital, despite the granary; it depended on lumber, woodcarving, lacquerwork, and related crafts, and those became the main tributes it paid to the distant Edo empire. The woodcarvers of Takayama were routinely exported to decorate temples and great pavilions. Fortunately, they left an imprint on their streets back home. The eighteenth-century buildings of Takayama are dark—the wood so dark it looks black under the burning sun—but the fine latticework over windows and at entryways is arrow straight and thin, light as a silk thread. There are eight old sake factories along here, each announcing its trade by means of a huge cedar globe suspended over the entrance. As the fronds dry out, the sphere turns from green to brown, signaling the maturity of the brew. We enter one or two factories, but no one much is around this afternoon, or else they are in the back somewhere, beside the vats, taking lunch.

It's difficult to hurry in these streets of the past, even though we have so little time. Once we are waylaid by three young girls who want us to snap their picture beside the figurine of *maneki neko,* the beckoning cat with the waving paw that merchants have adopted to bring fortune and friends into their shops. Since this is our favorite emblem—and this specimen, carved from a large block of black wood, is unusual—we can hardly resist. The girls giggle. Each lifts a curved hand to her ear and sits down, striking the pose of Japan's most ubiquitous cat. The tale of *maneki neko* comes in several versions; in the most popular, a grand lady of Yoshiwara is saved by her favorite feline who is killed defending her from a venomous snake. She carves its likeness in wood as a memorial and a charm, but the connection between such a sweet story and the attraction of money is obscure. A deeper connection exists in Japanese folklore, where the cat is portrayed as the figure who seduces the passerby—who entices the customer. The alluring cat is then unmasked as an enchantress of another order: as a witch, a geisha, or even a vampire.

We avoid traipsing through the shops ourselves, save one on a side street. Without a clue to what is for sale, we go in. A craftsman sits cross-legged on a raised platform against one wall. He is bent over some small aspect of his work, and it is clear he doesn't want to be disturbed; neither can he turn us out. He is neither a master carver of wood nor an artist of the clear lacquer for which Takayama is famous; rather, he applies woodblock prints to fabric and paper. He concentrates on shaping and decorating just two everyday items: cloth animals of the zodiac, which then are stuffed solid with sawdust, and exquisite papier-mache pencil or candy trays, light as balsam, ideal for a desk or table top. The trays are tough; we guess that they begin as newspaper pulped with resin and dried over a mold. The bottom is sealed in a dark brown craft paper and the inside is lined with a block print. The block prints are unpretentious and distinct folk scenes of Hida-Takayama, with solid black outlines and two or three colors: blues, yellows, greens, or reds, depending on the subject. The colors are so pale they seem extracted from mountain roots. The scenes are of a rice festival float, dabbed red, or of a fisherman in a wild river canyon, with greens and yellows, or of a village under faint mountain peaks, or of the inside of a farmhouse with a woman and her cat by the open hearth; or of a horse hauling a sled loaded with pottery from a mountain kiln.

We can't tell what the artist is doing, but it is clear we shouldn't disturb him until we select our trays. His head is bent into the detail of his work. The process takes us back to primary school, the last time we used papier-mache ourselves. Margaret remembers fashioning a mold from her own face—a paper mask of herself. I remember shaping the skeleton of a small horse from a wire coat hanger and fleshing it over with wet newspaper shreds, the smell of the glue, the blond desk with the open shelves beneath. We did no woodcuts to decorate our creations. I used bright paint, green and red. It was a rounded horse, without features, artless as a club.

We pick out a dozen trays; the craftsman nods, rises, and writes down the total price, shows us the numerals, counts out a dozen matching wood-block stamped sheets of wrapping paper, and carefully slides everything into one large shopping bag embossed too with a matching mountain woodcut. When he gives us back too much change—a most unusual occurrence—we return the excess, but immediately regret it; he acts stunned, perhaps even losing a little face.

Back on the narrow eighteenth-century lane, a shopkeeper in a long sturdy brown apron dips a gallon ladle on the end of a wooden handle into the gutters and sprinkles down the sidewalk. Two old women in heavy kimonos pass on geta. The concrete road, lined by the two-story black houses and moat-like gutters, is so narrow it seems to float on a hidden river.

✳ ✳ ✳

In Takayama, the gods of rice came down from their mountain dwellings just twice a year, spring and fall, to mingle with the farmers. The farmers charmed them down with Shinto magic, as well as with the promises of riotous and elaborate entertainments. This was the origin of the festival, or *matsuri*, here as everywhere in Japan—a means to placate the gods of fertility and sustenance. With the ascendancy of the merchant and artisan class, especially during Japan's centralization in the Edo Period, the farmer's festival came into the city and became a spectacular display of wealth as much as faith. Because of Takayama's isolation and stability, it has retained not only a large degree of festival tradition, but a large number of the original festival floats, which to this day remain the property and responsibility of the neighborhood families that originally built them.

The Takayama festival is centered on the Hachiman Shrine, which dates back to the fourth century, but was enlarged and rebuilt in its present image in 1683. We crisscross small streams, lined by the backs of houses, more idyllic than anything in Suzhou or the other "Venices of the East," and find the Hachiman shrine. On its grounds is the museum of festival floats where four of the twenty-three are enshrined in a rotating display. Come April and September, the 65,000 residents of this high mountain village somehow accommodate 300,000 guests for two days of *matsuri*, offering prayers for a bountiful harvest in the spring and a thanksgiving as winter drives close. We're here out of either season, but on the right day to find a Ms. Suzuki, an English-speaking docent born in the village.

The tall floats of Takayama are among the most splendid in Japan. Most are two and three centuries old, each owned by a neighborhood. The kids in the new suburbs were always jealous of the kids in the old town, Ms. Suzuki remembers, because they had no floats of their own. The town kids were allowed to don dragon masks and lead the parade of floats in a dance. Some of them were chosen to ride on the floats as well. A thousand locals put the parade in motion. Dozens of families own the wide-shouldered ceremonial jackets, skirts, and round straw hats of the samurai who escort the procession across the many crimson-railed bridges.

The floats are built on wheeled carriages that require as many as twenty strong backs to pull. Even the immense wagon wheels are decorated with gold plate and wooden carvings. The floats look like two- and three-story pavilions with balconies and enclosed chambers. The friezes and mounted statues on the lower tiers recount local legends and many of the great myths of Japan; the top tier is typically an airy cupola capped with a curving roof, where sometimes marionettes perform. Ms. Suzuki tells us that the tapestries which form the walls of the float chambers were woven not on a loom but on the fingernails of weavers who produced at the rate of an inch a week.

The most marvelous of the floats is *Hotei Tai*, named for the pot-bellied god of good fortune who rides just below the top story. On the top story, three large wooden marionettes, wearing silk and brocade, prance out on a beam, spin and dance and perform the most lifelike feats before they tumble into space, landing on the shoulders of the god below—who then waves his military fan and releases a streamer on which the year's special message is imprinted. Inside the float are eight master puppeteers who manipulate thirty-six invisible strings on which the puppets prance, leap, and somersault as though enchanted.

This is entertainment today for the crowds from the cities, but once it was for the delight of the gods. The stories the puppeteers of Takayama tell on these floats are of mountain hermits, beautiful maidens, and laughing gods. Their origins are in the indigenous Shinto worship, but Ms. Suzuki says there's not much religious meaning left. Perhaps she's just too close to see. To us, it is still a mix of Japanese history and its spirit culture, straight from Shinto, from the roots of nature. The floats carry representatives of emperors, empresses, and their ministers and courts, of swords and armor and drums, of celestial horses, phoenixes, dragons, and cranes, of plum blossoms, dogs, turtles, and leaping carp. Another order of floats—the *mikoshi*—carry the gods themselves. These portable floats are shouldered by the Shinto priests and monks. The Takayama festival begins, in fact, when the neighborhood priests transfer their shrine gods into these festival palanquins. The gods have been lured down from the hills and trees by a variety of rituals—purification by water, incantations, even the zigzags of white paper pasted on the floats which act as magnets through the ether. A round mirror represents the shrine god, and that is what the priest carries from altar to portable shrine. No one is allowed to look at the mirror as it is ferried through the streets.

What would one see in this mirror of the gods, this inner-looking glass? In any outer mirror, one would merely see what Japan has undertaken to reflect today: the once distant modern world. But whose face is in the inner mirror? What do the gods really look like? Is it their inhuman faces that lie behind all that Japan has mirrored, East to West, from China to America? And why these mirrors and the act of mirroring? Without reflection would there be nothing at all?

The lions dance to the sound of music from the Imperial Court and the beat of drums that once accompanied cockfights. The samurai reappear as escort. The farmers push and pull on the high floats. The pretty puppets advance like perfect little robots on hidden sinews, tiptoe to the edge, and jump.

*　*　*

We have missed the festivals of Takayama, which carry into the night, illuminated by a hundred lanterns on each great float. The sun is setting. We rush back through another neighborhood, less antiquated but containing the thick-walled garages with locked doors twenty and thirty feet high where most of the floats are stored. The boys play baseball out front and yell "hello!" as we pass. Our dinner is waiting in the main matted room downstairs. There are two other couples at the low table and a businessman. One couple is young, early twenties, unmarried, but it seems acceptable to travel that way these days. The middle-aged couple who own the *minshuku*, which is their home, certainly don't mind. They serve us an elaborate, largely vegetarian meal, then pass out hotel registration forms. Since our reading of Japanese is poor, we seek help from another couple, who turn out to be from Hong Kong. After dinner we all gather around the open hearth, the *irori*, where tea is heating on the coals and the kettle is suspended from an iron hook. The hook is decorated with an enormous trout, a traditional icon. Nearly all Japanese houses once had the open pit for cooking in the middle of the room, and the fish represented the presence of water which might douse the fire should it threaten to burn down the house.

Only the Japanese businessman is fully comfortable in the inn, I think; he alone comes down as one should to sip tea, outfitted in his *yukata* and slippers, having bathed. The rest of us—Americans, Hong Kong Chinese, young unmarried Japanese—are breaking our knees trying to relax on a mat around a smoky fire. The businessman is snap-

ping away on his camera, so I bring mine down to see if he can fix it—
or at least make a diagnosis, which he can't. . . . It is a black box and
records no images.

None of the three couples speaks the others' languages fluently,
and so we are reduced to working from what we share. Hong Kong
and Japan share the characters of a written language, but the characters receive different sounds and often very different meanings between the cultures. Of course, nearly everyone can read a little English—not just from school, but through the bombardment of American pop culture and marketing. If we can't make the best cameras,
cars, and VCRs in the world, at least we can market them like no one
else, with unrivaled athletes and performers at our command—an
arsenal of glitz.

The couple from Hong Kong turn out to be a journalist and a
newspaper editor. We know Hong Kong well enough to chat with
them for days, and so when the man from *The Japan Times* comes by to
take them out on the town, we're invited. We must first clear everything with our innkeepers; they must agree to keep the doors unbarred
until midnight. We promise not to require a bath when we return, and
while they are shocked that we would skip it, they are relieved. We
make a joke about Cinderella and midnight, and everyone suddenly
shares a word and story in common.

Of course, we end up spending the whole evening in a bar. At
least it is not a bar for men only, nor does it offer the sing-along flesh-
pot videos. There's some good *yaki-tori* and a rather raw supply of
spring sake served as it should be in square wooden boxes. When we
get back, we talk about the Japanese reputation for cleanliness and
agree that it isn't perfect at all, at least at the level we travel, on the
bottom; and in fact Japan is not entirely clean in public, either, where
litter and garbage are rather common. Perhaps the Japanese, and travelers from polluted cities of their own, have the ability to tunnel through
to beauty wherever they turn, but we do not; our eyes open wide and
perhaps do not focus on beauty alone as they should.

When we retire, Margaret examines the quilt that covers our futon
mattress on the floor. The sheet on the futon is clean enough, but there
is never a top sheet as in the West, and so we are at the mercy of
whoever or whatever has slept under the top quilt before us. The quilt
has its own cover, but it is too fancy to wash every day. Sometimes the
pillow—occasionally hard, filled with beans—has an uncleaned cover

as well. Walking the streets, one sees quilts draped out of windows on sunny days, freshened by nature, if not by detergent.

I sneak down the hall after midnight and locate a cabinet door. I extract a clean quilt cover to serve as a top sheet and steal back in, the black floorboards giving me away with their nightingale calls. . . . We hear the Hong Kong couple talk half the night, as if they haven't bedded down at all.

In the morning I wake to the chime of a bronze bell. I slide back a screen and from the *minshuku* window look down upon a small temple, its curved roof tiled in metal for the mountain snows. The temple backs into a graveyard, as most do, and in the middle of the graves is the unwalled pavilion housing the temple bell. This bell tower has the most graceful sweeping roof I've seen in Takayama. It is a Buddhist temple, that much I can tell—there's a shaven-headed young monk down there calling to a white cat—and there's an older monk up in the tower striking the morning bell with a stick.

VII.

Sado:
Island at the End of the World

Our innkeeper in Takayama insists on driving us to the train in his station wagon, which turns out against all odds to be a Ford. Add a top sheet, subtract the cobwebs, and it's a fine B & B, all for about the price of a night in a Swiss chalet, where you can wake to bells, too—those worn by cows. It's natural enough to think of Switzerland here, in Japan's Alps, not just because of order and mountain scenery, but because of what it costs the rest of the world to visit.

For Americans the meter is always running in Japan. It's an experience similar to visiting New York City from a small town and finding there are no Motel Sixes or fifty-nine-cent hamburgers. In visiting Japan, we have come to rely on bottom-of-the-rung inns and *minshukus*, noodle shops, vending machines, bakeries, and supermarkets or Circle Ks for processed cheese, crackers, cartons of milk, bags of cookies, overripe bananas, and bread. With our limitations in mind and our pocketbooks calibrated to a month's circuit back to Tokyo, we leave Takayama after a single night knowing it's a mistake—Takayama is the first town in Japan we immediately regret not staying twice as long in—but something is pushing us on, something that can eat at a traveler like worms, urging him onward regardless of what he discovers, beyond all sense, like a father who never stops the car on vacation. We are charging on, perhaps because we don't know where we are going; maybe, up ahead, we will find out. "Go far from Tokyo," our poet said. We have. But we still haven't heard the laugh of ghosts nor reached some Zensational vanishing point.

We board the 7:44 for Toyama and it pulls out of Takayama at 7:44. At 10:03 we reach Dino's nondescript town again and switch east for Niigata—land of rice now, the modern Kaga—arriving at this seaport barely in time to find the bus to the harbor. There the ferry boat to Sado Island pulls away at 15:45, arriving two hours twenty minutes later. Tickets are about thirteen dollars apiece. There's a jet boat that makes the passage, too, takes an hour and twenty minutes less, and costs almost exactly three times as much—nevertheless, a popular choice. Sado Island, the historical outpost of those exiled from the civilized capitals of the south, the hoary prison in the bitter northern Sea of Japan, has become a leading summer getaway for those now imprisoned in the high-rise cells of Tokyo. A lavish color brochure describes the Sado Island Jet Liner Service, Tourist Area No. 301, just three hours from Tokyo via the Joetsu Shinkansen bullet train and jet foil, disembarking at the port of Ogi where villagers still take to the inlets to scoop up seaweed, shells, and abalone from tub boats—round wooden washtubs looking like California redwood hot tubs. For four hundred yen, Tokyo tourists can even board a tub and try a little Sado fishing, and, according to the brochure, "Your heart will warm at the peaceful, unsophisticated village life." There are, in addition, placer gold mines where today's visitors can rent their own wooden gold pan.

Fortunately, we've arrived before high season, and our fellow passengers seem to be locals rather than sightseers. Our ship, a massive modern car ferry capable of cruising at 22 knots, is a bit of a shock inside. Not a chair or bench in sight. The interior has been stripped of seats and tables and everything has been lowered to the floor-level, Japanese style. The expansive passenger saloons are outfitted with rectangular platforms like raised garden beds, carpeted in green. We select a platform, remove our shoes, and sit down. Blankets are for rent, and we spring for two. The procedure here is to spread out your blanket, grab a plastic pan as your pillow, and take a nap or have a picnic. There's nothing to see on the voyage; at this reclined level, at least, the portal windows are too high to permit a view of anything but the sky.

When we dock at Ryotsu, the island's big city, the sun is setting, but we have a glimpse of two large mountain ranges, the peaks in snow, lending to Sado a substantial dimension: this is no small island. It must have been a fierce place of banishment for the ex-Emperor Juntoku and the Buddhist priest Nichiren in the thirteenth century, or

Two jizo statues in the snow at the Koyasan graveyard.

Nara's Todai-ji Temple—the world's largest wood structure.

Kyoto's Golden Temple.

A craftsman at Kanazawa's Kutani Pottery and Kosen Kiln.

Fish vendor at Wajima's morning market, Noto Peninsula.

A Western saying, carved in wood at Nikko.

Cherry blossom season in Tokyo's Ueno Park.

A typical downtown shopping arcade in Ueno, Tokyo.

Joggers greet the foreigners in Fukuoka.

Potters' graves in Okawachiyama's village of the secret kilns.

A Confucian shrine in Nagasaki.

The steaming crater of Mount Aso.

Shinto priest at Kumamoto's Suizen-ji Garden's Temple.

Samurais seated at Yatsushiro's Myoken festival.

Horse running during Yatsushiro's Myoken festival.

Mount Sakurajima erupting above Kagoshima.

for the homeless of Tokyo who were conscripted to toil in the gold mines by the Tokugawa shogunate three hundred years ago. What survives are simple folk traditions—dances, songs, and festivals, thought to have been passed on from as far away as the southern island of Kyushu and the ancient capital of Nara ten centuries ago and preserved here. We are too early in the year to attend these rites: the tub boat festivals, the lion dances or the *Mano Ondo* where the dancers take to the seashore with hundred pound *Jizo Bosatsu* statues (guardian of young children) strapped to their backs. Nor will we see the *Tsuburosashi*, surely one of Japan's most ancient rites, in which a man in a white mask and red-splashed kimono dances with two goddesses and a Shinto priest as he holds erect from his pelvis the two-foot wooden *tsuburo*, a holy dildo of fertility.

By this point, it is certain that we have condemned ourselves to being the sort of travelers who miss everything. An insistence on journeying out of season, a refusal to wrap ourselves up in a package tour, a lack of wealth and inside connections, avoidance of many of the top attractions: is this why we sense only the disappearance of Japan? We think not. We believe that by traveling along the edge we are less likely to fall into the great mirrors, the beautiful copies of America and China that dazzle the unwary outsider or delight the Japanese themselves. At the same time, we do not live here, we plant no roots, and we do not go far enough inward to become even for a moment Japanese. Instead, we rely on motion, we ride the waves of change, from place and event to place and event, closing a circle, looking in toward the center when permitted. The motion of our travel creates its own tenuous order, but of course it is not necessarily the order of truth. We too undergo an enchantment which blurs our vision, one eye East, one eye West, past and present always parting, with the darkness of evening in between dulling the sharpness of island peaks and the white razor-edged snows.

Out of the darkness we are met unexpectedly by the manager of the seaside inn we booked from Takayama; he drives us out of Ryotsu in his tiny van, along a narrow unlit highway. We try out our spoken Japanese, expanded only slightly these past weeks, but growing more natural; when we switch to English, the conversation sinks. The lobby of this resort *minshuku* has filled with villagers who partake of the hotel's large public bath before dinner, families with children, a raucous bunch. There are electronic games popping and booming off to one side. Our room comes with balcony, paper towels and even

Kleenex, disposable pre-pasted toothbrushes, and, best of all, its own deep tiny tiled and quiet bathtub into which we later pour ourselves, one at a time, knees drawn up, elbows in. Dinner, an additional fifteen hundred yen each, consists of pickles, Sado's own renowned Wakame seaweed mixed with sliced cucumber and a sauce of vinegar, sugar, and salt, not to mention grilled fish, raw fish, fried fish, and a boiled fish with vegetables and garnishes in a clear miso soup. We swim back to our room and into our futons on the floor. On the wall are posted instructions for an emergency:

If an earthquake occurs:
Obey the instructions we will be a worker.

In the morning we walk back down the coastal road to Ryotsu. Low clouds have closed over Sado Island, from which a foggy mist is squeezed. We board a local bus that takes an hour to cross the waist of the island to Aikawa on the western shore. At the dawn of the seventeenth century, only ten houses stood here, but gold was discovered in 1601, and the new Tokugawa Shogunate was quick to exploit the strike, conscripting miners among the floating population of the capital and shutting them up in the mines. Aikawa boomed, reaching a population of 100,000, making it for a time one of the larger cities in Asia. When the veins were stripped, Aikawa declined. Ten thousand people remain today. The narrow road to the gold mines is lined with temples and ends at a miners' cemetery. Nearby is Golden Sado, a drift mine once owned by the Imperial Household, where conscripts by the thousands dug and bailed out water from the shafts; bought by the Mitsubishi corporation, it is active today, and caters to tourists by means of an underground display of old mining methods demonstrated in fine Japanese fashion by life-sized robots in period costume.

We decide not to visit the puppets in the cave. Instead, we examine the schedule at the Aikawa bus terminal and catch a ride north to take in the celebrated seascapes of Senkaku Bay. Our plan is to wander via the local bus lines as far up the coast as we dare, grabbing the last possible bus back before dark. The shoreline is volcanic, a rough lava terrace honed by the cold wind and waves into a spectrum of reefs, cliffs, grottoes, and sea castles. In the early spring, it wears a desolate expression. The farming and fishing villages along the edges seem forlorn, deserted.

For perhaps an hour we allow the bus to move us north along this unknown coast, without any destination in mind, stopping on the shoulder of the road at each stop, picking up and disgorging no more than a handful of locals along the way. Finally, checking my watch, we elect to get out at a village of no discernible importance, attracted merely by its ideal setting in the arms of the sea cliffs. For most of the way, I have been lulled by the familiarity of the spectacular scenery, for it is almost a carbon copy of the Pacific I know along the Oregon and Washington coasts, the states of my birth and my home—as if here, even nature has conspired to mirror the world beyond, the empire thousands of miles away.

Hardly a soul stirs in this seaside town. Long wooden open boats for fishing are tied, empty, on the shingles of the shore, where massive concrete forms the shape of jacks have been piled as riprap. The village practices intensive agriculture all the way down to the water's edge, with greenhouse frames the shape of low Quonset huts now bare of their plastic wrappings, stacked like ribs between the tile-roofed houses. There are a few barns in town, but we can't see what animals lounge within. A farmer or a farmer's bent-back wife passes us as we nose about, keeping a shy distance. Up the hill, we spy a worn stone stairway to a torii gate, guarded by the rain-savaged statues of two temple dogs, and the modest temple itself beyond, with two stone lanterns on either side. The temple is closed today or at least at this hour, a wide bamboo shade pulled down over its entrance. The wooden walls have been blistered a seaside gray by the salt winds and sideways rain that blow in here for weeks at a time.

I know the terrain and I sense something of these small rural towns, too, having been raised in the midst of them, albeit on a different continent in a different society. Yet the bleakness, the remoteness, the simplicity, the shyness of farmers, the harshness of this old life and the closeness of uncultivated nature, contained by the sea to the west and the steep hills to the east, a modern road between, the weathered houses close and nearly indistinguishable from weathered barns and weathered outbuildings—all of this would have been understood instantly by my grandfather, who farmed and mined and logged in the equally unnoticed and dim country places where the Pacific ends. Here, the North Pacific announces its beginnings, drumming against the first island shore it meets.

The villagers have done the neat job of channeling the natural seascape to their benefit, a feat we would expect of the Japanese: from the hillsides down to the sea they have dredged and lined with hand-fitted stone a series of beds for runoff and irrigation, slicing up the town, the fields, the houses. Looking north from the main road toward the sea, I notice the patchwork of low rice and vegetable fields, fenced off with twisted posts, mats of straw laid against the rails as wind break, and in the distance, where three monolithic towers of cooled lava rise from the sea and seem to point inland, right at the edge of the shore I can make out some stone and tile buildings, a temple or shrine, and running along the beach like flecks of ink from a brush the outlines of the town's grave markers.

Not a soul speaks to us; we hardly pass anyone. There's nothing that looks like a store or noodle shop. The village is too real, perhaps, for the mere traveler. For me, it is enough to be here. The sun breaks through and warms us as we wait for the returning bus. We wait twenty minutes, then twenty more. The schedule we carry and the times affixed to the bus stop sign do not match what we observe. No buses pass. We begin to worry about spending the night in this village. No taxis here, and hardly a car has passed. The village itself is indifferent to our fate, nearly unpopulated, but we sense that it could become hospitable once we admit our distress. As the bus from the north suddenly rounds the cliff and bears down on us, empty of passengers, I can still see the graves along the beach, small towers in sympathetic reflection of the great towers left standing in the wake of the waves which have raked and sawn this tilted end of the earth long before human thought became aware of itself, aware of its fate: not just to change, but to die; not just to die, but to be pulverized and obliterated, leveled without a trace; as a species, unable to outlast even these dumb sea stones.

Oddest of all is the silence of this village. Subtract the traffic of the road, its silence seems so deep as to be unconscious. We both feel for a moment that we've reached the most remote point on earth, though it lacks walls of ancient ice or the dark heat of the jungle's belly. This coast is a familiar place we can't name where we walk like ghosts through a stranger's dream.

VIII.

Nikko:
The Perfect
Colouring of Passionate Life

We turn south, closing the final quadrant of our circle, crossing the sea back to Niigata. At the ferry docks, we are slow to find our way to the shuttle buses, which are chock-full and leave us standing alone on the curb, save for the two bus men who have been directing passengers. They motion to us not to worry. They complete their paperwork, remove their uniforms, and head for the parking lot, bidding us to follow. We all pile into a station wagon. Later we think they were just curious about us, the two Americans out of season, and during the thirty minute ride to the train terminal, we exchange limited English and limited Japanese.

One step from Tokyo, our destination today is the fabled city of Nikko, "one of the paradises of Japan," according to that great Victorian traveler, Isabella Bird, who, single and middle-aged, reached here on June 13, 1878. She was on her way north—very far north—to the remote island of Hokkaido where she would mingle with the Aino, Japan's aboriginal people. Compared to her, we are the tamest, most ordinary travelers, passengers on a comfortable train confined to the beaten track.

It was otherwise for Isabella. She set out north from Tokyo eleven years earlier than our previous phantom traveler, Percival Lowell, and this was well before any train could assist her. Distance had not yet been annihilated, although there were plenty of imitations of Western ways in Japan, which drove Ms. Bird as far from Tokyo as she could travel. The Tokyo she observed in 1878 already teemed with copies of two worlds: "red mail carts like those in London," a "squadron of

cavalry in European uniforms and with European saddles," the ministers, the military, the civil service, the police, all in European costume. It was as if she had landed in Edinburgh, in her native Scotland,
and found everyone, including the servants of Her Royal Majesty,
donning kimonos and getas, toting swords, shaving their foreheads
and knotting back their hair, and doing so with perfect seriousness.
The intrusion of Western ways in nineteenth-century Japan provoked
no favorable reaction from Ms. Bird. "Carriages and houses in English
style, with carpets, chairs, and tables, are becoming increasingly nu-
merous," she remarked, "and the bad taste which regulates the purchase of foreign furnishings is as marked as the good taste which everywhere presides over the adornment of the houses in purely Japanese style." At Nikko, she had the chance to reside in one of these
"purely Japanese" houses, and to see the temples that, to many, represent the highest achievement of Japanese architecture and adornment.

In preparing for her sojourn, she faced what she dubbed the "Food
Question," of what to take into the Japanese wilds where "the fishy
and vegetable abominations known as 'Japanese food' can only be
swallowed and digested by a few, and that after long practice." In
retrospect, however, she made amends for this slight. "After several
months of travelling in some of the roughest parts of the interior," she
stated, "I should advise a person in average health—and none other
should travel in Japan—not to encumber himself with tinned meats,
soups, claret, or any eatables or drinkables, except Liebig's extract of
meat."

✳   ✳   ✳

In the end, however, Isabella Bird did not travel light over the
unbeaten tracks of Japan. She packed a store of that strange extract of
meat, four pounds of raisins, some chocolate, and "brandy in case of
need." She took with her a folding chair, an air pillow she used for
rickshaw travel, "an india-rubber bath, sheets, a blanket, and last, and
more important than all else, a canvas stretcher on light poles, which
can be put together in two minutes; and being 2-1/2 feet high is supposed to be secure from fleas." There was more: her own Mexican
saddle and bridle, for instance; candles, of course; a map and a dictionary; "strong laced boots of unblacked leather;" a bamboo Japanese
hat; and money and a passport. She was accompanied by Ito, a ser-
vant she had just hired. Her outfit weighed in at 110 pounds; Ito was
allotted twelve more pounds. To traverse the ninety miles to Nikko,

they engaged three rickshaws (*kurumas*). The journey required three days, without a change of runners.

Every night at an inn along the road she was attacked by armies of fleas and by a terrifying lack of privacy. She had to sleep "under a fusty green mosquito net which was a perfect nest of fleas." The shoji screens were pocked with holes "and often at each hole I saw a human eye. Privacy was a luxury not even to be recalled," she wrote. The servants, "who were very noisy and rough, looked into my room constantly without any pretext; the host, a bright, pleasant-looking man, did the same; jugglers, musicians, blind shampooers, and singing girls, all pushed the screens aside . . . ." Yet Isabella could shake off these annoyances. "A traveler must buy his own experience," she declared, "and success or failure depends mainly on personal idiosyncrasies."

This is true today. The busmen have transferred us from ship to train in their own car, and as we transfer ourselves from Shinkansen to local train and back again, the station officials are invariably helpful. We reach Nikko in the late afternoon and make reservations by phoning the Nikko Kanaya Hotel, a historic edifice that offers rooms for less than the trendier pensions that abound, such as the Pension Turtle, the Logette St. Bois, and the nearly irresistible Pension Lambchop. Before undertaking the walk uphill to the Kanaya, we peruse a museum near the station where I see my first pair of geta ice skates, wooden platform sandals with metal blades.

Out on the street, we follow a young woman with a T-shirt in mysterious English that reads:

FELINES
IN
HAPPINESS
Metaphysical Cat Couple
Since 1980

Isabella Bird began her exploration of Nikko from the village of Imaichi, eight miles away and connected to the city of shrines by a "colossal avenue of cryptomeria," planted in the seventeenth century by Matsudaira Masatsuma to honor Japan's first shogun. Thirteen thousand of these stately Japanese cedars survive today. As for Nikko a century ago, Ms. Bird thought that its main avenue possessed a "sort of Swiss picturesqueness" with steep roofs amidst snowy mountain peaks. The shopkeepers stepped out "to stare at a foreigner as if foreigners had not become common events since 1870, when Sir H. and Lady Parkes, the first Europeans who were permitted to visit Nikko, took up their abode in the Imperial Hombo." The main street of Nikko was clean in those days, "a doll's street with small low houses, so finely matted, so exquisitely clean, so finically neat, so light and delicate," Ms. Bird wrote, "that even when I entered them without my boots I felt like a bull in a china shop, as if my mere weight would smash through and destroy. The street is so painfully clean," she continued, "that I should no more think of walking over it in muddy boots than over a drawing-room carpet." The main street we now ascend is as steep as ever, and retains a few quaint shops, but is no longer as clean as a matted room. Cars, trucks, and tour buses have rendered it a typical modern street with which Ms. Bird would not have put up for a moment.

When Isabella arrived, she sent Ito ahead with a note in Japanese requesting accommodations in a samurai house. It was a private house that had been receiving a few foreign guests since 1873, when Dr. James Hepburn, who created the first system for transliterating Japanese into Roman letters, advised its owner, a Mr. Kanaya, to dabble in the hotel trade. Kanaya's cottage in Nikko constituted the forerunner of the landmark hotel he was to build later, across the river—the Nikko Kanaya Hotel where we made our reservation.

When Ms. Bird first met Mr. Kanaya—"a very bright, pleasant-looking man"—he made a deep bow of welcome. His cottage was "a Japanese idyll," pleasing to the eye, gentle on the ear, in every way fine and refreshing. The two-story house stood on a stone terrace; a street from the mountain behind passed through a garden; and there was a view of the deep river valley across the way. Ms. Bird's description of the interior is a perfect portrait of everyone's dream of things Japanese: two "highly polished" verandas, mats "so fine and white that I fear to walk over them, even in my stockings," shoji screens serving as paper windows, panels "of wrinkled sky-blue paper splashed with gold," two vases with a single azalea and a single iris, and a folding screen with a landscape scene in washed ink.

The life of these innkeepers seemed pastoral as well, yet Isabella soon learned that "Kanaya deplores the want of money; he would like to be rich, and intends to build a hotel for foreigners." Kanaya achieved his goal. The Nikko Kanaya Hotel where we are staying is a vast European chalet on a steep hillside, itself now elderly and worn. Our room is neither in the traditional Japanese style nor sleekly ultramodern, but a piece honed out of the Continent, replete with heavy oak furniture (a writing table, a bureau with mirror, large leather-covered chairs). Foreign celebrities who have stayed here range from Albert Einstein to Shirley MacLaine. The furnishings certainly haven't been changed since the appearance of the General Law of Relativity. We like it.

The next morning we cross the river and enter the very room in Kanaya's cottage where Isabella Bird spent her idyll. The interiors have lost some of the polish upon polish that glazed Isabella's descriptions, but none of their charm. Little has changed in 115 years—deliberately so, since this is a private museum that visitors can tour by arrangement with the hotel's front desk. We make such arrangements, but when we are greeted at the door by the housekeeper, she does not seem to expect us. Speaking no English, she nevertheless plays the role of hostess deftly. We move from room to room, treasure to treasure—Western musical instruments, family photo albums. The river between Kanayas is like the sword edge of time. Kanaya's cottage is a relic of another era in Japan, but so is the Kanaya Hotel that succeeded it. Both the worlds in which they were born are already historical, solidified ashes of styles and traditions, models of earlier and earlier Japans.

❋   ❋   ❋

More ancient still is the Nikko of mausoleums and shrines, the Nikko of the tourist, site of what many call the finest sacred art and architecture in Japan. The most important single figure in recent Japanese history is Tokugawa Ieyasu (1543-1616), the man who founded the Tokugawa Shogunate. The shogunate lasted 250 years, during which Japan was united, the samurai class solidified, Tokyo built, and the nation closed to the outside world. It was at Nikko that Ieyasu the first shogun became Ieyasu the god.

The choice of Nikko for burial and deification was not without foundation. Ever since Shodo Shonin (735-817) dedicated the region of Futarasan (the two unruly mountains) to Buddhist mountain worship and Ennin (794-864), a priest who had learned his Buddhism in China, converted the region to Tendai Buddhism, Nikko had been recognized as high sacred ground. No better place for the shogun's mausoleums—one to his body, one to his spirit; no better site to insure his ascendancy as a divine spirit, a *kami*, and as a human incarnation of the Buddha, a *gongen*.

A year after his death, Ieyasu's ashes were carried in a great procession for burial at Nikko, and in 1634 his grandson, Iemitsu, the third shogun, began construction of the complex of shrines and mausoleums, Nikko Toshugu, that has become the most expensive, most ornate creation in all of Japan. Iemitsu engaged fifteen thousand craftsmen and rolled out enough sheets of gold leaf to cover six acres.

The formal entrance to the shrines of Nikko is the Shinkyo bridge, a vermilion arch over the wild Daiya River that separates the two Kanaya inns today. Twelve hundred years ago, Shodo Shonin was ferried across this river on the backs of two serpents during his journey to Nantaisan, one of Nikko's sacred mountains. In 1636, the crossing was commemorated with construction of Nikko's famous red-arched bridge and passage upon it was limited to the shogun and his envoys. Destroyed by a flood in 1902, the present version of the red bridge still exacts a toll: pedestrians must purchase a ticket to cross. Computing the current market value of our humble feet, we cross instead on a free public bridge and walk up to Rinno-ji, a Tendai temple founded twelve hundred years ago. Like most important temples, Rinno-ji has been rebuilt and spruced up countless times. It is wide and monumental, with a vast flowing tile roof. The entrance is clogged with a Japanese tour group, dressed in suits, ties, skirts, and heels—at a distance, they are more formally Westernized than any sightseeing group from the West could ever hope to be.

We press on, passing under a large torii gate of granite beside a five-story pagoda, then through the Nio gate, with its carving of *baku*, the being that devours dreams. We pause at the sacred stables, where visitors feed sections of carrot to a white stallion. The protectors of the stables are three monkeys carved in relief above the stable door, a trio that we in the West recognize instantly as the source of our popular saying: hear no evil, see no evil, speak no evil.

The path rises, parting the drum and bell towers, monuments born in the cities of China. We are near the heart of the grand monument. "The whole style of the buildings, the arrangements, the art of every kind, the thought which inspires the whole, are exclusively Japanese," Isabella Bird wrote after standing here, "and the glimpse from the Nio gate is a revelation of a previously undreamed of beauty, both in form and color." The logic of this arrangement, if any, is beside the point. This is a passage into thicker and thicker levels of detail and decoration, from pagoda to stable, from gate to a revolving sutra library containing seven thousand Buddhist scriptures within. One spin of this huge octagon is equivalent to a devoted reading of the entire canon—speed-reading at nearly the speed of light.

Above the next courtyard stands the single most ornate creation in Japan: Yomei Gate, known popularly as *higurashi-mon*, the Gate of Twilight. Yomei is a massive pass-through of two stories, painted bright reds, blues, and greens, gilded heavily in gold leaf, lacquered, and carved to the absolute hilt with a Noah's ark of subjects: lions leaping, dragons unfurling, flowers blooming, birds flying, and the sages, immortals, and children of Tang Dynasty China leaning out from the brackets. This gate is the zenith of ancient Japan's decorative arts, a masterpiece of convolution. Within the Gate of Twilight are more courts and shrines, all elaborately carved and gilded. "To pass from court to court is to pass from splendour to splendour," Isabella wrote. "One is almost glad to feel that this is the last, and that the strain on one's capacity for admiration is nearly over." There are buildings to house the portable shrines that encase the divine spirits of the first three shoguns, paraded during annual festivals; there are shrines and a mausoleum for the spirit of Ieyasu; there is a Chinese Gate, *Kara-mon*; and last, carved on the struts of an opening in the wall, *nemuri-neko*, the sleeping cat, who keeps the shrines free of mice and rats.

Squeezing through this hole in the wall, we are suddenly outside the vast shrine, on the first rung of a staircase of two hundred stone steps twisting up the hillside among the ancient cedars. There is less artifice out here, and at the top of the stairs is a modest platform where "the dust of Ieyasu sleeps in an unadorned but Cyclopean tomb of stone and bronze, surmounted by a bronze urn." The first shogun's tomb is enclosed by a wall and balustrade of white stone, and at the entrance monks are selling small wooden plaques featuring paintings of a cat at rest. We buy one of these wooden petitions, known as *ema*, and hang it on a rack, praying for the soul of our cat, for a safe crossing of the river of ice said to lie between us and the gates of heaven.

✳   ✳   ✳

For Isabella Bird, as for generations of visitors to Nikko, these shrines "are the most wonderful work of their kind in Japan." She praised especially the masterful carvings of peony, lotus, and bamboo, which "in all the perfect colouring of passionate life, unfold themselves amidst the leafage of the gorgeous tracery." For me, however, the beauty of Nikko is strained. It is art in overdrive. The spare Zen gardens of Kyoto can whisper to the soul, but the shrines of Nikko scream to the senses until they burst. As Isabella Bird admitted: "I am beginning to appreciate the extreme beauty of solitude in decoration." Still, all her descriptions of Nikko form a lush litany to the contrary: to a chaos of decoration in a land renowned for its devotion to order. What of Japanese restraint and conformity? Nikko confounds by its sheer abundance of the unregulated individual life.

The mad rush of images that gorges Nikko seems to have nothing to do with the reserved personality of the Japanese; and yet from a distance these shrines, wrapped in three-hundred-fifty-year-old cedars, are perfect of their kind. Elsewhere perhaps it is only the mask we see, composed and stoic, efficient and robotic—the uniform face of Japan. But here we peer beneath the surface at another life, a secret life, opening like a flower. Unable to break through over the centuries, it has become hopelessly entangled in the dark—except here, in the shadow of the cedars at Nikko, where the hidden soul of Japan is carved into high relief.

Nikko is a scroll for the dead, but also the mirror of life turned inside out.

IX.

Ueno:
The Mood of Dust

We close our first circle of Japan at Ueno, the northern district of Tokyo—the old Tokyo of small neighborhoods, a few of which survived the 1923 Kanto earthquake that killed a hundred thousand and the 1945 Allied firebombing that annihilated an equal number. It's a long walk from the Nezu subway stop to the Sawanoya Ryokan. We stop at a police post and ask directions, take a right at the umbrella shop, and then it's another three blocks along low-rise shop fronts and houses, almost to the rice mill.

Sawanoya Ryokan, popular with independent travelers, foreign and Japanese alike, is clean and cheap, with a common dining room on the first floor where everyone gathers for a reasonably-priced Western breakfast and finds out who is who. Our room is typical of such inns, with barely enough room on the matted floor for two futons, a coin-operated black and white television, tea service and thermos. There's one novelty here on the second floor: our personal fire escape, a rope coiled on the wall like a hangman's noose, worthy of Rapunzel. In deference to foreigners, one can take a morning shower on the first floor, but one must also clear out during the afternoon, giving the place the regulated feel of a youth hostel.

Tokyo is in a drizzle and it's cherry blossom time. We grab our umbrellas and head for Ueno Park. When Edo (Tokyo) was being built out of the marshes by the first Tokugawa Shogun, Ueno Hill was the unlucky gate to the north, the entryway for devils. The second Tokugawa Shogun, Hidetada, asked Tenkai, the priest-designer of Nikko, to erect a guardian temple town of Ueno. By the close of the seventeenth century, Ueno contained a cluster of seventy-two halls and shrines to this end. Most of these buildings came down in 1868 when the samurai were crushed at Ueno by the Imperial Army, marking the beginning of the Meiji Restoration. On the grounds of this sudden, decisive breach between the Japan of shogun and samurai and the new industrial and military Japan, Ueno Park was born—a vast plain of lakes, national museums, and winding lanes where those who drink to cherry blossoms congregate in the spring for *hanami*, the cherry blossom festival.

Ueno is Japanese eclecticism made visible, a theme park without a theme. There's a national museum of Western art housed in a sweeping but unmemorable building designed by Le Corbusier; the statue of a samurai in a crewcut walking his dog; a temple engulfed in dolls presented by parents whose prayers for their children were answered (the dolls burned in an annual ceremony to prevent overpopulation); gates marking the burial places of two early shoguns (their mausoleums destroyed by our side in World War Two); a large pond that was once an inlet of Tokyo Bay; and a shrine where modern Japanese students pray for success on their examinations, a custom that dates back to ancient China.

We pay a quick visit to the massive Tokyo National Museum, Japan's greatest storehouse, and while the Japanese exhibits fail to enthrall us—with the exception of the warrior costumes and weapons—we linger over the Chinese treasures, reminded of the Middle Kingdom where we traveled as intensely as we have in Japan. I'm no longer drawing so many connections between old China and Japan as when we started out. The farther into Japan I go, the less substantial these connections become. In fact, no two nations, no two cultures could be further apart. Although many Japanese surfaces duplicate those of a disappearing China, there were never the deeper linkages I sought. After so many days in Japan, I feel what is Japanese, not what is copied. While no other nation looks as Chinese and as American as Japan, its minutest flourish is entirely its own.

The mist accelerates into downpour. Ueno Park is preparing for the great spring festival. The flowers of the Ueno cherry trees fall in delicate pink streamers, signifying the transitory life, the reality of extinction, the marriage of impermanence and beauty. Along the paved pathways, companies have roped off their squares. Junior office workers have been sent to stake out their company's plot for the evening's ceremonial drinking of sake under the tumbling blossoms. We are hailed by a drunk who engages us in a discussion of America—the greatest country in the world, we're told, and also the worst. This is the cherry blossom express, the long drunk to the failure of perfection, the chance to dance and holler in public as the tiny, scentless cousins of the rose are shred by the sword of short duration.

Ueno is ideal for *hanami*; even I, a complete outsider, can see that. The nearly bare black boughs, fringed in pink blossoms, arch over the paved lanes. Vendors plant their wooden pushcarts and raise their roofs against the rain. Red and white banners line and sometimes cross the avenues. Everywhere there are men in suits and expensive full-length rain coats sloshing left and right, and mothers with children. Some of the kids are dressed up in holsters and toy guns, chaps and boots—American cowboys. A dozen men sit on a blue sheet under a transparent rain tarp anchored to the branches of a cherry tree, drinking and laughing, their shopping bags and unsheathed umbrellas at their sides, their shoes removed. A man sits alone on the tiniest lawn chair we have ever seen, a foot off the ground, hunched over a comic book, the square he is guarding outlined in white twine weighed down at the four corners with rocks. The pigeons circle.

We have to pick our way carefully over the causeway, past steles and bibbed statues, as the mud thickens in random puddles. I look out on Shinobazu Pond, this caged body of water once the very waters of the Pacific, long landlocked and developed, its connection to the sea filled in and blocked by dozens, even hundreds of tall concrete office buildings. Looking into this lake, I am saddened. The fate of the world is reflected in the still gray surface, the trimmed edges, the streets and rooftops. The Tokyo-Shanghai-Los Angelesation of the earth is unstoppable, the human sprawl that squats and rolls and levels the boundaries in its way until the surface of the planet is filled in, the nations and cultures locked together like puzzle pieces; and the little spaces, green and blue and brown, shrivel under a dung heap of converging colonies as the globe spins through the vacuum between the banging stars. This is the next century, the final hodgepodge, and I feel it soaking into my bones here in the cold firebombed clearing where Japan disappeared into the West.

＊　　＊　　＊

We are scant blocks from the Daimyo Clock Museum, a large collection of feudal Japanese timepieces from an era when the hour was not constant. The total hours of daylight were decreed to be equal to those apportioned to the night. Thus, in winter, an hour of daylight could be half as long as an hour of night. In summer, an hour of day could stretch to twice the length of an hour after dark. I'm trying to imagine what these adjustable hours felt like, and I see some sense in it beyond insuring the full employment of clock keepers to constantly recalibrate these instruments. For who has never wished to expand an hour of a summer's day or shorten an hour of dreary winter rain? The old clocks were perfect, but have no place in today's world, and certainly no place in Japan.

✳ ✳ ✳

Our last days in Ueno are sweet, but die too quickly. This is a neighborhood on a human scale, and we feel human in it. Across the street from our ryokan is a window shrine to cats, with two beckoning *maneki-neko* figurines, a painting of a large yellow cat, and a scroll of messages written in Japanese. We investigate. A fat yellow tabby turns up, and Margaret bends down to pet it. We linger until the cat shrine owner appears in the doorway. She's a *gaijin*—a blond foreigner from New England.

This is indeed a cat shrine of sorts, Elizabeth says: its message is that the citizens of Japan should treat their cats with care and concern, not dump them at temples or drown them by the bagful. Elizabeth's husband Itsuo concurs: the Japanese are absolutely rotten to animals. Hence, their admonishing window.

Itsuo is an artist, Elizabeth a journalist. They have been in this neighborhood for a few years, but he is finding the Tokyo art scene far too stifling. They are aiming for Boston. Itsuo speaks enough English to thoroughly lambaste the ruling Liberal Democratic Party for its lack of democracy and imagination, for its stifling conservatism. They invite us to a cherry-blossom party that evening, promising a frolic in a nearby graveyard, and give us directions to a second-story beauty shop where the celebration will begin with a feast. We're to bring nothing. They also encourage us to explore the neighborhood, dangling before our eyes the most tantalizing descriptions of old wells, rice mills, paper shops, and the local public baths.

We set off on foot, nosing about with no direction, covering block after block at no pace but our own. These are the kind of residential streets where futon covers are hung out the windows to bake in the sun, but also where cars are parked on special platforms—like bunkbeds—so that two vehicles can occupy the space of one. The old wooden houses and shops are co-equals with the new concrete squares and rectangles. Back stoops are stacked with potted plants and tiny washing machines (but never dryers). There are open lots where bulldozers and cranes are knocking down and chomping up whole blocks of the wooden tenements and counting houses, replacing the creaky past with the streamlined future. The history of the Shitamachi District—early Tokyo's region of outcasts, prostitutes, black markets, and lowly laborers—is being recast in the modern Western image that is blinding the world.

In a series for the *Mainichi Daily News* entitled "Vanishing," with detailed illustrations by Itsuo, Elizabeth Kiritani has recorded some of what will be lost in Ueno. At a penny-candy toy store run the last forty years by a mother and daughter, the owner tells Elizabeth that she "likes the cracks and drafts in this old house. . . . The new building next door," she continues, "may have the same dust as we have here, but in an old house dust has a mood."

No doubt that store will someday face the same fate as the better-known monuments of Tokyo, such as the redbrick Tokyo Station. "A thirty-six-floor intelligent building," Elizabeth writes, "may make more money and will provide more space, but at some point in every civilization, pride in the past, a sense of continuity and aesthetic values transcend materialism and pragmatism." I wish she were right, but Japan has not reached that point; it continues to banish its past without regret, remaking its architecture every decade.

Elizabeth and Itsuo live in the margins of this city that never looks back, in a compact four-and-a-half mat room shoe-horned into an apartment house of decaying wood and tile. Upstairs, a 75-year-old retiree from the Post Office lives alone, thundering away on a metal press all day. At night, he drinks and smokes, singing at the top of his lungs, shaking the straw floors and paper windows like an air hammer.

❋　❋　❋

The Taito-ku municipality into which are tucked Ueno, our ryokan, a metal press, the cat shrine, and much else, consists of 170,000 residents, to which are added 5,000 foreign residents (considered a hefty number). In addition, it has been determined that on the average in a single day three new babies are born here, but four other residents expire; that whereas twenty people move into the precinct daily, almost twenty four move out—all yielding a loss in population, which must be made up somewhere else in Tokyo, in the new tenements farther from the center. Four marriages are performed each day here, but just one divorce is granted—hardly an American statistic. There are three traffic accidents a day and a fire every forty-eight hours. Earthquake drills are as common in the schools here as fire drills are in America. Elementary schools are visited by earthquake simulators: that is, by a room with a wall removed, containing a school desk and two chairs, mounted on a flatbed truck. Once a student or two climbs aboard, the earthquake simulator rears and kicks like a barroom bronco.

* * *

Imeyasu's great-great-grandson, Tsunayoshi, a shogun and an unsteady Confucian, is buried at Ueno. He was a Japanese Caligula, obsessed with young girls and boys, but also a devoted follower of certain Buddhist wise men.

Unable to produce a living heir, he was persuaded that he was being punished for the sins he committed against animals in a former life. Therefore, since his birth year was that of the Dog in the Oriental zodiac, he set about erecting palaces for canines all over Edo; and those who killed a dog were meted out the death penalty.

Tokyoites found his "Edict of Compassion for Living Things" the maddest law ever promulgated.

* * *

The hairdresser's shop is at the top of the back stairs and by the time we locate it we can tell we're late: there's a pile of shoes on the landing so dense we can barely ford across. The long table, crowded with guests on either side, is jammed with dishes and bottles. Elizabeth presides. She teaches English, and these are her students. We immediately fall prey to the high spirits, the sake and brandy, the array of snacks. Itsuo crowns me with a bowler hat; someone snaps my rosy-cheeked portrait.

The students are ordinary workers, mostly women, young and old. Few will ever see America; they're not the rich of Japan. One works at McDonald's; she tells us her salary. Another works in her husband's business; she downplays her role as co-owner.

Rain is pounding the Yanaka cemetery nearby, one of Tokyo's largest, a spot that escaped the three disasters of this century: earthquake, bombardment, and development. Itsuo wants to lead a cherry-blossom delegation there to toast the wasted blooms. We don't go with him to the graves. We're too comfortable at the table. The beauty shop equipment on the edges of the room is discretely covered in white sheets, as though the proprietor were on a Grand Tour in another part of the world.

Tomorrow, we will complete our own minor tour, and for the first time we're not looking forward to home. We have stayed in this neighborhood long enough so that we are acknowledged by its residents: an old man strolling the streets in his robe; a mother watering her curbside plants. We've met a number of Japanese who crop up in the dining room of our ryokan: a professor of Library Science who wants us to polish the English in his conference papers; a cook who writes poetry. Through the cold, cutting rain we feel everywhere the warmth of Japan melting through the constant reserve, the withdrawn eyes.

Back in rainy Oregon we will receive letters and postcards from Ueno. Kentaro the cook sends us a photo album in which we are pictured at the Sayanawa Ryokan and at the hairdresser's party. He also includes shots of himself at Ueno Park under the cherry blossoms and two portraits of a round-faced little girl in white bobby sox, unlabeled. She must be his daughter. His final postcard is a poem in English:

Cloudy and rainbow.
of Oregon!

It's our last day in Japan. For the first time since we arrived in Tokyo, the sun is out for good. We lock our luggage in Ueno Station and walk east into Asakusa, a famous amusement district since Meiji times. We walk all the way to the Sumida River where restaurant barges and two-tiered glass tour boats cruise. As with many urban rivers in Japan, the Sumida's banks are reinforced with concrete; a park lines the embankment. The cherry blossoms detach in the heat of the sun, and under the trees people spend a Sunday on stiff benches. At a cascading fountain children remove their shoes and wade in. There are baby strollers and playgrounds and a few quiet *hanami* parties. Block after block of modern buildings hug the riverway.

At the heart of Asakusa, we prowl through the Kannon Temple grounds, known as Senso-ji. This is Tokyo's oldest temple, established in 628, but it has been rebuilt countless times over fourteen centuries. The first Tokugawa shogun made it his prayer hall in 1590. We bombed the main hall in 1945, and it wasn't rebuilt until 1958. Tokyo's oldest temple is now cement.

Between the great gates of this complex is a long promenade of shops and stalls selling everything from dolls to crackers, packed this morning with Japanese families. Perhaps some of them are thinking of Basho's famous lines:

Through clouds of blossoms
Is that the bell of Ueno
Or of Asakusa?

The haiku does not translate well into English, or into the Western mind; but every day at 6 a.m. the bell sounds from Senso-ji and today there is a cloud of pink blossoms wherever we turn.

From the temple we can see rides in an adjacent amusement park, Hanayashiki, which is not one of Japan's spiffy, ultramodern, high-tech pleasure lands, but a leftover from the American occupation. The skeletons of two high rides tower above the temple roofs. One is a simple steel column like the shaft of an enormous umbrella from which six little gingerbread houses dangle on cables, houses complete with chimneys and tiled roofs. The houses go up and down in a slow circle; we can't understand its meaning. The second ride is an enormous bleacher raised on a metal arm and swung back and forth, back and forth, as if on the arm of an oscillating clock. The ride is painted red, white, and blue, and it is capped by a replica of the Statue of Liberty. It is strange to look up in the sky and see the Lady there, translated from another continent. The air swells with the cotton candy of cherry blossoms.

❋   ❋   ❋

Ages ago we set out from Tokyo to Koyasan. So it seems; and so it seems as if we have traveled far. In reality, we've traversed very little space or time; but there are other distances, more difficult to quantify. When we first entered Tokyo from the Narita Airport, we knew nothing; we've come a ways. It was on a winter's night that we arrived; the airport bus took nearly three hours to reach our hotel. We moved through the darkness in a baffled freeway shaped like a tunnel, soundless save for the staccato conversation of two businessmen. Across from the Misty Hotel I spotted the aftermath of a minor auto accident, a fender bender attended by five police cars and at least fifteen policemen. At the time I did not know how labor-intensive, how curiously inefficient Japan could be.

We stayed our first few days at the Tokyo Prince Hotel, in the Shiba Ward, not far from Roppongi. It was a telling location, could we have read it then: a modern blocky hotel next door to an ancient shrine next door to the Tokyo Tower transmitter next door to a golf driving range—the chaotic layout bisected by streets, arcing ramps, and freeways. We had nothing with which to compare this jumble. It turned out to be typical.

At the Tokyo Prince a major renovation was under way, and the hammers were pounding discreetly. Just down the hall from our room,

Daniel Barenboim was a guest. He had come to Tokyo with the Orchestre de Paris to give three concerts in commemoration of the 200th Anniversary of the French Revolution. Why the French Revolution should be commemorated in Tokyo I did not know. *Cats* was also beginning its roadshow run. The Japanese buy the best of the West, and they love it.

As we passed Mr. Barenboim's door, we heard exquisite music, uncanned, unrecorded, untransmitted. We wanted to linger in the hall but couldn't. The Tokyo pace had already seized us by the scruff of the neck. Locked in fast-forward, we zipped from our hotel to the grounds of Zojo-ji Temple, its tiled two-story gate standing since the time of Shakespeare. This was formerly the family temple of the Tokugawa shoguns, but we had no notion of who these shoguns were. Instead, it was the oddities that first captured our attention, in particular the huge chorus of child-like *jizo* dolls. We would not again see this many together, thousands neatly arranged in long parallel tiers. Each little statue was identical; each wore the same red crocheted cap and bib; each was positioned in front of three containers—a large fluted urn for flowers, a tiny cup for incense, and a long tube designed to hold a pinwheel. Each *jizo* had its own pinwheel, and as the wind blew we could hear the petals of the wheels fluttering, fluttering, beside the *jizos*, their eyes closed tight.

That first afternoon in Tokyo we discovered a cheap new stand-up cafe in a building striped in bold yellow and green. The windows were emblazoned in English with the set prices—COFFEE ¥200, SOUP ¥200. The cafe sign, complete with tall firs as emblems, read ROCKY FROM OREGON. Inside, salarymen stood in neat suits and ties at tiny round high-tech tables. But no Rocky from Oregon came forth to greet us.

Leaving Tokyo for Koyasan, we grabbed a snack at a pastry shop where each little item rode across the counter on an assembly line. We snatched what we fancied as the plates clacked by. The chefs worked on the other side of the tracks, near enough to converse with—but no one was taking the time to chat. The wheels within wheels were rotating at top speed. There would be no time to jump the tracks. The only time was that kept inside the cyclotron, regular as the pulse of an atom.

Now, waiting for the Skyliner to take us to Narita Airport, we plot our second circle of Japan. Although we have traveled from cold

Koyasan to the far shores of Sado, we failed to hear the laughter of ghosts, to locate the vanishing point in the mirror. The closest I could come to satori in a Japan that disappears at every turn was in Kanazawa where, browsing in a department store, I began to read the messages stamped on T-shirts.

The most complex of these shirts contained a school pennant labeled ZIT-AM, with a motto reading WAO-SENSATION. Above the pennant in block letters was a three-tiered headline:

DRAMATIC STREET
NEW - FE
TAKE & USE FOR SELF

Underneath, a four-line subhead:

PRASTIC - 1
BIG SENTIMENTAL
N5879Y-2703Z
BEAUTIFUL CITY

The meaning nagged at me as a Zen koan might. The mysterious text hinted at a real world, a found poetry of registration numbers, advertising claims, and paragraphs of prose that had slipped their moorings. No one in America was writing prose like that; no one could.

These postmodern haiku probed the depths. One shirt asked:

WELCOM SPOOKY GOLF CLUB
BEST CONDITION?

It was another question I could not answer, one I would never have thought to pose.

Finally I encountered the ultimate shirt-poem, fashioned expressly for the end of our century:

MIXTURE RHYTHM &
MELLOW SOUND STRIKE
Your heart. Now
Drift in the fusion wave

It was pop physics at its best. I tried to swing with it.

Now, about to leave Japan, adrift in the fusion wave, unfused to anything, I barely notice the stainless steel cars of the Skyliner train as they slide up to the platform. The cars are empty. I see no engineer, no conductor. We are in a subway somewhere in the bowels of Ueno Station. A black American is beside us, attaché case in hand, waiting for the doors to open. The interior of the train car is spotless, the seats unripped, the walls unmarred, the floors unlittered. All the seats face the wrong way; but at the flick of some invisible switch, the seats swivel 180 degrees in unison to face the airport. The doors slide open automatically. The black traveler beside us shrugs and laughs. "Yes," he says, "We must be in Japan."

We see our faces reflected in the window glass, faces we don't recognize, making us laugh, as if we, too, had vanished somewhere inside our long travels and been replaced by our emissaries.

X.

Interlude:
The Dead Center of Gravity

Twenty hours later we're back in America, standing in the bus depot in Portland, Oregon, our long journey's luggage in hand—
slammed back into an alien culture, our own. We find seats near the
back of the Greyhound as it fills up; in fact, it's oversold, illegal standing room only, and the aisles are packed. No robots and computers in
charge here. An agent boards and offers refunds plus free tickets for
those who will get off. Everyone's grumbling aloud, but volunteers
do come forward, including one young woman in cut-offs who barks
as she saunters down the aisle, "I've got a free ticket and I don't care
how long I got to wait. I'm going to get my twenty-nine bucks."

After immersion in the Japanese way, the American way seems
completely uncouth. Our driver comes on a half-hour late and announces on the loudspeaker that his bosses are nincompoops. He tells
us that he was awakened and ordered to drive this shift. We're back in
the land of frank and incensed speech, on the open road. There's not a
circle in sight, only an endless freeway.

As the bus pulls out, all eyes are on a young black man who has
dragged his baggage on and parked it in the aisle—a large, clear plastic bag four feet tall, crammed to the brim with unfolded clothing. The
driver orders him to stuff this amorphous parcel in the open bin overhead, and he complies, without bowing. As we hit the freeway, his
plastic bag begins to ooze out like the innards of a lava lamp, its substance falling ever so slowly toward its owner's head. He is blissfully
unaware of this attack from above, and no one is about to warn him.
Everyone is settling back, measuring the progress of doom. The bag
pours from the rafters lump by lump like heavy dough. It is a scant
twelve inches from striking his head when he glances up. He rises

and stuffs his sack back in with a vengeance, griping about the driver—that asshole. His audience turns away, disappointed.

We are grateful to be sitting together. We won't have to share our life story with a stranger in the next seat, or listen to the private soap opera that so many bus passengers seem to carry with them and sing at the slightest provocation. On an American bus one is likely to hear stories that most Japanese wouldn't know how to tell, stories from the heart, the country-western heart full of the blood of divorce, betrayal, and bad fortune, of a night in jail or the loss of a job, mixed with the mournful longing for the trucker's open road, for true love lost, for a three-bedroom house with a two-car garage and a faithful hound baying in the bed of a pickup. We're a nation of mongrels, of lonely dreamers, fluid as ectoplasm in a canning jar.

✳　✳　✳

The Japanese are different. For one thing, as David Mura writes in an account of his year in Japan, "the Japanese place far more value on surface, on beauty and appearance, than the depth-seeking, psychologically and morally conscious Americans." He is correct. And yet the Japanese can plumb the inner depths, too. Mura quotes the Butoh dancing master Ono, who says: "When you are sad, it is not just your single self who is sad, but all the dead people, the great number of souls who are living inside you. . . . It's the relationship between what is living inside me and the living realm of the dead that is dance. . . ."

So what exactly are the differences? David Mura cuts to the heart: "For Americans unacquainted with Japanese culture, as I had been, it is difficult to comprehend the enormous differences between the two cultures, how their concepts of what constitutes both a human being and a society are fundamentally unalike." The reflections in the mirror—the modern cityscapes and clothing, the technologies, the politics, the pop of pop cultures—are Western and familiar, but the life behind the mirror is alien. "In the end," Mura decides, "the society felt to my American psyche too cramped, too well-defined, too rule-oriented, too polite, too circumscribed." He is speaking of the real differences felt by outsiders inside Japan.

The first outsiders from the West to see Japan were a few missionaries and traders who arrived four hundred years ago.

The Japan they saw was Oriental, a copy of golden China; a Japan of Zen and tea; a Japan of elaborate ceremony and order; a Japan the opposite of ourselves. For a full century after the first Westerners began reaching Japan in 1543, the year one of their ships was wrecked close enough for rescue, they were struck by their differences from the Japanese, at once peculiar and extreme. The Japanese, in the words of Father Alessandro Valignano, practiced "rites and ceremonies so different from those of all the other nations that it seems they deliberately try to be unlike any other people"; sixteenth-century Japan "was a world the reverse of Europe."

The Japanese were not simply polite, for example; they were the most polite race on earth. "Even the common folk and peasants," Valignano wrote, were "so remarkably polite that they give the impression that they were trained at court." Politeness, in turn, made their language unique. João Rodrigues, who sailed to Japan in 1576 at the age of fifteen, and became a masterful translator among his fellow Jesuits, felt that "what distinguishes Japanese and makes it different from all other known languages is the way in which respect and courtesy are nearly always expressed in their speech."

Added to politeness were other virtues practiced to an extreme. For example, modesty and restraint. ("They keep their anger and rage so tightly under control that rarely does anybody show vexation," Valignano claimed; in Japan, "everything is done quietly and in good order.") Or a fascination with mechanical inventions. (Father Luis Frois, who died in Nagasaki in 1597 after thirty-four years in Japan, could entertain the fiercest warlord in Japan with nothing more than an alarm clock from Europe.) Or a taste for novelty. (Jorge Alvares, the trader who gave the first eyewitness account of Japan by any European, noticed that the Japanese liked "seeing black people, especially Africans, and they will come 15 leagues just to see them and entertain them for three or four days.")

The most extreme difference, however, was the Japanese standard of cleanliness. It pervaded their lives like a national aesthetic principle then, and it does still. Oda Nobunaga, who reunited central Japan in the late sixteenth century, used to drop in on the Jesuits unannounced "so that he could inspect the cleanliness and neatness of our houses," Father Gaspar Coelho noted in 1582. "A great enemy of dirt and disorder," Nobunaga kept his palace so clean that, as one Jesuit noted, "the gardens and corridors were such that one could not spit in them," a great inconvenience, apparently. When Father Luis Frois visited Nobunaga's castle near Kyoto, even its stable "was so clean and well-kept that it seemed rather to be a fine chamber for the diversion of nobles than a place to lodge horses. The four or five youths who looked after it went about dressed in silk and carrying daggers in gilt sheaths," he said. Their Lord Nobunaga kept "35 shaven men who did no other work save walking around and sweeping with their brooms and cleaning all these houses an hour before daybreak; this they did with as much care and perfection as if each day were a solemn festival, because the thing which pleased him most and to which he always paid great attention was this extreme exterior cleanliness."

We found this extreme exterior cleanliness in modern Japan— and the simplicity, order, and precision that underlie it. Four hundred years earlier, it was manifest as it is now in the most mundane ways: in the use of chopsticks as a means to eat "in the neatest possible way"; in the leaving of shoes on the landing so as not to soil the inside of the house; in the sweeping and sprinkling of the streets of Kyoto twice a day; and always in the bath, for the Japanese were already the champion bathers of the world. Father Rodrigues declared that the Japanese exceeded "everybody else in this matter, not only in the frequency with which they bath during the day, but even more so in the cleanliness and dignity which they observe in that place." Rodrigues went on to describe the sine qua non of Renaissance hygiene, a Japanese privy at the end of a stone path: "New clogs were placed there for the guests to use in wet weather, and new slippers are also to be found there. . . . The exterior of their privies is kept extremely clean and a perfume-pan and new paper cut for use and placed there. . . . A ewer of clean water and other things needed for washing the hands are found nearby, for it is an invariable custom of both nobles and commoners to wash their hands every time after using the privy for their major and minor necessities."

From courtesy to the privy, there are always these elaborate forms to follow, difficult for an outsider to unravel. "The Japanese have such innumerable ceremonies that nobody knows all of them," Father Lourenço Mexia complained. "They make use of seven or eight just to drink a little water [he meant tea] and they have more than thirty regarding the use of the fan; and there is an infinite number regarding their way of eating and sending gifts and their social dealings."

Reading now about the first appearance of Japan in the Western experience, it is as if nothing has changed. All the ceremonies, all the differences which first appeared to Westerners, persist to this day.

Except that now there is a second Japan. While a Jesuit of the Renaissance returning to modern Japan might find everything still in its place, he would scarcely know what planet he was on. The old windup alarm clock has become a pachinko parlor; robots work side by side with men. He would know enough to remove his shoes before he went into a house, but he might not know the house. In its very interior is a second Japan, a copy of America, co-existing with a Chinese version twelve centuries old.

By the time the first Westerners arrived, Japan had imported this new formal culture, labeled the pieces, and fit it together so that even the seams were invisible. It was a supreme copy, occupying Japan like a standing army. It was a perfect China, tended by supreme copyists. Much of this Oriental Japan still stands, in art and architecture, in ceremony and thought, and it is this Japan that the first Western missionary and merchant knew. The Japan he would not know is America.

While our predecessors witnessed the intricacies and contemplated the mysteries of the Japan that turned itself into a China, we are watching Japan attempt the same act of presto-duplication with America. It should be no surprise that Japan is doing a masterful job with a foreign model. Now, in a single generation, as the high technology of the West moves East, Japan has molded itself to new shapes and forces. Japan is doing with its image of America what it did with its image of China—reproducing it, perfecting it, taking it to extremes.

Today everyone arriving from the West will see themselves in the mirror of Japan. We are everywhere, around every corner, in every house. It's not what we would have seen in the sixteenth century—we weren't being reflected then. The view is more confusing. It's jarring. We find the old differences that were once fresh, and we find new differences that are familiar.

＊　　＊　　＊

When we first went to Japan, we left a nation without rituals and arrived in a land riddled with ceremony. The Japan of the Orient, of the past, embraces ritual, and those rites exist side by side and sometimes deep inside the new Japan of the West. It is difficult to know if an ornate procedure is a reaffirmation of the past, an attempt to reintegrate with the future, or mere picturesque formalism. Tea drinking is one of these nodes where either much is being created or else much is being dissolved.

A number of the first Westerners in Japan observed that the Japanese seemed to drink water by a set of rules; they were not yet aware that the drink was tea, and that its ceremonial form, *cha no yu*, borrowed from China in the fifteenth century, was reaching its apex at the very time these Westerners were visiting Japan. In Kyoto in 1587,

Toyotomi Hideyoshi, who completed the unification of Japan begun by Nobunaga, convened a ten-day tea festival. He served tea in the pine groves with his own hands, pitching a plush tea hut, trimmed in gold leaf. Such a luxurious display was frowned upon by his celebrated companion, Sen no Rikyu, who laid down the aesthetics of *wabi cha*, poverty tea, the austere and rustic ceremony that has come down to us today.

At the heart of Rikyu's tea ceremony is the nonmaterial, the undifferentiated, the tranquil, the silent, the utterly natural. Father João Rodrigues, who often served as an interpreter for Hideyoshi himself, left an account of a sixteenth-century tea ceremony he witnessed. At the appointed hour, those invited would shave their heads and pull on new stockings, enter a low gate to a forest, change into clean sandals, and follow newly-rinsed stepping stones into the woods. There they would contemplate the arbor, wash their hands in a "rude stone trough," and reaching the tea house, remove their fans and daggers, step out of their sandals, and stoop low to pass through the tiny entrance like a womb. Inside, each guest would meditate upon the flower arrangement in the alcove (*tokonoma*), read the scroll hanging there, and then inspect the house, the hearth, the reeds of the windows, the grain of the wood. When everyone was seated, the master entered the hut and began the preparation of the tea.

As Father Rodrigues observed, "Everything employed in the ceremony is as nature created it—rustic, unrefined and simple, as would befit a lonely country hermitage." The "effects of wealth are moderated" by the style of the cottage—thatched with straw and reeds, framed with rough timber, so that there is "no artificiality or gentility apparent, but only decrepitude and naturalness." The tea vessels are likewise not finely wrought or embellished; rough Korean rice bowls became most prized. This was part of *mitate*, of seeing beauty where it is not expected.

The tea ceremony shares much with Zen, and tea is said to have come into Japan with Zen from China in 1191, imported by the monk Eisai, founder of the Rinzai sect. Eisai hoped to keep Zen novices awake during their long and arduous meditations. Blurring distinctions, looking into nature, finding new objects of beauty, concentrating on the immediate as the true—these are aspects of a tea-and-Zen way of life not without a Chinese basis, but pushed to the limits in Japan. In 1591, Hideyoshi ordered Rikyu to commit suicide, no one knows why—

light green powder whipped to a froth, wild flowers in the simplest arrangement imaginable, the soul scrubbed clean.

Sen no Rikyu left seven fundamental rules for tea; extracted, they form a code of conduct for Oriental Japan:

(1) "Make a delicious bowl of tea" (meaning define what's to be done, simply and directly).

(2) "Lay the charcoal so that it heats the water" (meaning give every component its proper part, waste nothing, be aware of the simplest procedure).

(3) "Arrange the flowers as they are in the field" (meaning do not neglect the beautiful; perfect form follows nature).

(4) "In summer, suggest coolness; in winter, warmth" (meaning come into correspondence with the seasons, blend with the situation).

(5) "Do everything ahead of time" (meaning create no misunderstanding, reach no shortfall, cause no inconvenience to others).

(6) "Prepare for rain" (meaning ready yourself for the worst disaster, always; for death, always).

(7) "Give those with whom you find yourself every consideration" (meaning harmonize; meaning recognize your true position in the universe and embody it).

This was the underlying code of Old Japan, and it has survived. In some ways, it is all of Japan that is left.

As for the tea ceremony, it is seldom performed anymore in China, but in Japan it has never been more popular. Philosophy and knowledge are no longer what bring so many through the low door; it's a matter of style.

Fifteen generations after Rikyu, there are three major schools of tea certifying tea masters and authorizing utensils. A multimillion-dollar franchise system has coalesced out of the tea huts on the hills of Kyoto. One school boasts over two million students. It is a finishing school for young ladies and wives, a mark of good breeding. Poverty Tea is Big Business, but old purposes persist.

"The purpose of this gathering to drink tea and of the conversation thereat," Father Rodrigues wrote, "is not for the guests to deliver long speeches, but rather that they may calmly and moderately contemplate within themselves the things they see there; this they do, not to compliment the host on them, but rather to understand in this way the mysteries which are enclosed therein."

These are mysteries that do not open to the West, even as it is the West that is being brewed and drunk while the last huts are downed, making way for steel-girded apartments. Still, there's no better tea in the world; it is delicious enough to make us think of what was once beautiful, of what has already died, of what we cannot find today in America or China.

Thus, and for a thousand other reasons, we decide to return to Japan. This time we will start far from Tokyo indeed, on the southwest island of Kyushu. There, we will board another cyclotron, but an older one, slower and nearer China. At its center are the volcanic peaks in whose craters the very first Japan was born.

And this time we mean to follow the supreme commandment of a Japanese artist, Noguchi Isamu. His dictum comes from a daunting note he once wrote to himself. It's simple, and probably impossible:

"Seek the dead center of gravity."

❋   ❋   ❋

Our journey back begins on Japan Airlines, where the passengers are almost all Japanese. As I doze, I am assaulted by idle questions:

Does Japan have a past? Yes, of course it does, but as Norma Field argues in her portrait of Japan at century's end, vast painful regions of the collective past, those involving World War Two crimes and the Emperor cult, remain in darkness. She is able to dissect the "death-in-life quality of daily routine in the world's most successful economy" as we cannot because she looks from the inside, among her relatives in Japan. She also pays homage to Japan's few but remarkable dissidents "who resist the comforts of amnesia and the lure of fabulous consumption, who insist on thinking of the past and present against each other."

Why do the Japanese love the cute, the exotic, even the grotesque, almost as much as they worship designer labels and prestige brands? Americans are not immune to the attractions in either category, of course, but perhaps the difference is in degree. Americans can resist the magnets of their culture; the Japanese seem to have nothing inside with which to resist.

Are Americans not more creative than the Japanese in business, science, and art? No, but Americans are the masters of entertainment marketing. Witness the success worldwide of our pop performers, athletes, and movie stars. For the Japanese, every new invention, wherever it originates, is just the start, not the end. They extend what's novel to a degree Americans can not reach and also are not interested in reaching.

Are Americans as lazy, as careless, as disorderly as the Japanese think? Our unruliness, our lack of conformity, our ethnic diversity terrify and repel them. Yet how they dream of our luxurious freedoms.

What is the source of this Japanese mania for order and neatness? It encompasses the way food is stacked in a restaurant kitchen, the way objects are placed in the most ordinary room. Neatness is neither an American nor current Chinese obsession. It must be a matter of national aesthetics in Japan. Where else in the world would so many men pause to scrutinize the artistic floral arrangements, *ikibana*, in a department store? Where else would department stores turn over so much space to displays of graceful arts? In America, the basic shopping mall display is of hot cars and brute pickup trucks.

The stewardess bows in our direction as she draws the curtain closed between steerage and business class; I keep thinking of questions.

Why doesn't America know how to sell commodities to the Japanese? America is not inspired to make copies of strictly Japanese products, refine them, and sell them back to the Japanese, but the Japanese are fond of concocting such reversals: televisions, VCRs, automobiles. They are the masters of the mirror; we're narcissists.

What is the essential difference between Japanese society and our own? Norma Field writes that "Japanese society in its educational pursuits offers a pitilessly thorough realization of American aspirations," namely, to achieve "lifetime employment with a corporate giant." But if Japan is a dictatorial corporation, then China is a dictatorial household, and America, a dictatorial child.

Why can't Japan accept other races and outsiders, at least to the degree we do in America? Black American journalist Juan Williams, who lived in Japan in 1991 under a fellowship from the Japan Society, feels that prejudice in Japan is "not a simple matter of black and white," but in large measure the result of how all outsiders are regarded. One black businessman Williams interviewed for *The Washington Post Magazine* explained that the Japanese "are less a racially oriented society than a hierarchical one. They want to know where a person stands, how low to bow, are you the general manager or president." Novelist Kyo Nobuko—born, raised, and married to a Japanese in Japan, but herself not a citizen and of Korean extraction—explains: "Living in a society of groups, if we act differently from the group people, it gets hard to live together.'"

You are either inside or outside forever.

What powers the Japanese economic machine? Japan's former prime minister Nakasone, in an interview with Juan Williams, predicted that " in the near future, Japan will more readily accept different people." Nakasone added, "We are very immature in dealing with foreign culture or foreign people." He informed Williams that he embarrassed himself with racist remarks about American minorities, but he has since studied the issue. "I learned that the energy of the U.S. is nurtured by different people coming together," Nakasone concluded. "It is the power of fusion." What he did not say was that the energy of Japan is nurtured by the ability of its one race to come together to the exclusion of all others. Americans might be as capable as the Japanese of making personal sacrifices for the good of the nation, but what could ever fuse them together as densely into a single element?

We cross the international date line, bent for Tokyo. . . . Perhaps Norma Field has put all my questions together in the notion that "the religion of Japan is Japaneseness, which is best practiced in daily life." Cultivated "to the point of invisibility by daily practice," she adds, "this religion is resistant to challenge. . . ."

As I contemplate the invisible ways of an invisible nation, I am distracted by a Japanese businessman skipping down the aisle in his socks. Emblazoned across the back of his white sweatshirt is a message in English: "Millions now free of acid indigestion." I sit up, laughing. It is so difficult to learn something true, true to the core. I lack the scepter of the seventeenth-century Japanese poet, Jozan, which is hollow down the center, the better "to express clarity of mind." By comparison, my scepter is as dense as a graphite rod.

Our plane is falling back to Earth.

❋   ❋   ❋

When Columbus first landed in the Americas, at San Salvador, he thought he was in Japan; sailing on to Cuba, he thought he had reached Cathay. Five hundred years later, I'm disoriented, too. China, America, Japan: I feel the poles of the world spin and wobble. This is the fabled island of Mu, a word for the perfect Void.

Thirty months have passed since I was in Japan. As the last decade of the century begins, I know how much the dizzying world has changed. The wall dividing Europe has melted down like pudding. The communist states of Eastern Europe and the Soviet Union, after which modern China tried to remold itself, have collapsed. America, which many saw as a declining power, is now preeminent, poised to dictate a "new world order" from the barrel of a gun—a robotic, electronic, cold and inhuman gun.

The Orient seems the least changed. In China, the motion of history has come to rest, countering by its inertia the currents sweeping much of the world. Tiananmen Square became the setting for a revolution, a democratic revolution presaging those of Poland, Hungary, Czechoslovakia, even Albania, but it died in the shock of storm troops and tanks on the fourth of June. Centralized, defiantly unfree and unrepentant, China is out of step—a big Burma, a gargantuan Cuba, a lion among little tigers.

As for Japan, the nineties open with a new phase in its imperial history. Hirohito has died, the era of the Showa Emperor is done, the new Heisei reign has begun, but corporate and social feudalisms are still enthroned. Today does not feel like a new era at all in Japan. The prosperity continues; Japan pulls alongside America; and visions of an all-out economic war with Japan enter the uneasy American psyche. While Japan, like most of the world, is in recession (the growth of its economic engines cut in half), employment has not been threatened, and the opposition parties are weak.

We return to Japan not as investigators of altered global and political realities, however; we return as ordinary travelers. We will not meet with notable Japanese leaders, celebrities, businessmen, or even writers. We will travel ordinary routes in ordinary ways. The Japan we're interested in is the daily one and also the invisible one which may not exist. We'll trace a different circle. We won't leave Tokyo's Narita Airport except on a connecting flight to the west. We will go all the way west to Kyushu, where the weather now changing from fall to winter will be more pleasing, the connections with China more intimate, the remnants of an older Japan more vital. Who knows? Carried far enough back into Japan, we might decelerate and vanish, transported on the back of a turtle to the submerged shores of Mu.

All this nonsense propels us on, but arriving in Fukuoka, Kyushu's capital, our plane dumps us into the midst of another Tokyo clone, a city of newly-minted granite, glass, and poured concrete.

XI.

Fukuoka:
The Great Wall of Japan

Since St. Francis Xavier first landed on the southern tip of the southern island in 1549, Kyushu has maintained a greater concentration of Christians than any other region of Japan. Never mind that the total enrollment of Christians is minuscule.

We happen to meet our first Kyushu Christian in a dingy waiting room at Narita International Airport, a room without grace, crammed like a boxcar with ticket holders, nearly every Japanese passenger lighting up a cigarette. There are so many cigarettes ablaze that the ashtrays smolder like volcanic vents.

We take refuge against a far wall. Beside us, also suffering from the smoke, a young woman echoes our complaint. Her name is Keiko, she speaks good English, and she is a Seventh-Day Adventist. There are twenty thousand Seventh-Day Adventists in Japan, Keiko says; and she should know: her father is a minister in an Adventist church near Fukuoka. There have been Adventists in Japan for a century.

Keiko lives in California and works at a hospital. The only reason she is returning home is to visit her mother, suddenly and seriously ill. By the time the spacious, smoke-free 767 comes to rest in the darkness of northern Kyushu, Keiko has invited us to stay in her family home, something we can not do, especially with her mother so ill.

We can see how the Adventist's prohibitions would be especially hard to swallow in Japan—no smoking, no fish—but when we ask Keiko why so few Japanese have converted to Christianity, she answers, "Because the Japanese are too well-off these days. They see no reason to convert."

※　※　※

Our hotel in the heart of Fukuoka bears the traditional name of Miyako, but it looks like Gumby in bell-bottom trousers. The Japanese have an amusing regard for modern architecture. Many of the new buildings are ridiculous, but fun, the sort of thing a teenage genius might design, spatially ugly but peppy and deflating. These new skyscrapers, office complexes, department stores, and hotel towers subscribe to an aesthetic the opposite of that of the miniature garden: they are blowups of shapes that might be graceful at a human scale, models you could hold in your palm, but enlarged, they become hilarious. There's something endearing about a ten-story beer bottle in which people live and work. A Godzilla architecture rises up on its hindquarters, lumbering across the cityscapes of Japan.

We spot our monstrous hotel from the Hakata subway station. We're as far south as the bullet train from Tokyo penetrates, its terminus our starting point, but we are hardly in the hinterlands. Tokyo-Fukuoka is the second busiest domestic air route in the world, traversed by five million passengers a year. Only Tokyo-Sapporo is more popular. It's midnight in Fukuoka; we're twenty-four hours without sleep. At street level, the false lobby we enter contains two escalators surrounded by a display of pottery, the craft for which Kyushu is most renowned. The upper lobby, the real one, consists of a no-nonsense check-in counter and two bellhops who do not attempt to separate us from our packs.

Our room is a double, all its accoutrements squeezed into place. Inside are more miniaturized spaces. The one window is a narrow strip, floor to ceiling, two feet wide, double-paned with built-in blinds. It affords a slight view of an adjacent office tower. A desk is built into the wall. A mini-fridge with night-switch is packed with liquor, oolong tea, and Pokari Sweat. There are three tiny curve-backed chairs, a coffee table, a lighted closet with a folding door, wide enough for three hangers. Between our two twin beds is a high-tech white plastic lamp/radio/clock; above it, an ink drawing of a nude. The bathroom is still more compact, and so tight that the handle to flush the toilet must be fixed to the side of the sink. A large hair dryer is mounted on the wall. There is room for a tray with shampoo, conditioner, soap, and two pre-pasted toothbrushes in cellophane. There are also three large containers of Kanebo Valcan hair products: hair tonic, hair liquid, and aftershave in a ghastly shade of green. Under a retractable laundry line, the tiny tub is painted with a blue ring signifying the high water mark, and a sign in English is printed on the wall: "Notice: Please don't use hair dye. Manager."

The inventory is by no means complete. Crammed into this room so small we walk sideways along the foot of the bed are the following: a hot thermos, a cold water thermos, two tea bags, two glasses, two tea cups, and a Panasonic color television. The TV offers NHK, RKB, and various satellite hookups, some with multiplex simultaneous translations into English and German. The pay sector provides (1) Golf from the Bridgestone Ladies Open with "shots of excellent techniques, the intensity of competition and the joy of victory of pro golfers"; (2) *Rainbow Kids*, a Japanese movie; (3) Harrison Ford in *Presumed Innocent*; and (4) "Special Video Programs," meaning two thirty-minute soft porn loops for adults. Charges vary; all are subject to the three-percent consumption tax.

It's as if a capsule hotel for drunken salarymen has exploded in here and reached respectable if pinched dimensions. These are Western accommodations, but with amenities for the Japanese businessman on a mid-level expense account.

Before bedding down I peer from a slit in the hide of Godzilla, trying to comprehend where I am. This could be any modern city. I fall back into the dark padded interior, deplaned but still flying. I dream of being chased by stiff-legged dinosaurs. When I wake it is still dark, and I can't remember where I am. It takes me so long to remember, to reconstruct the last few stages that brought me here, that it requires considerable willpower to keep from crying out in the dark.

❊ ❊ ❊

The oldest Zen temple in Japan, at least of the Rinzai sect, is said to be Shofuku-ji, within walking distance of our Fukuoka hotel. It was constructed in 1195. The priest Eisai had just returned from China, bearing Chan Buddhism (in Japanese, Zen Buddhism). At the main gate, a stele engraved to verify Zen's introduction to Japan still stands. Shofuku-ji prospered; it became Kyushu's largest complex; but after war and fire, it has been reduced to a fourth of its original size. At this site, Eisai is also credited with planting the first green tea in Japan, yet another item the Japanese borrowed from the high culture of ancient China. Scriptures in Eisai's own hand reside in the inner recesses of this temple, as does an old Korean bell, commemorating the main route by which Chinese civilization traveled to Japan.

Today, the temple grounds are as subdued as the yellow cat dozing in the sun in front of the closed side gate. The weathered wooden halls and shrines are sealed, but we encounter a few citizens of Fukuoka out for a quiet stroll, and at the rear of a particularly splendid wooden temple, we observe a gentleman in a camel hair sports coat and tie practicing the flute. The flute case lies open on the stairs, but he is not a street musician playing for coins. Everyone keeps their distance. It is quiet enough here to hear each note as it trembles on the breeze. The rock walkways are immaculate, not gaudy, the white gravel margins neatly raked. There are a few small wooden lean-tos, shrines with sandstone statues of pilgrims draped in bright red aprons and an exquisite memorial garden of heaped rocks, statuary, and steles. A brown-robed monk in a straw hat is bowed over, weeding the ground under a tea hedge. Lost in thought, he does not look up.

By lunchtime, we have wound through the city to its great central park, Ohori Koen, modeled after China's most celebrated body of water, West Lake. Here, however, the copyists have failed, or the likeness is too reduced and subtle for us to recognize. Ohori looks rather more like a shrunken Central Park in New York City, thoroughly urban, ringed by peaks of modern concrete buildings. Causeways connect small islands in the lake, once part of a castle moat, and we cross the bridges faithfully, but to no purpose; the scenery is uninspiring. Perhaps we have been walking too long, our first day outside in Japan. The din rolling in from the horizon reminds us that we are locked inside a huge metropolis; the old castle at the edge of the park is gone. A man is bent down feeding a gallery of pigeons. Four young schoolgirls join him, all smiles, two in navy pinafores. A young couple, their bicycles parked nearby, sit on the lake shore. He lies back, napping; she sits upright, reading a book. They have brought their pet to the lake, a white rabbit on a string. Cranes roost on an unbridged island, but against a backdrop of gray and redbrick apartment towers, they seem like residents of a zoo. Skirting the far arc of the lake, we are waylaid by a gaggle of schoolgirls wearing identical red track suits. Before jogging off in unison, they insist we take their photo—smiles, the V for Victory sign, the chant of "cheese."

Beyond the temples of Zen, jolted back to the modern, we sit on a bench at a children's playground. For the first time in Japan, we have a long look at two homeless men. They are not young. One has a bicycle, a woman's model, on which he carefully straps his bindle over the rear tire. His bedroll is protected by a clear plastic bag. To the handlebars he ties white plastic bags. Both men seem a bit lost, but not unhappy. One has opened a book and is singing to himself.

Back at the main parking lot we notice the stray cats sitting in the sun on the hoods of expensive cars. An old woman leaning on a plain wooden cane, assisted by her daughter and granddaughter, creeps around the edge of the lake and bends down to chat with a line of nursery school children outfitted in uniforms, cute as stuffed animals.

Famished, we dive into the nearest department store and make for the food floor in the basement, where we are arrested by a demonstration of Chinese dim sum, prepared by college students. It's a formal demo: three young women stand by in matching red suits, skirts, high heels, and bowler hats; they are draped in wide white sashes, as though they have just won a beauty pageant. We are not sure what is being promoted, but the store manager pops over to invite us to take more pictures.

Only a few hours back in Japan and we remember what a completely natty and wonderfully coifed nation modern Japan is. The kimono is disappearing from the streets, but a model 1960s Jacqueline Kennedy world of fashion reigns, children dressed up like dolls.

Given a choice between the suited life and the one among tea hedges, between rush and Zen, consumption and contemplation, we have no difficulty; but we are used to choosing; and here, both monastery and department store are severely circumscribed worlds. Nearly everyone wears a defining uniform, even in the guise of "free" Western fashions, so that schoolchildren, secretaries, salarymen, perhaps even tramps are fashioned to their group, dressing in front of the same mirror.

✳   ✳   ✳

At Fukuoka did Kublai Khan the conquest of Japan decree. In fact, it was at Fukuoka that China launched its two great military invasions of Japan. The first attempt failed in 1274, but seven years later nothing less than a divine wind—a kamikaze—would be enough to repel the Chinese Armada. With 4,400 ships and 140,000 soldiers converging on Hakata Bay, the Khan's forces dwarfed those of the more famous Spanish Armada, and southern Japan, which had been the first point of contact with China since the second century, was the last unclaimed kingdom of the East for the Mongols, who ruled the Orient as far west as the Black Sea.

In the first invasion, Kublai had marshaled nine hundred ships with forty thousand Chinese and Korean soldiers to bring Japan to its knees. The invaders reached Hakata Bay and completed one day's military campaign before a typhoon threatened. The fleet put to sea where hundreds of ships sank, thirteen thousand troops drowned, and the campaign ended. The Khan was not pleased.

Meanwhile, the Japanese built a wall of stone, their western barrier to the next invasion. Only twelve miles long, the wall ran through nine regions, and each local leader was responsible for erecting his domain's sector. It was not a copy of China's Great Wall: just six feet tall and eight feet wide, it could not have been visible from space; yet the fortification was fated to hold. In 1281, the advance contingents of Chinese who landed at its foot were unable to penetrate Japan. The Japanese mounted a resistance force of a hundred thousand. The Mongols employed poisoned arrows, lassos, and spears; the Japanese countered with wooden shields and swords. By the end of July, the invaders withdrew to the sea, joining up with the main fleet that had arrived late after months of bureaucratic delay.

All Japan, from the Emperor down, mounted elaborate programs of prayer at Shinto shrines. A priest at Fukuoka, Nichiren, although calling the Japanese to task for past sins, prophesized supernatural doom for the outsiders. Indeed, a divine wind did strike in August, taking down four thousand ships and as many as a hundred thousand of the Chinese. Saved a second time by typhoon, Japan kept intact its record of never succumbing to invasion; and Japan would not be occupied by a foreign military force until this century, when a second great empire, the American one, unleashed its own atomic wind, flattening the old gods forever.

Segments of the stone fortification against the Mongolian invasion still exist on Hakata Bay at Ikinomatsubara, Mazu, and Nishijin. We reach the wall by train, half an hour from central Fukuoka. Tourists venture out to the coast here, but there are no others this afternoon and not a single vendor. We hike through twisted pines and sea brush, following signs to the exposed portions of the wall. These prove to be uninspiring ruins—just a long lane of rocks fitted by hand, little more than a fat country fence. The old wall has been excavated and resides in a pit. The pit is surrounded by a cyclone fence. There's a slight breeze coming in off the sea. China and Korea are close, due west. Kyushu is as close to the edge of the Oriental mainland as Japan gets. That's what drew us here—the point of first contact. As we circle Kyushu we will also come to other points of contact, where Christians and Europeans first came ashore.

But China was near. A few Japanese had left Kyushu and seen China for themselves, returning with Zen, tea, calligraphy, and customs of the greatest empire in the world. (Later it was said that the folding fan was the only purely Japanese invention that was not imported from China.) Yet even in Kyushu, the Chinese connection could be tenuous. Decades passed in which the sole intercourse was by trading ship, and usually it was the Chinese who came to Japan, not the reverse.

We walk both sides of the excavated wall. There's not a soul in the vicinity. The pine trees have a battered, cowered visage. We locate a formal path to the sea, where a work gang is taking down some of the old pines, loosened by the latest typhoon. The wood is sawn into segments and neatly stacked on a tiny red trailer with tank tires. The three workers, two men and a woman, greet us shyly. We walk through a torii gate to the beach. The sand is strewn with debris. The storm six weeks earlier has washed garbage far inland; it nestles in the entangled tree trunks, still uncollected. West along the shore is a brick path, a cement seawall, and another fenced excavation of the Anti-Mongolian wall. We turn back on a second littered path and reach a busy street. At an immaculate graveyard of marble terraces and markers we watch a brown, black, and white calico meander up and down the blocks of the dead. The cemetery is trimmed in a wire fence. Opposite, in the garden of a house, an old woman is bent over pulling up onions, another cat at her feet.

✴   ✴   ✴

On a rare day in winter, after a storm at sea, one might still find a glass float torn loose from a Japanese fishing net, washed up on the shores of Oregon. Sometimes whole ships, broken in storms, demasted and rudderless, drifted across the Pacific on the same long route and reached foreign lands, their crews still clinging to life. The kamikaze of a typhoon could turn back invasions from China, but Kuroshio, the Black Current, could propel Japanese sailors into distant exile.

During the Edo Period, 1603-1867, when the Tokugawa Shoguns ruled, it was forbidden upon the penalty of death for any citizen to leave Japan or indeed to return to Japan from any other country—but castaways did both, none was ever executed, and the first Japanese on record to visit America was just such a drifter. His name was Captain Jukichi. His ship was slapped by a storm southeast of Nagoya in October, 1813, and for a year and a half it drifted across the empty Pacific. Most of his crew died early on. Captain Jukichi stored their corpses on wooden boards next to his own cabin, but in the end he had to consign the flesh and crumbling skulls to the sea, carefully cleaning the room afterwards. By the second year adrift, he and the two surviving crewmen were living solely on soybeans.

On March 24, 1815, the *Forester*, one of John Jacob Astor's fur-trading ships, happened upon the drifters and took them aboard, where Captain Jukichi was served food he could not recognize. He assumed his rescuers were Dutch and that he was near Nagasaki, where the Dutch maintained a trading post. When the ship made landfall, however, Jukichi was transported by horseback to a small village where there was not a single Japanese resident. The following morning, he returned ashore with some of the sailors. They came to a herd of cows in a field. Using axes, the crew slaughtered the cattle; with long kitchen knives, they stripped off the hides. Jukichi, a vegetarian Buddhist, wept. Later he wrote, "This could not be Nagasaki. I must have come to animals' hell."

In fact he had arrived in California; he was somewhere near the present site of Santa Barbara. After eleven days in California, Jukichi's rescuers sailed north to Alaska. It was four years before he managed to return to Japan. After his long ordeal in strange lands, Jukichi, like a Japanese Gulliver, had become strange to his own people. He did not allow his wife near him. Raised to the rank of samurai, he ignored all worldly demands save one: to build a memorial to his deceased mates. He toured temples and begged for funds in return for displaying the artifacts of his foreign travels. Then he resigned as a samurai, plunging his family into poverty. His wife left him; so did his only son.

Finally, in 1824, a large stone ship with the Buddhist prayer of supplication etched on its mast in Chinese characters was placed in a temple; on a square base were the names of the doomed sailors. Jukichi's monument is on display today at the Jofuku-ji Temple in Nagoya, where Katherine Plummer, who has brought the stories of Japan's long distance drifters to Western readers in *The Shogun's Reluctant Ambassadors*, visited it in 1981. Ms. Plummer points out that although these "unwitting emissaries" returned with valuable information about the outside world, few Japanese were interested. In fact, the relation of stories about life abroad was illegal in Tokugawa Japan. Captain Jukichi's story was narrated in secret to a local scholar and circulated underground. This account would remain virtually unknown to the Japanese public; one of the few copies left is at the temple in Nagoya.

Pre-modern Japan was as xenophobic as its ancient cultural model, China. As Engelbrecht Kaempfer, a Dutch scholar, wrote in the seventeenth century, "The voyages and travels of the natives into foreign countries, of foreigners into Japan, were judged prejudicial to the publick tranquility, forasmuch as they serve only to breed inclinations inconsistent with the nature of the country, and the genius of the Nation."

XII.

Okawachiyama:
The Secret Kilns

L eaving Fukuoka, we board a local train westward to Karatsu and south to the pottery village of Imari. Tons of schoolchildren in uniform, dressed like sailors from the past, board along the way and give full rein to a wilder streak they control at school. Although they are curious about the American couple aboard this morning, they do not heckle us, keeping to their groups. In their arrogance and unruly energy, they remind us of American school kids; but belonging to the group makes them less self-conscious. One seat ahead of us a boy is bent over, picking his schoolmate's pimples.

Another group on these faraway trains consists of adventurous senior citizens, all smiles, their teeth golden, out together for an excursion. They chatter away, holding each other's arms. Their windbreakers match, of course, and so do their cotton tennis shoes. Some carry modern metal walking sticks, claw-footed for support. They are having a ball, Margaret whispers. One extremely old man gets on at a village stop smoking an unfiltered cigarette, forbidden in our car, and consumes it—no one, not even the conductor, pointing out the rules. Like the other oldsters, he dons a white duckbill cap. They seem so happy and innocent as tourists that one forgets the history they must have lived through, the whole century, the war, the occupation, the rebuilding. We know nothing of what they suffered, except that it was considerable. Between them and the new students there is a gulf, as there is between centuries, now between generations, even in Japan—or so we imagine until we think where the school clans are headed in the new Japan: most to lives of narrow choices: salarymen and housewives, many moving east to Tokyo.

Karatsu, where we change trains for Imari, seems a wild west town. The name means "China Port," and it was from here that Japanese porcelains were first exported. As the train slows down, we pass the Log Cabin Restaurant and then a trailer court of covered wagons. There's something called the Sound R.V. Park and then the Magic Garden Trailer Court, places we're told later where young people come and rent space to listen to loud music—audio love hotels for adolescents.

The students are gone now, and most of the trekking seniors, too, leaving few of us on the leg to Imari. There are some fastidious white-collar workers aboard, eyes always cast down, their lips reciting lines in a whisper, as though they are on their way to give a speech in English. An old lady across the aisle is futzing and futzing. She adjusts her lunch, untying it from a scarf and repacking it. She rearranges and refolds her towel until it is just so. She empties everything from her purse and puts it back in better order. Along the tracks the roofs are tiled, except a few in straw. White cranes dot the rice fields. The fruit trees are bare this autumn, their leaves stripped. The lady has removed her shoes and put her feet up on the facing seat, but the vacuum holds for a moment only; she can't stop filling it.

We pull into Imari, a deliberately quaint town where even the manhole covers are exquisite: tableaus of junks laden with pottery, sailing from the kilns of Imari upon a river to the sea—where, via the straits of Malacca and Africa, Japanese ceramics first reached the West.

✳   ✳   ✳

Imari, at the center of Saga Prefecture, became a term synonymous with Japanese pottery in seventeenth-century Europe. Japan's trade with the West originated in such ports, and during the 1600s the Dutch East India Company hauled tons of Imari ware to Europe. The route became known as the Ceramic Road. Imari ware was not Japanese in origin, however; it was the product of master artisans forcibly removed from Korea, then contained for life in pottery towns. Potters of Korean ancestry still live in this region. There are 700,000 Japanese-born Koreans in Japan today; many have not adopted Japanese names, a requirement for becoming citizens, and are registered as aliens.

The best preserved of these Korean pottery villages is a few miles into the mountains from Imari. When we disembark at Okiwachiyama, the Village of the Secret Kilns, we find a group of craftspeople in the parking lot packing up the stalls, displays, and wares from a five-day festival. Later, waiting for the return bus, we notice how the clean-up is organized. Everyone knows everyone else in this tiny hillside town, and the work is friendly, informal, cooperative—in the older sense of Japan, communal.

Okawachiyama is too cute to be real, and it is no longer what it was, a camp where captive workers filled the treasuries of the Lords of Saga with fine exports. Today, it is a pleasant, steep outdoor shopping mall for tourists from Tokyo, although the hill houses are real enough and one old kiln looks as if it is still fired by wood. In the early afternoon, few tourists have made the trek, fewer still of the festival-weary potters have opened their doors, and for the most part we are climbing uphill alone, in a silent town under a dark blue sky. After Fukuoka, we don't mind this at all. The kilns at Okawachiyama were built in 1675 upon the order of Lord Nabeshima, and here, using the celadon clay of the mountains, there evolved three distinct new wares, including Nabeshima-Sometsuke, whose pacific blue designs frequently depicted scenes from classical China (which in turn is the initial source of much Korean pottery).

Hideyoshi, who completed the unification of Japan in the late sixteenth century and was to be succeeded by the first of the Tokugawa Shoguns, launched two invasions of Korea, in 1592 and 1597—Mongolian Invasions in reverse, since Hideyoshi's ultimate goal was the conquest of China. His forces failed miserably, but many of the generals from Kyushu, fanciers of the tea ceremony and connoisseurs of Korean tea vessels, compelled hundreds of Korean potters to return to Japan. The invasions became known as the Pottery Wars, and particularly in the creation of porcelains, Japan was victorious.

In 1615, a captured Korean potter, Ri Sanpei, came upon kaolin, a white clay, and porcelain production began in Saga—by coincidence at a time when European demand for similar Chinese porcelain was high and China's ability to fulfill it low. The Nabeshima clan established well-guarded communities of Korean potters at Okawachiyama and Arita.

The largest brick kiln at Okawachiyama today is by no means ancient, but its form is traditional—that of the climbing kiln (*noborigama*), introduced from Korea. The linked chambers are built on a slope and fired from the bottom up. Fuel is added at each chamber, and it takes days to reach the 1300-degree mark, hot enough to fire the porcelain. Red pine is the favored wood. Under a rude wooden shed, the climbing kiln is cool and quiet now. Hardly a resident appears on any of the streets that twist into the mountainside. There are no restaurants or inns in this village, and that helps preserve it. We follow the undulating stream back down, its bed sculpted in curves by cemented stones.

The bus will not be back for hours. We walk to the exhibition hall, but it is closed. The public rest room is as inviting as a temple: a roof of gray tiles, an enormous blue and white tile mosaic of a mountain village forming the wall between the men's side and the women's. Three women are cleaning up the stubble of a rice field near the rest house. Across the highway is the river and a wide hillside cemetery.

At the entrance to town, on the far side of the highway, is the rebuilt barrier gate that once confined the Korean artisans, and beyond it, over the river to Imari, is a chime bridge, where bells on a post ring in the wind. Across it is a straw-roofed pavilion known as The Crusher, underneath which three enormous wooden teeter-totters, as large as dugout canoes, fill with water, pivot, and empty into the river, snapping back to rest with a thrashing force. Beyond the old machinery is Okawachiyama's true monument to its secret past, Potter's Field—the pyramid piled high with the 880 gravestones of Koreans who lived and died in the village, crowned with a Buddhist statue, arms uplifted in compassion. Nearby is the grave of Ri Sanpei himself, and the white statue of the goddess of mercy, her hands folded in prayer. This potter's pyramid of uniform, engraved stone tablets is one of the most affecting in Japan. Across the river the village and its score of kiln chimneys are folded into the steep blue mountains as into a curtain. One can imagine the subterranean tears of these exiles, generation after generation, for whom there is never a slip of hope for return, unless it be beyond the grave, the other side of stone.

XIII.

Nagasaki:
The Glass Hand

Margaret masters the Japanese railway timetable on the limited express southwest to Nagasaki. We see hints of the damage inflicted by Typhoon Number 19. In monetary terms, Number 19 was the second worst typhoon ever to hit Japan. Six weeks after this ill wind, tile roofs remain ripped open, fields scoured, fruit trees empty, greenhouses uncovered, and in Nagasaki, stained glass windows on a historic church blown out, the entrance gate to a Buddhist temple smashed in.

We walk from our Nagasaki hotel to the harbor. This is a picture-perfect city, a tourist's port of hills and streetcars often compared to San Francisco. In all of Japan, Nagasaki boasts of the longest connection with the Western world. For us, Nagasaki has a another face, of course, translucent, with darker bones beneath the skin. Here is where we dropped the second atomic bomb. I'm uneasy. I've come to Nagasaki to face a fear fated to be mine since birth, to walk across the ground zero of this disemboweling century, but now that I'm here, I'm losing my nerve. I mean to postpone this mission as long as possible.

The harbor is busy with ships and tankers under fresh blue skies. The air smells clean, as if it has washed across a bay of flowers. We circle the Monument to the Travelers to Nagasaki, a grouping of six life-size figures in bronze, representative of the two thousand young men who journeyed here to study before Japan opened to outsiders in 1859. These are the students who laid the foundations for the Meiji Restoration, the end of Shogunate Japan and the beginning of a modern nation.

We are alone this December except for the five tour buses in the far corner of the harbor parking lot. A handful of the passengers joins us—five schoolgirls in dark blue middies, black nylons and shoes, their hair all cut the same medium length. Their teacher, in a gray blazer, explains in English that they are on a field trip from Tokyo. Nagasaki is a favorite of school groups from all over Japan. Planeloads of school kids descend on the city year-round. She tries to prompt the girls to practice their English, but they are shy. We ask what grade they are in. They answer the eleventh grade, but they seem much younger. We ask what sight they enjoyed most in Nagasaki: the Christian churches, Chinese temples, historic bridges, the Dutch Island, the Atomic Bomb Museum, the Madame Butterfly House? No, they all agree, the best sight in Nagasaki is the shopping.

After they rush off to the buses, shopping bags swinging, we notice that two of the Travelers to Nagasaki figures are missing, severed at the ankle by Typhoon 19. Only their feet, pinioned by steel bars, remain in place, one pair facing west, one pair facing east.

*　　*　　*

We head north along the Nagasaki harbor and buy tickets for the scenic boat tour on the Ohato Pier. At first we are alone aboard a large vessel, but at the last moment the pier fills with uniformed schoolchildren, whole schools of them, blue-coated boys as well as girls, boisterous, held in check by a few teachers and two young lady tour guides decked out in red jackets with white blouses and black ties, red pleated skirts, black high heels connected by white nylons, and the silly black bowler hats that are all the rage in Japan. They carry the flags identifying their tour company; all day they rally their group around them at sight after sight.

As we pull away from the wharf, a loud speaker cranks up and bellows forth a recorded narrative of Nagasaki Harbor in Japanese, complete with an occasional ballad sung by the female narrator. We escape this blast by standing outside on the high observation deck. Nagasaki's harbor, one of the Orient's largest, is Japan's chief shipbuilding location, as it was in 1945 when we targeted it for the second atomic bombing. We ended up hitting a point well north of the harbor, in the next fold of steep hills. We also leveled a Catholic Church.

The dry docks are massive; the red- and white-striped cranes, long and muscular. Here the big vessels are built, the container ships and super-tankers. These are the dry docks of the Mitsubishi Industries, Ltd., Nagasaki Shipyard and Machinery Works. One dock, with a one million ton capacity, is said to be the world's largest. It is situated in the harbor on Koyagi Island, named for Kobo Daishi, who lit incense on the spot before leaving for China in the ninth century. The stone stairway of a small temple leads down from the island to the water; the Chinese merchants of Nagasaki still come here to pray for the souls of Chinese sailors lost at sea.

One of the students is brave enough to corner me on deck and pummel me with questions and answers lifted from his English language primer. He speaks very, very slowly, and he speaks clearly. His history teacher rescues me. The teacher speaks rapid-fire English with holes in it, difficult to follow. These students are on a field trip from Hokkaido, the northern island of Japan.

Mostly, we are left alone. Japan is a fine country to tour because Westerners are mostly left alone. It can be a cold country in that way, but if one makes the first move, relations quickly thaw. I like being left alone, standing over the water, waiting to see what comes up next—a Japanese Navy boat, a freighter from Panama with a Japanese name, a tiny island where shiny steel wind turbines sing low. Turning back, we have fine views of the city tumbling down the hills to the harbor. It is a low-rise city, no skyscrapers, a town-city. A couple with a child ask me to snap their portrait using a disposable camera. They are a Japanese couple, but they are from Brazil, and their child has grown up in Brasilia. They all speak Portuguese.

In the afternoon we eat lunch on a back street near our hotel. Most of downtown Nagasaki is a series of cramped alleyways laid this way and that. Old women on motor scooters bomb by without a glance, brushing us back. A man in tie and suit gallantly helps us buy bananas from a sidewalk vendor. Across from the bench where we spread out, munching on breads and pastries, sipping from a plastic carton of milk, is a two-story building over a small driveway where preschool children are at play. A metal tower rises from the driveway, a skeleton of steel bars topped by a turret with a siren. It take us twenty minutes to recognize that this is the neighborhood firehouse and that the firehouse keeper's family lives inside.

✳　✳　✳

The port of Nagasaki dates from 1571 when it was created especially for foreign trade. The local leader, Omura-Sumitada, had converted to Christianity; in 1580, he put a large section of the port's village under the control of the Jesuit fathers. Seven years later, Japan's strongman Hideyoshi confiscated the Christian town and put it back in the hands of the Japanese. This did not stop European ships from converging on Nagasaki. Chinese silk and Japanese silver were the coveted items of exchange at the time, and since Japanese sailors were prohibited from leaving the shores of Japan, these foreign intermediaries were necessary to keep Middle Kingdom luxuries in supply.

In the early days of foreign trade, the Portuguese held sway at Nagasaki. If they hadn't pushed Christianity so hard, the Portuguese might have stretched the "Christian Century" beyond 1639, when they and all other Europeans except the Dutch were banned from Japanese ports. The ban held for several hundred years, but for a few decades the Japanese at Nagasaki copied Portuguese fashions and frills at a furious rate, cultivating such foreign delicacies as card games, tobacco, bread, and a sponge cake called castella (*kasutera*) that remains Nagasaki's key confectionery. The Nagasaki upper crust also enjoyed dressing up Portuguese, in capes and puffy pantaloons. But as the crackdown on Christians intensified, Portugal's Nagasaki days were numbered. In the end, only the Dutch—who alone seemed uninterested in proselytizing—ended up with a Japanese outpost: a compact artificial island in the harbor, joined to Nagasaki by a guarded bridge. The island was called Dejima. There the Dutch maintained a quarantined trading village from 1641 to 1854—the sole European presence in Japan across three centuries.

Dejima survives, albeit as a shrunken copy of itself. We find the Dutch traders' old island by walking a few blocks up the Nakajima River from the land-filled harbor. What remains of the real Dejima—a few stone cannons painted in dark rust on stone wheels, a warehouse, a small field in which shards of pottery and debris are being excavated—is next door to a scale model of the isle, reduced fifteen times. We stride like giants around this fan-shaped replica, looking down on the tiny brown two-story wooden houses with shoji screens surrounded by a tile-roofed wall. There are tiny trees, too, and a moat.

Another field-tripping school group in red baseball caps has joined us. We circulate clockwise. Looking toward the harbor I can see a line of concrete buildings topped by a huge sign with the three red diamonds of the Mitsubishi logo looming over this bonsai of the past.

※　※　※

The Chinese started to settle at Nagasaki five centuries ago. Straight up the hillside from Dejima, east of the river that splits the city in half, is the Teramachi district, the domain of Buddhist temples, most of which were built by and for the Chinese. The first of these,

Kofuku-ji, was constructed in 1620; its main hall was rebuilt in the late 1800s by craftsmen from Nanjing. The most famous of Nagasaki's Chinese temples is Sofuku-ji, constructed in 1629 under the eye of Chaonian, a monk from Fuzhou who here introduced the Obaku Zen sect to Japan. Some of the best of China's Ming Dynasty architecture is preserved here: the main hall was built in China and reassembled in Nagasaki in 1646. We find it nearly uninhabited. There's a school and playground within its walls, and a few schoolchildren wave at us from the top of some long stairs. The temples are old enough to pass for those still left in China, save for their wealthier, cleaner appearances, a few Shinto decorations, the ladle and wooden basin, and the stone graveyards attached to the main temples like arms.

In 1689, the Shogun moved the Chinese into a walled compound in the southeast section of Nagasaki—a looser form of the Dutch Dejima. Two wooden halls remain in Nagasaki's small Chinatown, as do scores of shops and restaurants. The Chinese population of Nagasaki is seven hundred, in a city a thousand times that big, but the number is considered significant in Japan, where few foreign enclaves exist. The Nagasaki Chinese exerted a lasting influence on the city and on Japan, introducing the dragon dance, painting techniques, and engineering principles. The Hong Kong-Shanghai Bank Building still stands facing the Nagasaki harbor; it was once the terminus of the only telegraph line linking Japan to China, and via Shanghai, to Europe.

The most ostentatious edifice of the Chinese presence in Nagasaki is the Confucian Shrine built with assistance from the Chinese government in 1893 and refurbished in 1983. It is blindingly overdone, with beaming yellow tile roofs and red walls. The main courtyard is lined with seventy-two marble statues of Confucian disciples—each figure spotlessly white and smooth as polished plaster. Nowhere in China have I ever seen such immaculate temple decoration, and I suspect that from Day One no idol in China ever started out this clean. Next door is a Chinese Museum with objects on loan from the People's Republic, including a few of the terra-cotta soldiers of China's First Emperor from Xi'an. It is a small collection that in its spiffiness makes me long for real China's dirt and grime.

The Buddhist temples slope down each to its own arched bridge on the Nakajima River. The causeways along these ten historic bridges make for a fine afternoon stroll. A few women are out in their kimonos and geta, and rickshaws weave through the motorcycle and small truck traffic. Everyone stops at Megane-Bashi, Spectacles Bridge, so named because its double arches, reflected in the river below, resemble a pair of glasses. The river is too low these days for such reflections. Spectacles is credited to the genius of a Chinese monk from the Kofuku-ji Temple, who imparted to Nagasaki the secrets of building the stone arch. Standing in one way or another since 1634, Spectacles Bridge is Japan's oldest stone arch bridge, although it is thought that it may have started out as a covered wooden bridge. What is certain is that it has been bashed by countless floods and typhoons from as early as 1647. On the night on July 23, 1982, Spectacles Bridge was so heavily damaged by flood waters that it had to be pieced back together stone by stone.

We buy ice cream cones from a woman wearing a white duckbill cap and apron. She digs a lump of ice cream from a chamber deep in a green pushcart. It looks wonderful, the ice cream, but it is no good—about as tasty as teflon. We watch the Japanese tourists cross the Spectacles Bridge, posing for pictures. Everyone snaps away.

Ducks gather downriver, and parallel to them an old man and his daughter descend the paving-stone bank to the edge. She is assisting him with obvious reluctance. They are carrying piles of sticks and boards, cardboard boxes and newspapers, stacking them up on the shore walkway. He drops his cane, squats down on the rocks of the low river bed, and makes a neat pyre of sticks. His daughter hands him piece after piece. He lingers over the newspapers, scanning the headlines before consigning them to the fire. We are not the only ones watching. Everyone's baffled as to his purpose. Even his daughter walks away with a puzzled air. What could he be burning by the river, and why? Something of his life, a life near its end, wrapped up in wood—no one can see what. We would have to look through lenses as large as bridge arches to know what he is burning. In the end, of course, it doesn't matter. One day everything will be carried to the sea by flood; even fire will be drowned.

❋　❋　❋

On February 5, 1597, twenty-six Christians were crucified on Nishizaka Hill in Nagasaki. They were nailed to the cross as examples, following the decree of Hideyoshi who saw Christianity as the vanguard of a Western invasion. The twenty-six were marched to their martyrdom overland from Kyoto. Twenty of the twenty-six were Japanese converts; six were foreigners, including four from Spain, one from Mexico, and one from India; and three of the executed were children. None, not even the children, renounced their faith on Nishizaka Hill.

In 1862, the crucified were canonized by Pope Pius IX. One hundred years later, a monument to the martyrs was unveiled on the plain hillside: a wide bronze cross on a wall, the twenty-six impaled upon it, all in robes, hands in prayer, halos radiating. The scale of the figures is roughly 1:4. There are visitors as we approach—again, schoolchildren out for a scenic education. To the right of the monument wall two utterly bizarre steeples pierce the sky. For a moment we are in Barcelona; these towers are exactly the sort one would now identify with Antonio Gaudi—living forms, tall collages pieced together as if by intelligent wasps.

It turns out that the spires and the memorial hall nearby are the work of Imai Kenji, a student of Spain's Gaudi. Imai Kenji collected ceramic, clay, and glass fragments along the route the martyrs walked in 1597 and pasted them to a wall of the Martyr's Hill museum. He decorated the courtyard with stone, slate, and shattered vessels. The mosaic is a marvelous hodgepodge, wild and swirling, emblematic and primitive, with all the inspired disorder of a child's collage.

The twenty-six executed here were the region's first great martyrs. Many followed. Foreign missionaries were forcibly expelled in 1614, and the Christians who remained were punished in ways that defy the imagination: by branding, by boiling, by burning in straw raincoats. Richard Cocks, an English businessman, reported another sixteen martyrs "in the Towne of Nagasaki . . . whereof five were burned and the rest beheaded and cut in pieces, and cast into the Sea in Sackes of thirtie fathome deepe: yet the Priests got them up againe, and kept them secretly for Reliques." Cocks reported the pulling down of churches across Japan, the opening of their graveyards and expulsion of Christian bones, the establishment of pagodas and Buddhist temples in former churchyards—all undertaken "utterly to roote out the memory of Christianitie out of Japan."

Yet a native Christianity flourished and did not die down until the Shimabara Rebellion in 1638, when forty thousand impoverished peasants and Christian converts were crushed in Kyushu by 120,000 of the Shogun's troops. Even then, the Japanese Christians held on. They hid in villages near Nagasaki and handed down the doctrine in secret. In 1852, before the ban on Christianity was raised, Nagasaki's daimyo sent a group of young Japanese converts to Rome, where the Pope received them. Then, in 1865, a month after the Oura Catholic Church, dedicated to the twenty-six martyrs, opened in Nagasaki, a group of hidden Christians introduced themselves to Father Petitjean. They had kept their faith underground for two centuries.

As a result of its history, the Nagasaki region contains twenty percent of all Japanese Catholics. Pope John Paul II visited in 1981 to conduct an ordination mass for fourteen new priests at the cathedral that had once been the largest in Japan; it was a rebuilt version, having been leveled by the A-bomb thirty-six years earlier.

The martyr's monument and memorial hall are, like Christianity in Japan, minor markers even in a city as ostensibly international as Nagasaki. In their austerity and relative unimportance as tourist sites, they retain a bit of dignity, unruffled by a thousand vendors, tour buses, and monolithic landscaping. Yet there's almost always a bizarre touch. Between the martyr's monument and the museum to early Christianity in Japan is a public rest room where, along one wall, a woman opens a cluster of plastic garbage bags stuffed with empty pop cans. She dons an apron and systematically feeds the cans into a vending machine one at a time. On the side of the machine is painted a parrot in a baseball cap and overalls, a can crushed in its beak. This is a can-crushing machine, and as each can disappears into its trapdoor mouth, a tiny ticket stub is coughed back out—a coupon redeemable for merchandise, Green Stamps for recyclers. What attracts us to the recycling machine is its annoying voice. As each can is inserted and crushed, a recording mechanism barks out its thank you in Japanese: "Arigato gozaimashita." This is the same phrase one is constantly assaulted with by the shop girls in the basement of a department store as one runs the gauntlet from counter to counter. The robotic version is harsher and even less stoppable, and the recycler seems hypnotized by its crushing monotony. "Arigato gozaimashita." Snap. Cough. Sputter. "Arigato gozaimashita." "Arigato gozaimashita." "Arigato gozaimashita." A nation so rite-bound in its politeness its machines must be taught to act Japanese.

❋   ❋   ❋

Nagasaki is an entangled city. We can only pull a few strands. We have no time to track down the banyan tree that Ulysses S. Grant planted here in 1879, and no purpose in finding it, either. We fairly fly up and down "Dutch Slope," where seven clapboard houses stand, apparently built as residences in the late nineteenth century for foreign employees of some company. The verandas and the latticework above the verandas were crafted by the Japanese, but the blocky style is every inch and bead European. All the houses except one are closed up, and the open one is a new restaurant. We peer in a window or two. Dutch Slope is a Wild West ghost town. The interiors are as vacant as a plain of sod.

We do manage a few hours in Glover Park, just above our perfectly-Westernized business hotel, the Nagasaki Tokyu. We climb the hill that passes Oura Cathedral, Japan's oldest gothic-style church, where the Crypto-Christians first revealed themselves after a mere 225 years of secret devotion in a society where privacy scarcely exists. Topping this steep grade, steeped in the aroma of sponge cake baked in a dozen shops, we arrive at Glover Park, the model village of Nagasaki's Western legacy, a collection of actual buildings and mansions from the past century, lived in by Japan's first resident entrepreneurs from abroad. The park grounds are spacious and green, landscaped in the Japanese style, with goldfish ponds and rock work. There are outdoor escalators cut into the grassy slope, lending to the whole display the ambiance of a department store.

As we ride up we are entertained by piped-in music—Scottish music, as it happens—and at the top we have a full view of the harbor and massive dry docks. When Kobo Daishi walked through Nagasaki and boarded a ship for China, there wasn't a single shiny escalator, nor a Western house, no docks or metal cranes, no hotels, no factories, no streetcars, not one Chinese temple—maybe a hut and a fisherman's family, a wooden boat or two.

Somewhere in Glover Park are fragments of Japan's first asphalt road and the nation's first tennis court, but we don't find either. Instead, we follow the path from building to building. The three most important mansions—those of Alt, Ringer, and Glover—are on their original lots above the harbor and possess sweeping covered porches, stately columns, immense wooden shutters. They resemble colonial bungalows, except for the Japanese tiled roofs and gardens. The interiors retain the original furnishings and knickknacks of Meiji Restoration days. The Alt House, home to tea exporter William Alt, dates from about 1865. Built of stone upon stone, it features a high Tuscan vestibule. Koyama Hide, a local master carpenter, did the house—built the Oura Cathedral, too. The Ringer House is a wooden version of the Alt mansion, finished the same year. Frederick Ringer was an Englishman, a tea inspector out of Canton, who ended up a trader in machinery and coal, but also had a hand in producing a Nagasaki newspaper and establishing the city water system.

The third house is the big one, the home of Thomas Blake Glover (1838-1911). Glover hailed from Aberdeen, Scotland, hence the Scottish music aboard the garden escalators. He arrived at Nagasaki via Shanghai in 1859, age twenty-two, an international arms dealer. His Glover & Co. supplied many a Japanese daimyo with gunpowder and warships. His house is the largest bungalow of the lot, and the oldest. Constructed about 1862 by the redoubtable Koyama Hide, it is the oldest Western-style home in Japan. Repeated again and again is the claim that this is the house that inspired the creation in the West of our best-known literary and operatic figure from Japan—Madame Butterfly.

No one knows the true sources of Madame Butterfly, but the setting is right, and certain aspects of Glover's pioneering life in Japan are highly operatic. He dabbled in every enterprise of the century, from coal mines and steamships to a brewery in Yokohama. He aided young Japanese students bound for Europe. He married a Japanese woman—rumored to be the divorced wife of a samurai—and they had a daughter and son. The old family photographs in Glover Park hint at a rich "colonial" life. In 1908, Glover received the Second Class Order of the Rising Sun from the government. His son, Kuraba Tomisaburo, stayed in Japan and was essentially Japanese, so much so that there, during World War II, when falsely accused of being a traitor to Japan, he committed suicide.

The interior of Glover's mansion is so crowded with Japanese tourists and tour groups that we enter by the rear exit. The rooms are furnished with period pieces and given over to life-sized waxen statues of their original inhabitants who sit forever fixed in parlors discussing the affairs of a vanished world. These polished puppets inspire keen interest, prolonged looks, and considerable contemplation. We elbow through for a close look at Glover and his wife, his daughter who left Japan, and his son who stayed to die.

We're surrounded by Japanese. If Nagasaki is Japan's international city—and by Japanese standards it certainly is—then one still needs a magnifying glass and a tour guide to find it so. In feeling and to most appearances, Nagasaki is a thoroughly Japanese city, prettier than most but not noticeably more cosmopolitan. In the center of Glover Park is an image of Puccini in relief; a wall decorated with music from his opera, Madame Butterfly; and a statue of Japanese opera diva Miura Tamaki.

There's no equivalent in America for Glover Park, none at all. We have houses, sites, and parks dedicated to immigrants, but their descendants have multiplied, not disappeared. Few, few indeed are the Westerners who ever came to Japan to begin new generations, to live and to die.

✳   ✳   ✳

Yet Westerners did die in Nagasaki, although not by choice. The oldest of the city's seven international cemeteries is across the harbor on the flanks of Inasa. Again we strike out on foot, an hour's walk, and locate Goshin-ji Temple. Behind it is a Chinese cemetery, established in 1602 for burial of Chinese traders, and still in use. The hillside is a series of fenced yards in which Nagasaki's various waves of immigrants are buried. To one side of the elaborate armchair graves, low walls, and paved courtyards of the Chinese are the Dutch and Russian plots. Since the mid-1600s, the Dutch have been burying their dead here. It is well-tended: a neat graveyard of large headstones. The gate in the high stone fence is locked, however, but we are alone and I find a way to climb in. It's Dutch, all right: swept clean, the headstones aging but legible.

Adjacent is the Russian sector, also fenced and locked. Established in 1859, it contains a stately mausoleum with a large rounded Orthodox dome—perhaps the final residence of victims of the Japanese-Russian war in 1904. The whole burial ground at Inasa received the brunt of the latest kamikaze typhoon. Headstones are toppled, tree limbs and trunks are shattered, the ground itself is blistered and unraked.

To the east of the Chinese, the Dutch, and the Russians is a tiny multinational cemetery, open, unfenced, and unvisited. This is the most humble of the collections. The markers are rectangular stone tablets laid horizontally upon the ground like doors to coffins. They lie among autumn leaves, pages of an unwritten historical romance. The blurred inscriptions are tantalizing enigmas; some have been rendered illegible by repeated storms; only a handful are fully decipherable. At my feet I try to transcribe as best I can a few stones. Where letters have vanished, I leave a space:

IN MEMORY
OF
CAPT. JAMES FAIRFOUL
LATE

OF THE BARQUE
EMILY G. _STARR_
DIED
JULY 1_ 1862
AGED 65
BORN IN SCOTLAND
HE WAS A CITIZEN OF
THE UNITED STATES

Nearby, another, more difficult, but more romantic still:

TO THE MEMORY
OF
MOHAMED SALAY
FORMERLYINTHEEMPLOY
OF M_ HIMJEL_
OFAPISTOLSHOTACCIDENT
DECEMBER 18 1859
AGED 24 YEARS

Was this death the result of a duel? Most likely. The grave beside Salay's, which we can barely read at all, is of an Englishman who died in the same year.

Altogether, thirty-one such markers remain in the field, some broken in half, others flaking into oblivion. The latest storm has erased a few more letters from the footnotes engraved here. One or two more big storms and nothing will survive but stone waiting to be ground to dust.

The Nagasaki-Nishi Lion's Club took an inventory of the graves and engraved the results on a wide red marble tablet in June 1990. The roll call reads:

POSITION OF GRAVESTONE	NAME	NATIONALITY	DIED(Aged)
A	JOAO RAIMUNDO	PORTUGAL	1868
B	HORRACE L. PETERSON	AMERICA	1867
C	LUIZ CORREA	PORTUGAL	1868
D	JOSEPH BIRKETT	ENGLAND	1868 (20)

E JOSEPH REED		1860 (24)
F SOLOMON M. KEELER		
G (UNKNOWN)		
H CIITO CAVIER	FRANCE	1860
I RANDOLPH NICKEL		186?
J (UNKNOWN)		
K (UNKNOWN)		
L JOSEPH ALLIN	AMERICA	37
M ANDREU MALCOLM	ENGLAND	1859 (23)
N MOHAMED SALAY		1859 (24)
O (UNKNOWN)		
P CAPT. JAMES FAIRFOUL	SCOTLAND	1862 (65)
Q (UNKNOWN)		
R JOHN DENBY	ENGLAND	1860 (64)
S GEORGE BUNKER		1867 (28)
T JOHN GREGORIA	ENGLAND	1860 (24)
U (UNKNOWN)		
V (UNKNOWN)		
W CHARLIE J. TERRY		1863 (8 mhs)
X HOAN LUE	CHINA	1860
Y J.W. DAVIS	ENGLAND	1866
Z (UNKNOWN)		
A' (UNKNOWN)		
B' HENRY D. TOOVEY	ENGLAND	1859 (29)
C' CHARLES COLLINS	ENGLAND	1861 (27)
D' THOMAS BARY	ENGLAND	1860 (21)
E' GUSTAR WILKENS		1869 (37)

Of the thirty-one foreigners buried here, nine are already stripped of their names. Most of the dead were yet in their twenties; one, little Charlie, was an infant. The greatest number were from England; others came to Nagasaki from Portugal, France, Scotland, and China. All would die far from home, at a rate of two or three a year. They began digging graves at this place from the opening of the port in 1859 and stopped ten years later, moving to another field. Of the two Americans, Horrace Peterson and Joseph Allin, nothing at all is known.

The Lion's Club inscription explains its mission:

OVER THESE MANY YEARS THE GRAVESTONES HAVE BE-
COME WEATHERED, OBLITERATING SOME OF THE NAMES, SO

THIS STONE WAS ERECTED ON WHICH ALL THOSE NAMES THAT WERE READABLE WERE RE-ENGRAVED FOR POSTERITY. THIS WAS DONE AS A SMALL TOKEN OF INTERNATIONAL FRIENDSHIP.

. . . its duty:

WE SOMETIMES ATTEND TO THESE GRAVES AND SAY PRAYERS FOR THEIR SOULS.

. . . its sorrow:

AT PRESENT, IT IS NOT AT ALL KNOWN WHETHER THERE ARE RELATIVES REMAINING IN THEIR HOMELANDS.

Indeed, this is a far place to die, homeless among wanderers, on a quiet hillside of palm trees, of crosses, of crosses with an oblique slash, of Chinese lanterns, of the exiles' stones in foreign languages— Dutch and Russian, Chinese and English—all facing a harbor in the western Pacific. Walking back down through the paved pathways to the street, I try to imagine the flash of light that grazed the dead on these slopes the morning America dropped the bomb. The exiles were lucky to die in Nagasaki the way they died, whether by drowning or gunshot, fever or age. Far worse deaths lay in wait, and it is toward their monument that we must move after all these diversions, these postponements. The dead bring us back to what we came here to see.

✳ ✳ ✳

When I wake Sunday morning I can not shake off the dream. It clings for a week or more. I am walking on the edge of a steep sand cliff which breaks off without warning, throwing me onto my back. As I slide into the abyss, I manage to propel myself back up the slope. I'm safe, but the dream stays with me as only a nightmare can.

On August 9, 1945, at 11:05 in the morning, an atomic bomb far more powerful than the first one at Hiroshima exploded over this city, Nagasaki, and killed how many people? No one knows, exactly. Says one tour book: 25,000 to 75,000. Says a more recent one: 150,000 (out of a population of 210,000). Numbers are meaningless, just something clean and abstract. A local bilingual tour book has it right: "Many people were burned deeply and died, crying and groaning for water."

To reach the hypocenter, the World Peace Symbol Zone, the Nagasaki International Culture Hall—better known as the Atomic Bomb Museum—we use the streetcars, transferring once. Nagasaki is one of the few cities left in Japan that run these relics down the middle of their main streets. They are cheaper, more scenic, and only slightly slower than the best subways in the world. We embark at our usual stop and are surprised to find an American aboard, the first one we've talked to in many days. Julie's just out of junior college in California and on vacation in Nagasaki before starting a job in the sales department of an Osaka Hotel. She's the only one in the car in shorts; the only one in a Mickey Mouse tank top, too. She hardly knows a word of Japanese, but those few she flings at strangers and pries open smiles. She's the real American, we suppose—loud, brash, fun, free, altogether very un-Japanese; she's also scared to death, of traveling alone, of Japan, of the future. She asks if she can tag along to the Atomic Bomb Museum; it just happened to be where she's going, you know?

What's worse than one's own countrymen in a foreign land? We try to be understanding, but it isn't easy. It does not seem that Julie is nearing the Peace Park with any knots in her stomach, no stretch of gray history in her mind where a city existed one minute and the next disappeared like paint in a fire. She's talking to a woman and her grade-school son, laughing and pointing. We disembark together at Matsuyami Machi, a long way north of the port. There are signs in the street that point the way. We become entangled in a line of pedestrians, all dressed in bright yellow gloves with matching hats and hard plastic sun visors. They are heading for the park, but everyone is carrying blue and yellow plastic bags. It's a group of neighborhood people out on a volunteer Sunday cleanup.

The Peace Statue is the first thing we see clearly today, the thirty-foot high bronze figure, right hand to the sky, left hand extended horizontally, right leg folded in lotus position, left leg forward and bent at the knee, eyes closed, a pacific expression. Pigeons sweep in huge concentric circles that shrink and expand. Sometimes they all come to rest at once on the Peace Statue's arms, knees, shoulders. Margaret finds it a massive, dull piece of work, but with the pigeons it takes flight, it expresses an impossible wish. Kitamura Seibo, the sculptor, has left a poem, written in the spring of 1955, expressing something of his intent:

After experiencing that nightmarish war,

that blood-curdling carnage,
that unendurable horror,
Who could walk away without praying for peace?
  This statue was created as a signpost in
  cause of global harmony.
Standing ten meters tall
  it conveys the profundity of knowledge and
  the beauty of health and virility.
The right hand points to the atomic bomb,
  the left hand points to peace,
  and the face prays deeply for the victims of war.
Transcending the barriers of race
  and evoking the qualities of both Buddha and God,
  it is a symbol of the greatest determination
  ever known in the history of Nagasaki
  and of the highest hope of all mankind.

In this conception, the hand that once pointed to heaven now points to mass destruction; peace resides over a distant horizon.

Next to a plaque bearing these words in Japanese and English—the two languages of concern in the event—a man in a tie has set up a card table, flanked on either side by a gallery of photographs, enlargements of the horrors of that day, worse in black and white than in color, skin fried off the face. Margaret can't go near; I don't want to either. We know what happened. Only Julie and the young Japanese men who follow her can scan the photographs from as close as the length of an arm. It is three of these boys who persuade her to pose in their photograph. She stands between two of them and puts her arms around their necks. It's a big CHEESE photo, high-spirited and raucous, with the Peace Statue and the pigeons looking down in the background. We are able to part with Julie by lagging at the Peace Fountain; she dashes on.

There's an inscription at the fountain written by a survivor, a woman who was a nine-year-old child when the bomb struck:

I was very thirsty and went out for water. I found that the water had something greasy all over it. People told me the grease had fallen from the sky. But I was so desperately thirsty that I drank it just as it was.

The fountain was built in 1969 to refresh the spirits of those victims who died in Nagasaki begging for a drink of water.

∗   ∗   ∗

The only starving beings in the Peace Park today are the stray cats, out in abundance. There are an exceptional number of kind people in attendance on Sunday; seated on benches, they provide leftover noodles for the cats.

We are walking down to the center of the explosion through the World Peace Symbol Zone, a corridor of outdoor sculpture founded by Nagasaki in 1978. The city invited each of the nations of the world to send a peace monument to stand on this rare ground. The works are various and inventive; a mother lifting a child in the air above her arched body stuns us. Beginning in 1978, statues were donated by Porto, Nagasaki's sister city in Portugal; by Czechoslovakia; by Bulgaria; by East Germany; by Middleburg, Nagasaki's sister city in The Netherlands; by the Soviet Union; by the People's Republic of China; by Poland; by Pistoia, Italy; by Cuba; by Santos, Brazil. Not a large response, except from the Soviet Union and Eastern Europe—from a communist world that has since disappeared. But America has not disappeared, except here, in the Nagasaki World Peace Symbol Zone. We're not contrite. We're all for peace, of course, but with the right kind of folks. Besides, the wars are over, and no one wants to remember this place.

∗   ∗   ∗

The Urakami Catholic Cathedral towers over the valley of the bombing on a hill where its ancestor church was first erected in 1584. During the three centuries of the Shogunate's ban on Christianity, the leader of Urakami Village resided here, and the secret Christians promulgated the faith in a greater concentration than anywhere else in Japan. When the Meiji Restoration formally assured freedom of worship in 1873, the hill was again open to the building of a large church. Completed in 1925, the cathedral was hailed as among the largest in Asia, seating six thousand. On August 9, 1945, the atom bomb leveled it, except for a few towering slivers of red brick. Eighty-five hundred of the 14,000 Nagasaki Catholics perished. The present cathedral is immense; it was inaugurated in 1981 by the Pope. What remains on the site from 1945 is a garden of headless statues. Their heads, severed by the blast, were never restored.

From Urakami Cathedral back down through Urakami town to the center of the explosion is a quarter mile. The town is completely rebuilt, modern and bustling. Everyone is going about their usual business on a Sunday afternoon. Across the Urakami river the path is lined with trees and paved down to a garden where a few simple monuments remain. We sit on a stone bench on the edge of a garden bed of azaleas and hydrangeas and eat the pastries we bought in the village, feeding scraps to a few stray cats. Just across the river is a new Love Hotel. From its windows lovers can view a cenotaph consisting of seven black marble blocks pointing in a direct line to the invisible point in the sky, a quarter mile up, where the bomb blew apart.

This spot in Nagasaki was not the primary target of the day. Our B29 was bound for an industrial city to the north, Kokura, but that site was hemmed in by clouds. Circling three times, the crew dropped back to the south for the second target, and as the clouds drew apart momentarily, the Mitsubishi Nagasaki Iron Works—an arms complex north of the ship harbor—appeared six miles below.

By Nagasaki's official count, the bomb killed 73,884 and injured 74,909—three of every five citizens. The landscape was scorched and completely leveled, leaving a flat crater of 2.59 square miles.

We eat our lunch under the bare cherry trees and feed the abandoned cats in silence. There's nothing to say here. Flowers and a rack of folded paper cranes have been placed at the base of the hypocenter. To one side are some architectural remains, transported here: a scorched spiral staircase from the iron works; the twisted, charred water tank on stilts from a school; a corner of the redbrick Urakami Cathedral, sliced off and bent ever so slightly by waves of unimaginable heat.

A father poses with his child for a picture by the hypocenter monument. Overhead, a small plane crosses, broadcasting an advertisement. I stand under the monument and look straight up into the formless air. At the center of the circle is a sub-microscopic black hole rent in the fabric of a blue heaven, a dead center of gravity for the dead from which no light can ever escape.

✳   ✳   ✳

We are climbing the stairway from hypocenter to Atomic Bomb Museum—officially entitled the Nagasaki International Culture Hall—when we are overtaken by a local, Maekawa Tomoko, who offers us a guided tour. Tomoko is a member of the Nagasaki Foundation for the Promotion of Peace. Since 1984, the foundation's purpose has been "to strive, from the point of view of all mankind, for the abolition of nuclear weapons and the realization of lasting world peace, and to contribute thereby to the welfare of humanity." Among other duties, members serve as guides at the Atomic Bomb Museum. Tomoko has also served as an interpreter for the international gatherings hosted in the name of world peace and nuclear disarmament in Nagasaki. She's unintrusive, answering our questions at length only as we pose them.

This is a museum of horrors—photographs, documents, relics of destruction by plutonium. One wide mural depicts the area before and then after: the earth before, the moon after. Tomoko tells us that Kokura, the intended target that day, was protected by a haze that came in part from the smoke of previous conventional bombings. Even the strike on the Iron Works was not in the plan, but the Nagasaki Mitsubishi shipyards to the south were also covered by clouds. Thus, the bomb was delivered far from the heart of the city, in this valley protected on three sides by steep hills. What were the conditions in the hours after the bombing, we ask. It rained, Tomoko replies, and the rain filled the reservoir with deadly radiation, but the hills helped contain the destruction; and three days later a typhoon struck, some-what cleansing the land. Is there radiation here now? She doesn't know. No one seems to know. Five decades have passed, but we feel we are standing in a zone of eternal contamination.

Pictures and remains bring the day closer. When the bomb exploded, the heat was intense enough to eradicate everyone near the hypocenter, at ground zero; to burn those standing a mile away; to burn the exposed skin of those two miles away. With the heat came the sheer force of the blast: shattering wood, splintering glass, hurling pieces of Nagasaki like poison-tipped spears. Simultaneously, the exploding waves carried radiation: alpha rays, beta rays, neutron rays, gamma rays. The radioactivity was fatal to nearly anyone caught within a half-mile radius. Those who entered the area to care for the dead and injured were subjected to unthinkable doses.

Many entered the death zone. The Nagasaki Medical College Hospital had been destroyed, but medical personnel streamed in to help. Relief stations were set up to treat the wounded. Survivors were placed on relief trains and received at hospitals in other towns. Many of the survivors are living today in Nagasaki. Seven years after the war, a high frequency of leukemia was recorded here, and in Hiroshima as well. Cancer of the thyroid increased. Some survivors who were in the womb on August 9 suffered microcephaly, a small head. Atomic-bomb cataracts were common. At present, no one knows how far into succeeding generations the after-effects will spread.

Among museum relics are roof tiles, their surfaces erupting in bubbles—tiles not only burnt but boiled. The heat on the day is estimated to have reached two million degrees centigrade. A large fireball was created—a second sun with a surface temperature of nine thousand degrees centigrade. It melted down houses, melted down bodies, and ignited a fire that spun through Nagasaki City, burning a third of it to the ground.

✳   ✳   ✳

On the fifth floor, Tomoko invites us into a room marked "Partly Office Room" to have coffee with a few of the other volunteers. They tell us that they regret the failure of both the Japanese and the American government to recognize and adequately aid A-bomb victims; regret as well both nations' reluctance to achieve complete disarmament. We're told that at a recent conference in Nagasaki, 205 autonomous regions of Japan declared their cities non-nuclear. They are heartened by the end of the Cold War, but they fear that little attention has been paid to the Asia Pacific region. They support a ban on all nuclear weapons at sea. They talk, too, about the Nagasaki A-Bomb Hospital and the Megumi-no-Oka Atomic Bomb Home for the Elderly. Among the programs Tomoko thinks most promising is the U.N. Disarmament Fellowship designed to educate young diplomats in peace. Since 1983, junior diplomats from twenty-five countries have visited Nagasaki each year to tour the museum, talk with survivors, and discuss the politics of disarmament. All the volunteers look forward to the building of a new museum once the peace fund established by the city in 1985 permits. At present the museum is an uninviting concrete hulk housing an uninviting collection that no one should ignore.

We see no Americans in the museum, but Tomoko assures us that many Americans come. We've never met any. Of the one million visitors each year, 950,000 are Japanese. Of course, in America, Hiroshima is better known. (Not that many McDonald's-Disneyland-Country-Western-crazed Americans would visit there either). Tomoko's reply to Nagasaki's second-city status is succinct: Nagasaki wasn't first, but it must be last, and therefore never be forgotten.

Were it not for Nagasaki's mayor, Motoshima Hitoshi, such a message would not have carried so far, nor been borne with such intensity to a world that would rather ignore the past or joke about it. As the Fiftieth Anniversary of the Pearl Harbor Bombing neared, President Bush ruled out any apology to Japan for nuclear attacks. A Navy pilot shot down by the Japanese during World War Two, Bush was not the sort to visit Nagasaki peace parks or hypocenters; instead, he went to Hawaii to attend observances of American losses there . . . this at a time when polls showed that three of four Japanese wanted an American apology and three of four Americans saw no need. This at a time when Senator Ernest F. Hollings of South Carolina told workers in Hartsville, S.C., that they "should draw a mushroom cloud and put underneath it: MADE IN AMERICA BY LAZY AND ILLITERATE WORKERS AND TESTED IN JAPAN." According to Mr. Hollings, this was a joke and he was glad that he made it.

The Senator's joke did not tickle Mayor Motoshima's funny bone. A tireless emissary on behalf of world peace and complete disarmament, the Mayor is a Christian and an Independent—unusual qualities in a Japan dominated by one political party, the LDP. Born to a family of secret Christians on nearby Goto Island, Motoshima became a wanderer; later, a student activist, but not a radical; later still, an officer in World War Two who ordered his men into battle; and lastly, mayor of Nagasaki. From that position, he has spoken to the world of the need for renouncing war, nuclear war above all, while evincing no anti-American feeling. Unlike Bush, he frequently apologizes, speaking of "the awareness of the Japanese people that Hiroshima and Nagasaki are a consequence of the war of aggression committed by us." Adds the Mayor: "We are aware that we were not only victims but also victimizers." Speaking at the United Nations in 1991, he reiterated this view of Japanese aggression and responsibility. Motoshima has also issued public apologies to the Koreans for war crimes.

During his third term, in 1988, Mayor Motoshima shook up the nation by announcing that the Emperor bore responsibility for the war. Hirohito died a month later. Right-wingers threatened the Mayor's life, and he was put under a round-the-clock police guard. Meanwhile he opened the city facilities to Vietnamese boat people in August, 1989, and in September confronted the U.S. Navy in the Peace Park Incident. This came about when Commander Peter Roberts, in charge of the frigate *Rodney M. Davis*, arrived on a "friendship" mission. Since 1974, no warships from countries deploying nuclear weapons had been allowed into the port of Nagasaki; but Commander Roberts assured the Mayor that no nuclear devices were aboard. The day Roberts laid a wreath at the Peace Park, the Mayor refused to appear. The wreath was stomped to pieces by a group of A-bomb survivors and their families, for which the Mayor apologized and was in turn roundly denounced by peace activists.

Mayor Motoshima is frequently chided by Nagasaki's Left: for dragging his feet in declaring his city a nuclear-free zone; for kowtowing to the arms producers (who, ironically, control what has become Nagasaki's number one industry); for not somehow continuing the supplement paid by the city to its bomb survivors. But it was from the Right that the death threats came, and in January 1990 an assassin struck. Wounded seriously, Motoshima managed to survive. That August he attended peace conferences in Italy and was granted an audience with Pope John Paul II. Later, he traveled to New York to speak at the United Nations on behalf of the banning of all nuclear testing. On April 21, 1991, at age sixty-eight, Mayor Motoshima, by a narrow margin, won his fourth term.

As a mayor of peace, Motoshima carries on the local tradition. On August 9, 1958, then Mayor of Nagasaki, Tagawa Tsutomu, attending a memorial for the bomb victims, appealed to the world for a universal ban on nuclear weapons. He urged the 312,000 citizens of his city to work for world peace. Ten thousand people gathered at the Peace Park; one thousand Catholics held a mass at Urakami Cathedral. At 11:02, church bells pealed, trains and buses stopped, the people conducted silent prayers, and the schoolchildren of Nagasaki released sixty pigeons from Peace Park.

* * *

Before the attempted assassination of Mayor Motoshima, Norma Field interviewed him for her book, *In the Realm of a Dying Emperor.* The interviews were not at all what one might expect from a tough dissident and tireless peace activist. Under constant guard, restricted in his movements because of threats, he told Norma Field he was engaged in a reading program concentrating on one topic—death.

"What I need to be studying now is how to die," he said.

The Mayor added that his life under siege had abruptly changed, destroying his routines. This turn of events had presented him with more free time and a new direction. "I've gotten to the age when I really want time to think about what I'm doing," the Mayor explained. "I want a new life, a renaissance!"

In a subsequent interview, the Mayor was more specific. "I want to go traveling."

"With a rucksack?" Ms. Field asked.

"No, this time with a Samsonite suitcase on wheels," the Mayor answered. "And hiking boots inside. You know, it's good to live in a place where you know everybody. But it would also be interesting to live in a place where you know no one."

With the Mayor's unintended blessing, we resume our travels, our thoughts on disappearance and death. We set out for another crater, another volcano; Japan is filled with them.

✳   ✳   ✳

Waiting for a Nagasaki streetcar the next morning, we watch two men at work, both smoking as they flap their black and white checkered flags. They toot on whistles like gym coaches and cavort in whatever way it takes to hail passing cars and induce them to enter their parking garages for the day. From across the street I can hear the steel rain of steel balls in a pachinko parlor. It is Monday morning all over Japan, and everything is untangled from the shadows.

At Nagasaki's downtown Mazda dealership the sales force is lined up two rows deep in the showroom, men in front, for the 9 a.m. pep rally.

The gas stations are outfitted with washing machines to keep the towels and chamois clean. Everyone gets their windshield wiped; car mats, too; the works—no boom in self-service here. As a customer pulls away with a full tank, uniformed gas jockeys bow.

The last sign we see leaving Nagasaki is on an office:

INSTITUTE FOR RESEARCH IN HUMAN HAPPINESS

Its venetian blinds are drawn shut, but I see a brilliant flash of light as if from an explosion inside an empty glass vault. Perhaps this is an underground entrance to a parallel cyclotron; but whether fashioned of aging wood or polished plutonium, I can't tell.

At the Atomic Bomb Museum the most haunting relic is a lump of glass in which the ashes of a human hand are embedded, " a grudging hand that remains forever," says the museum brochure—a handprint on the century.

XIV.

Mt. Unzen:
The Volcano Channel

From the moment we clear the rim of hills girding Nagasaki and descend into the valley beyond everything seems to change, to belong to a new zone of the world ruled by volcanoes and craters, onsens and hot springs. We are on an early morning bus heading east across the Shimabara Peninsula. On the near horizon is a cluster of volcanoes known as Unzen, active again after two hundred years. There's a hint of smoke, smeared sideways, from the tallest of Unzen's cones, Mt. Fugen. Just five months earlier, Mt. Fugen convulsed in full eruption. Ten thousand people were driven from their homes; forty were killed. Shimabara Peninsula was pelted with rocks and coated in dust, suffering for weeks in what the newspaper termed "a choking poisonous fog."

Seated across from us is a retired gentleman who peppers us with a smattering of English. He's on his way to take the waters—the volcanic hot spring waters of Unzen Onsen—and as he sings along with the recorded songs on the bus loudspeaker, he laughs and taps his wooden walking stick with authority, as though he's sized us up and sees through us. He tells the bus driver who we are and where we're from; the driver broadcasts this information in Japanese to the other passengers. Our informant smiles ever more broadly. He's on his second can of sake, purchased from a vending machine, and perfectly soused, he bubbles over with mirth.

Until the recent eruption, all the tourist pamphlets assured visitors that Unzen was an extinct volcano. Now, the tourists have ceased coming to Unzen at all—save a few merry old men with canes and caned sake. As a result, the three great hot springs—the old spring of Furuyu, the new spring of Shinyu, and the geysers and pools of Kojigoku, known as hells—are deserted. The three dozen fumaroles, solfataras, mud pots, and geysers of Unzen Onsen are shrouded in warm vapors, undisturbed by sightseers. For a thousand years this village was the setting for a remote temple and monastery. Three hundred years ago, the waters were converted to serve the national passion of the bath. In the late nineteenth century, Unzen Onsen became an R & R hill station for Europeans and Americans who were conducting the China trade from Shanghai and Hong Kong. Until then, Unzen's chief claim to fame dated from 1627 when some thirty converts who refused to renounce Christianity were boiled alive in its volcanic pools.

These days dozens of modern resort inns pipe the magmatized waters indoors to soak their Japanese clientele. There are the usual claims all spas make as to the health benefits of the natural hot springs. When we arrive, the hells are deserted, save a family or two and a few old women selling eggs boiled in the springs. I sample one for lunch, an odd sort of communion.

Every hell has its story. Great Shout Hell, a noisy spring, reminds listeners of the screams of the damned; Oita Hell appeared about the time a Shimabara woman of that name was executed for the murder of her husband; Sparrow Hell tweets like a bird; Seishichi Hell recalls a Christian martyred there; and Hachiman Hell resembles the location in Buddhist topography of the inferno devoted to any who have given in to one or more of the 84,000 lusts. Deposits of solidified gas and acid ring the steaming outlets, white and yellow sulfur flowers that emit a frightful fragrance; these embroidered pools, in turn, are ringed by small rock retaining walls. Paving stone paths with log rail fences link hell to hell, vendor to vendor. In Japan, even a valley of sulphur and gas can be shaped into a stroll garden.

We walk up to the bus depot, buy tickets for the ride to Unzen's active peak, Mt. Fugen, and while waiting, wander down to a toy store the likes of which we have not seen in America since our childhoods: a five & dime run by an elderly lady. The items are all priced low: a tiny metal train and track, a Groucho nose and glasses, a tin sheriff's badge. As we browse, we see the old man with cane and sake pass, alone, in robe and wooden getas; he disappears into the Unzen public bath, pleased as a clam.

❋ ❋ ❋

The first American to trod on Japanese soil was a ship's captain, John Kendrick. He feigned shipwreck in May 1791 and bluntly tried to open the fur trade with Japanese Buddhists. He was expelled, but natural calamity followed promptly, reinforcing the belief that the home gods were upset by foreign incursions. In 1791, it was Mt. Unzen that expressed this divine wrath; its eruption took out twenty-seven villages and buried thousands in lava, smoke, and stone.

I cannot help recalling this curious little coincidence as I step onto Mt. Unzen almost exactly two centuries later. The local bus to Nita Pass has wound up the flanks like an iron donkey, switching back and forth, affording wide high views of the Shimabara Peninsula and the surrounding harbors, the dots of lava islands. Beyond, to the east, in the center of Kyushu, lies the most famous of the island's volcanoes, Mt. Aso, our eventual destination today.

In autumn, with the maple trees on the slopes burning red, Unzen is said to impart the most beautiful views in Japan—a charming exaggeration, no doubt. We disembark at the top. Overhead, smoke pours steadily from a cone, thin as steam. We are a bit afraid this close to the volcano, but no one else seems to be concerned. Of course, there is almost no one else at the top. A tourist or two pokes about; a couple of vendors; a cable car operator. The air is sharp, on the verge of frost, and the sky is hazy, oppressively so. A tram leads up from the asphalt parking lot for a closer view of Mt. Fugen's spout, but it is a thousand yen for a short rise, an outrageous fee. The trail to the same point and to the Fugen temple and caves is closed, the gate locked, the torii arches invisible in the clouds, so all we can tell, looking up to the crater rim, is that it is still belching smoke, blotting out the eastern sky. We walk around the parking lot where a few hardy vendors, leaning against their carts, smoke cigarettes or chew on cobs of boiled corn.

Looking south, we consider hiking down to the golf course, Japan's oldest public links, opened in 1913. We saw it on the way up. The caddies were ladies in bonnets. Groups of nattily attired male golfers were nonchalantly teeing off across yellowed fairways into the flanks of a killer volcano. We could hike all the way back down to the hot springs village, but I don't have the heart for such a descent. From the top, the trail down appears to be unremarkable, little different from taking the road. The autumn colors are fading into gray, or perhaps they were squeezed dry by the summer eruption. We wait for the next bus, pacing back and forth to keep warm.

All the way down to Unzen Onsen, wherever we wind across the western spine of the mountain, we see downed forests, snapped not by the force of the volcano but by Typhoon 19. One needs a scorecard to keep up with the ravages of nature this year. Kyushu is more directly exposed to the extremes of nature than Honshu, the central island of Japan, and it is no wonder the big cities, the masses of people, have migrated there, clustered and safe, far from their mythic origins on Kyushu.

That evening we are surprised to see Mt. Fugen steaming away on the television news. For two days, the peak has been acting up. Scientists surveyed it from a helicopter today and concluded that molten lava could begin flowing down the slopes at any moment. They have issued a warning that the dome could collapse. It is unthinkable that we tourists were allowed at the dome today, a dome in danger of eruption or collapse a scant few months after it killed forty. "There must be no liability in Japan," Margaret says.

"Everything is an act of God—or of the gods," I answer. Except that the volcano has no more gods. In the port town of Shimabara at the eastern foot of Mt. Unzen, modern communications technology has evicted the divine guardians of the volcano and instituted a sort of geological C-SPAN. Cable Television Shimabara (CTS) has installed cameras at the crater and broadcasts live images of the mountain twenty-four hours a day. Homes, offices, and restaurants subscribe, as do Shimabara bars. As drinkers imbibe, they keep a wary eye on the screen, spouting pop geology.

The Unzen locals claim that live cable in the volcano gives them a sense of ease rather than anxiety—they can monitor developments from dining room or bed. The postal service no longer stations spotters around the volcano to ensure safe mail delivery. Everyone now watches the screen for danger signs, for the red globe of a pyroclastic flow. Our eyes are focused on electronic probes inserted into the crater of nature. These robotic extensions never blink, never think, but obliterate the volcano gods that once terrified us. Raw nature once terrified us, too, but it seems pacified by the televison probe. Natural disaster has been converted to live rock video. Unzen is the world's first living room volcano.

XV.

Mt. Aso:
A Bowl of Ash

The important thing about Mt. Aso National Park is not its volcanic cones; it is the cows. Aso is the Japanese Wild West, Kyushu's Chisolm Trail, an Oriental high chapparal of chaps, bed rolls, and branding irons. But here, too, the frontier has been tamed—by tour buses, visitor centers, and the Japanese version of pensions.

We leave Unzen Onsen in the afternoon, departing Shimabara Peninsula by ferry and catching a bus to Kumamoto, the main city west of Aso. Before resuming our circle south, we will make a detour straight to the center of the island, to Mt. Aso. We take a trolley to the Kumamoto train station, buy tickets on the next local to Aso Station, and visit the tour desk to book the night's accommodations.

There are whole villages of pensions surrounding Mt. Aso—sparkling new bed & breakfasts with European exteriors, gingerbread and lace, designed to attract the throngs and fulfill the fantasies of young unmarried women who want to visit Swiss chalets without leaving Japan. The names of pensions do not strike most Japanese as absurd; rather, they sound delightful, cute and frothy. The tourist desk hands us a list of possibilities near Aso Station, and we ask the women to translate some of the lower-priced options. There's the Starry Pension and the Pension Snoopy; there's the Champagne de Alice and the "Wendy Umbrera" (which turns out to be Windy Umbrella); there's the Aso-no-Morning Salad and even the Pension Smile Penguin. Since the Smile Penguin is closed for the season, we settle on the Pension Aso-no-Tokeidai, meaning Clock Tower, located at the Otohime Pension Village.

The train to Aso makes every stop it can on the way up to the vast Mt. Aso caldera in which the pensions and volcanic cones are ensconced. On our way up we pass a real steam engine, black as caked oil, on its run back down. Its cars are old-fashioned, maroon and silver, and the conductors are dressed in cowboy boots. This is "Aso Boy," steam train to the volcano.

At Aso Station, Tokunaga Yoshiharu, the owner of the Clock Tower Pension, picks us up in his Ford Fiesta. He also owns a Ford Bronco. The Clock Tower is new, family run, friendly, and the upstairs rooms resemble the dorms in a Swiss chalet: fresh and spartan. Downstairs there's a breakfast bar, a piano in one corner, and stuffed animals on the window sills. A carefully prepared dinner is delivered to our table: consomme, salad, rice gratin, vegetables, and steak. Coffee's the drink. The only other guest is a school administrator.

After dinner, we take our bath. When we emerge, steaming hot, Tokunaga invites us for a drink. Room is made at the table next to the fireplace. We're served cup after cup of Kyushu's chief liquor, *shochu*, more popular than sake, which it resembles. Distilled from potatoes rather than rice, using a process said to derive from the Dutch community in Nagasaki, *shochu* is less subtle than sake, but does not pack the kick and burn of red-eye whiskey. We throw back a few and speak English with our hosts. They want to know what is the most beautiful place we have seen in Japan, and in the world. We tell them where we are headed in Kyushu. We learn that our host plays the viola in the Kumamoto Symphony Orchestra. We meet his children. His wife offers to hang out our laundry in the morning. We look through a picture album of previous foreign guests. Our host has never visited America, although he's more at home in our language than we are in his. When I press him, both he and the college administrator admit they'd love to visit America but lack the courage.

Before we depart for good, we will all be posing for pictures outside the Clock Tower with the family and their shaggy dog, the peaks of Aso rising, rounded and dusty gray on the horizon.

After a breakfast of corn soup, a fried egg, lunch meat, salad, rolls, and coffee, Tokunaga drives us to Aso Station where we catch the local bus to the volcano. Ancient Mt. Aso was beheaded in a massive eruption that created the caldera which is now the grounds of a large National Park—said to be the largest volcanic crater in the world, some seventy-five miles in circumference. As the bus rises we can see the circle of cliffs that mark the ancient caldera, the hundred-square-mile floor of old Mt. Aso. Sprouting up from the crater are five more recent volcanic cones, including one that is still steaming.

The Aso caldera is paved lava fields and grass plains where cattle herds graze. The bus stops for quick views now and then, and at one point there is a tie-up where all the tour buses and cars have pulled over. The attraction is cattle, ordinary cows on a patch of range—a rare sight in Japan where livestock is normally confined to the insides of barns or the tiniest of corrals. The Aso cows stand near enough the road that I can see their brands. No Rocking R's here; Aso steers are branded in Chinese characters.

It is a scene out of the newspaper advertisement running in *The Japan Times* that features a cowpuncher with lasso and Stetson, longhorns grazing, snow peaks in the background, and a headline for 100% NATURAL BEEF AND BUFFALO . . . FROM ROCKIES TO YOUR TABLE. These old west cows contain NO GROWTH HORMONES, NO ANTI-BIOTICS, NO STIMULANTS, AND NO ARTIFICIAL ADDITIVES—JUST 100% NATURAL 100% HEALTHY ROCKY MOUNTAIN BEEF. As for the buffalo, the advertisers boast that BUFFALO MEAT IS LOW IN FAT AND CHOLESTEROL, AND ESPECIALLY HIGH IN VITAMIN B, AND IRON. THESE BUFFALO ARE RAISED 100% PURE AND NATURAL IN THE ROCKY MOUNTAINS, WITHOUT ANY ARTIFICIAL ADDITIVES. I try to imagine a reverse ad in America for 100% PURE MT. ASO VOLCANIC BEEF . . . RAISED IN THE LARGEST CRATER ON EARTH, but no one in America knows Mt. Aso and few could afford a steak dinner imported from Higo Prefecture, Kyushu. The clincher for selling buffalo steaks in Tokyo comes at the end of the ad: THIS IS THE MEAT THE AMERICAN INDIANS ATE, AND THE HEALTHIEST MEAT FOR THE FUTURE.

✳   ✳   ✳

At the bus terminus, Aso-zan Nishi, everyone rushes off to buy tickets inside a grim cement station for the *kakonishi* cable car, a five-minute ropeway to the summit of Naka-dake, the only one of Aso's five peaks that remains active. We take a look at the Naka-dake's flat top from the Sanjo Shrine, a humble wooden temple to the volcano with its statue of a grimacing Buddhist deity that looks as much Mayan as it does Oriental. The walk to the top won't be far. As we ascend along a winding paved road, we meet lines of schoolchildren returning to their tour buses.

The crater is one of the most active on earth and has stripped the surrounding slopes and valleys of all life. Naka-dake is the latest expression of Mt. Aso, whose history covers thirty million years. Every day Naka-dake puffs and growls; its most recent serious eruption was in September 1979 when it coughed up a rock fall that reached a distance of a half mile, where it crushed three sightseers to death.

In 1958, when an eight-year cycle of eruptions began, darkening the skies of Kumamoto thirty miles to the west, a series of concrete pavilions were erected around the crater rim as shelters. They dot the white sulfur-ribboned landscape like yurts pitched on a black desert dune. We're surprised to discover that the floors of these shelters are littered with broken glass and trash.

The crater rim is immense—nearly two thousand feet across, over five hundred feet deep. There's smoke in the belly. No fences have been built here, but there are a few makeshift shrines where crude little Buddhist dolls may be purchased and tossed into the fire. White smoke sweeps up from the pit and merges with the low gray clouds. The wind is swift and cold.

I decide to make the hike from Naka-dake crater, at 4,341 feet, to the summit of the next cone, Aso's tallest, Taka-dake, at 5,223 feet. From that summit, I will continue down through Sensui-kyo, a volcanic gorge that leads to the ancient Aso Shrine. I will be retracing the trail that Aso pilgrims once took, perhaps as long ago as eighteen centuries. It's a trail that leads in and out of the fire at the very center of Kyushu.

Margaret decides to take the bus back to the station and wait for me to come out some six hours later. I set out down the side of the crater across a wide field of black ash. The trail is virtually unmarked; I have only the most general of maps; but at the top of the next low slope, I can see a marker. There's no one crossing this plain but me. I'm not quite sure where the big peak, Taka-dake, is, but I expect that to become obvious. Once on its great summit, I expect that a moment of wisdom will unfold itself at my feet, that I will find the Japan that underlies Japan, a light where the fires of creation once burned.

The farther I wander from the crater, the more I am lost. I top the next slope and locate the marker, a bare wooden post without inscription. The terrain ahead is no longer dust; it's rocks. Moreover, there's no peak, just a slope tumbling into a valley of clouds. I turn ninety degrees and keep on the ridge line. I come to a cairn of stones and another wooden marker, but again I can find no message, no arrow pointing anywhere.

I've wasted an hour. I retrace my steps and recross the crater's plain to a road that ascends the far side of Naka-dake. I pass some tripods holding seismic equipment and eventually have a view of the

Naka-dake crater from its eastern rim. There's more smoke than before, but I'm not advancing. The ceiling of clouds is lowering. I turn
back a second time. There's only one direction left that I haven't tried.
Now that I look closely, I begin to see yellow arrows painted on rocks;
they point straight up to a sawtooth peak. This must be the wall of the
tallest cone; on the other side is the hidden gorge leading to Aso Shrine.

I begin to climb this wall of loose rock, of brown and red pumice,
of yellowed ash. The way is so steep I have to bend down and pull on
the outcroppings. I stagger forward, then slip back on the gravel. This
will take an hour or more. I glance up to the craggy summit now and
then to memorize its position. Fog is sweeping over the top. I'm halfway up when the fog thickens and lowers. I can no longer see even
the outline of a summit.

My chance is slipping away; the peak is disappearing. I can wait
for the fog to retreat, or I can keep going in hopes it will lift. Once to
the top, the gorge of the pilgrims might very well be backlit by the
afternoon sun. I weigh my chances; I stare into the faceless fog. I look
for a marker, a distant point in a mirror coated with frozen breath.
There's nothing ahead but heaven's sea—no islands, no towers—and
the sea of mist is starting to roll down the cone. Soon I will be buried.

It comes to me that I must turn back and descend. I don't know
this mountain. I pick up my pace to outrun the fog. The fog charges
over the summit like eighteen centuries of pilgrims, a procession of
smouldering fire. Should this cloud overtake me and swallow the wide
field ahead, I would be lost, lost for hours, perhaps all night. No light
could find me; no sound could be heard.

I quicken my pace across the pumice plain. Partway to the summit of old Japan, space has closed up, swallowing whole mountains.
In another hour, nothing will be visible.

✳   ✳   ✳

"Did you make it over the top?" Margaret asks when I show up
early at Aso Station.

"Nope."

"Did you find the Great Absolute?"

"Absolutely," I answer. "Nature abhors a vacuum."

For that matter, civilization abhors a vacuum, too, filling in the
hyocenter at Nagasaki with gardens and love hotels just as fire and
smoke plug the throat of Unzen or fog and cloud paint over the heights
of Aso. Blank space cannot endure; shapeless, it becomes the universal magnet.

"No more craters for a while," I swear, slumping onto the station bench. Across the tracks I stare at an playground on a narrow strip of grass parallel to the platform. There are wooden and rope jungle gyms, swings, teeter-totters. Someone in a Harvard sweatshirt tees up a golf ball and receives a lesson. Along the log fence, in English letters a yard tall, the park name is spelled: WESTERN GARDEN. On the horizon, the sun is setting fire to the dust cliffs of old Aso rim.

Margaret has been chatting with Yumi Corrigan at the tourist desk. Yumi's married an Australian; in fact, they were married in the Aso Shrine I utterly failed to reach. Yumi has known the priest there since she was a little girl. The Aso priesthood is hereditary: the priest traces his position back ninety generations: the same family, no break. Every spring, there's a fire festival at Aso Shrine, she says, and it coincides with more than myth and gods. The straw fields in the old Aso crater are also set afire on festival day to kill off the ticks.

On certain hillsides within the caldera, farmers arrange to burn fields in the pattern of the slashing character for fire, *he*. It's a branding of the earth. In the beginning, the word was fire.

XVI.

Kumamoto, Hinagu:
Spa in the Sea

The next morning we leave the center of Kyushu on the slow train back down to Kumamoto where we stay the night at the cheapest *minshuku* we can find. Its proprietor, a wiry sixty-six-year-old, picks us up in a station wagon and whisks us to his home. He loves entertaining foreigners. The walls of his fire pit dining room are lined with portraits of his guests from around the world. We talk all evening. He and his wife serve tea, tangerines, and *mochi*—a sugary rice cake that gags us.

An American flag is unfurled on the wall. There's an Australian flag, too, in honor of the other guest who has joined us. He has left his wife and children in Australia for a month and is touring Japan for pure pleasure. He has plenty of advice. Rely on the tourist desk at each train station to book a *minshuku*, he says. It never fails. Even at Narita Airport. He prefers to travel close to the earth, the way we usually do. Or maybe, like us, he's just too poor to travel any other way.

The Higoshi Minshuku is run by a laundry fanatic. Our host has a big automatic washer, and in the morning the clothes lines sag under reams of sheets and towels. He's at the ironing board with the *yukatas*, singing to himself. He's no great shakes as a housekeeper in general, but the single sheets on our futons are not only pressed; they're starched. The towels in the shared bathroom are fluffed.

The bathroom contains the standard Japanese soaker tub and rinse-off showers, but otherwise is strictly Western. The toilet is the sit-on model, a rarity in out-of-the-way family-run Japanese inns. When I sit on the toilet I'm face to face with a neatly lettered sign that reads:

To Our Foreign Guests,

No worries when you use our western toilet—to
make you feel comfortable we have provided wet
paper towels which you may wipe the toilet seat
with—please use them if you like . . . just wipe
the seat and off you go!!!

Happy times . . . The Management

When we check out in the morning, the owner is nearly in tears
that we must leave; his wife gives us each a hug; we're presented with
a box of sesame crackers they refer to as Cracker Jacks; then it's off we
go.

✳   ✳   ✳

Before leaving Kumamoto, we stop at the city's celebrated garden. In 1600, the daimyo Hosokawa Tadaoki, an ancestor of the builder
of the Ryoan-ji Zen Garden in Kyoto and himself a follower of Sen no
Rikyu, Japan's greatest tea master, ordered the death of his wife, Gracia.
She was then thirty-seven and Japan's most celebrated convert to
Christianity. Locked in a brutal battle with forces hostile to the
Tokugawa Shogunate, her husband feared what his adversaries would
do to his wife if she were captured; he spared her that possibility by
providing a good death. Later, the Shogun awarded the victorious
Hosokawa clan with Kumamoto, where they ruled for fourteen generations. Their chief legacy is Suizen-ji, a masterpiece in the tradition
of landscape gardens, which the Hosokawas laid out in 1632. We reach
it early in the morning on a streetcar named San Antonio.

Only at the gates to the garden do we realize that today is
Shichigosan, the annual Seven-Five-Three festival, when girls aged three
and seven and boys aged five are taken to the local shrines to receive
divine protection. Most of the kids are dressed up in traditional bright
robes and kimonos, towed by parents and grandparents to the Shinto
priests for their blessing; but a few of the honored children are attired
in Western suits or dresses. We witness the first hours of the ritual at
the garden's temple, the Izumi Shrine, dedicated to the divine spirits
of the Hosokawa clan, including the soul of Gracia. Izumi dates back
to 1878; lost in fire during the last war, it was rebuilt 1973 to look older,
more venerable.

The attraction is the stroll garden, tiny compared to Kenroku-en in Kanazawa, but no less an achievement in miniature outdoor sculpture. The theme is the Tokaido Highway, Japan's great Edo era roadway connecting Kyoto to Tokyo and immortalized in the block prints of Hiroshige. In the nineteenth century, the popular "floating world" portraits of geishas and gamblers, whorehouses and bathhouses, had evolved into illustrated travel books. Hiroshige's *Fifty-three Stations of the Tokaido* was a runaway bestseller and the Suizen Garden in Kumamoto is a three-dimensional realization of that ukiyo-e picture gallery: Lake Biwa is rendered as a pond; Mt. Fuji as an artificial hill; the circular gravel path with stone bridges through the garden, a microcosm of scenic overlooks along the old Tokaido Road. Art becomes theme park: a ribbon of nature reduced to human scale, trimmed and stylized, enwraps a garden of clever, showy allusions. On one edge of the spring-fed pond is a dilapidated teahouse and souvenir stand, said by some to have been shipped from Kyoto and reassembled here. It is the four-hundred-year-old teahouse where Sen no Rikyu himself perfected the tea ceremony, priceless beyond all calculation—or, as is said by others, it is a replica of Kyoto's great teahouse, built in Kumamoto in 1912. I am not expert enough to tell copy from original, nor even to separate a work of the twentieth century from the seventeenth. All I know is that I cannot trust guidebooks, tourist offices, or other experts when it comes to dates and records. Everything is suspect; nothing is exactly what it appears. Children, who care least for historical accuracy, pose undisturbed on the teahouse porch under the straw roof while their parents snap away on disposable cameras.

We walk to the far edge of the picture garden. Along this margin is the Yabusame riding ground where every October locals dress up in samurai archer's garb and take three shots at targets from galloping steeds. Today, there are just some stray cats. We feed cats in the way others feed pigeons. At the end of the archers' road, back of little Mt. Fuji, there is a sandlot where oldsters in safari hats are whacking croquet balls through square metal wickets. Their mallets are lean turnings of high craftsmanship. Swarms of little girls and boys catch up with us, sucking on ice cream cones. Two boys are dressed in gray suits, red ties, short pants, black shoes, and high white knee socks— future salarymen; the girls in kimonos, their future compliant wives. The borrowed scenery on the garden's horizon is a soiled twelve-story concrete edifice topped by a sign in English—GREEN HOTEL—awaiting its miniaturization in an asphalt garden of the future, a station on the New Tokaido Road.

* * *

Kyushu has crowned itself Japan's "Silicon Island" and set up shop not as the birthplace of Japan but as the breeding ground of the nation's high-tech future. This aspect has not been much in evidence on our travels, but the electronics and computer industries do exist somewhere in this cyclotron. A recent extension of the silicon dream is the technopolis, a sort of research park with an insatiable appetite. One has taken shape at the Kumamoto airport, but it is as intangible as ozone, as impalpable as a computer byte—until, consulting the official Kumamoto guide map, I read as follows:

KUMAMOTO NEW WAVE

Kumamoto Technopolis consist of 2 cities, 12 towns and 2 villages including Kumamoto City which is main city in Kumamoto. It has a population of about five hundreds and fifty thousand and the area of this city is 95600 hectare.

Kumamoto Technopolis Project as for kernel propel position is constructed by Prefecture and is administrated by Kumamoto Technopolis Foundation. It preparate the latest equipment, plays an important role as Men of Ability Center or The Information Center.

Besides Kumamoto Prefecture go on the adjustment of Techno Research Park as most important project of Kumamoto Technopolis. It is research development position of Kumamoto Technopolis Project, contain Technopolis Center, The Applied Electronics Research Center, university-industry cooperation center and soft-ware house and so on.

Thus Kumamoto Technopolis aim at realization of harmonious city with the extremity industry, industry, science, ours life environment and unfold activity.

Immersed in the prose of full robotic harmony, I waive all further questions.

* * *

The young woman at the tour desk in the Kumamoto Train Station is going down the list of *minshuku* and ryokan for the town of Hinagu Spa for the twelfth time. She's called half the inns in Hinagu already and they all have excuses: they are closed for the season or full up. It dawns on us finally that we are simply not wanted, we're too much trouble. Hinagu is a spa town for the Japanese: no chain hotels, no Japanese inns that cater at all to foreigners, no tourist desk, no brochures in English. That's why we've picked it, but Hinagu has not yet taken to us. A policeman, standing by the counter, whiling away the time with the young women who work there, is now putting in his two cents worth. Turns out he's from Hinagu and knows the inns. They finally ring up one he approves of, Kotobuki Ryokan, a fifteen minute walk from the station. Its price is higher than we've ever paid at a ryokan or *minshuku*, even with meals, but we've come too far to turn back and lose face. Besides, we don't want to give in to hostility.

Forty-eight minutes by train south, we pull into Hinagu Station and deduce that a small back street, parallel to the main coast highway that rips through the town, is the one with the inns. The hot springs at Hinagu were officially discovered in 1409, erupting from the seabed at nearly ideal bathing temperatures (no hotter than 113 degrees F). Spa and fishing made the town. Hinagu remains small and poor, largely uneffaced by sprawling new buildings—a town of dark, weathered wooden houses, green vegetable gardens, orange trees, and small shops. There's not much English anywhere. Inn after inn is labeled only in Chinese characters and we're not sure how to read ours. Fortunately, a couple insists on guiding us along—tourists, too, we think, since they don't really know the way. But at last they spot our name on a chalk board. This is our inn, with sliding doors, two golf clubs and a plastic practice golf bowl stationed outside. We remove our shoes. Inside, the reception room is nearly black: a torn vinyl couch, fresh fish in a basket, glimpse of a smoky kitchen. We are expected. A smiling woman speaking not a word of English leads us to the third floor. The room is old. We bow. The thermos of hot water, the tea cups and pot, are worn. We do have a private bath, Eastern style, and a sink, located on a strip between the bedroom and the hall.

Our ryokan does possess three friendly cats, with one named Chibo ("Little Boy"), and the people are friendly enough, but we are a curiosity. Our hostess, after spreading out the futons and preparing our quilts, returns, embarrassed but laughing, and with plenty of bows tucks in the bottom sheet securely. After she leaves, laughter peals from the kitchen below where they are still debating how Westerners want their beds turned down. A room over, there is a convention of men, not making much noise.

We don't really know what to do, now that we are in a real spa town in Japan, and there's no one to ask such a basic, abstract question. We do what we usually do in stranded circumstances: explore the town from top to bottom on our feet, walking from a high shrine on the cliffs—empty, unremarkable—to the seaside. We are looking for some huge outdoor spa carved out of the mountainside or the sea rocks, but there is nothing. Maybe the action is in the public baths; but we see and hear little there. We conclude that each hotel has piped in its own supply of the spring; there's no open central spring anymore.

The Hinagu causeway is cement, with a hefty seawall. Small open fishing boats tie up on the wharves. Fishermen in baseball caps and white cotton gloves squat to mend the nets. Along the seawall the hotels have put out clotheslines of metal pipe anchored to cement blocks; they are filled with spa towels. For us, Hinagu Spa is a lonely place; we talk more to cats in the street than to people.

We cross the highway back to our ryokan. There's no sidewalk, just a line of wooden storefronts. Back at our room, we surprise a man using our toilet. He's a guest who just couldn't pass by our open screens without relieving himself.

There's nothing to do in Hinagu but eat and bathe. We eat a spectacular dinner. Our hostess removes us to a private matted room on the second floor facing the street. She's protected her black blouse and skirt with a pressed white apron; her socks are embroidered with lace. There are pillows on either side of the low table where we squat down. She brings up the courses one by one, each in its own specially shaped dish. Her gold capped teeth are blazing. She even places coins in a small black and white TV and turns it on for us. We turn it off as soon as she's gone. Dinner is fish, fish, and more fish, in particular *name sakana*: raw fish. Clams in butter boil in a ceramic hot pot over a sterno flame (*tobanyaki*). In the soup there are quail eggs. The *name sakana* with horseradish is perfectly sliced; so too the *name* eel. The raw eel of Kyushu, served in the pattern of a flower, I especially relish. *Name sakana* with quail egg arrives. Cooked trout with head and tail. Prawns tempura with vegetables, also tempura. Fluffy rice, as much as we want. Tea. Beer. And something Margaret describes as "custard with things in it."

We retire. There's nothing to do after dinner but take a bath. The *ofuro* downstairs has no showers with it. We know that one does not enter a tub without a thorough cleaning, so we end up scooping buckets of tub water and scrubbing and rinsing. I plunge into the hot spring basin. . . . I begin to hear voices singing, drunken voices from above. It is not the gods who sing tonight. It's the men next door, one of whom has already peed in our toilet. They sing all night. Outside, others pass on the back street that rises in a gentle curve along the sea cliffs. They too are singing, and we lie on the floor awake, looking up into the darkness, not knowing the words to their songs.

＊　　＊　　＊

The ryokan breakfast is tofu and grated radish, slices of tomato, cucumber, and ham, soup with more tofu, strips of *nori* (dried seaweed), rice, and a hearty raw egg—a traditional power breakfast, just what we need for the morning train to Yatsushiro.

Yatsushiro is set to conduct its festival tomorrow, one of Kyushu's best. We haven't been to a festival yet; we can't claim to have an acquaintance with even the most elementary of interiors of Japan without joining a city's celebration. The gods will be there, along with the drunken horses.

Having had our fill of traditional futons, mats, and squat toilets, we book a Yatsushiro business hotel, but otherwise traveling cheap we forgo the ease of a taxi and inquire about the route of the city bus. The woman at the info desk tells us how to find our way; she also assures us that the big festival will definitely be held tomorrow at the train station. Come back about ten o'clock. The brochures, on the other hand, claim that the festival is held at a shrine near the river.

The city bus fails to dump us anywhere near our hotel. We seek it in vain, waylaying a few pedestrians. They draw us maps; they point; if they know the way, it is beyond expression. We bump into two Russian sailors, drunk and penniless, poor souls. I think they want us to take them out for a round of drinks, but we can't, and they don't press us. They're happy, but Japan is a lousy port to be in without money. They look like American transients next to the neat and well-to-do Japanese. At least these sailors are young; that's worth something, especially when you have to kick around, when you can still believe money doesn't make a difference. We finally sight our elusive hotel a few blocks away, next to a covered arcade that seems to run like a metal shaft through the gut of the city. The desk assures us that the festival, Yatsushiro Myoken, is held at a distant shrine, that we should come down in the morning and book a taxi.

We take possession of our room with modular bath, then walk down a block to the shopping arcade. The shopping snakes for blocks, emptying on one end near the YKK zipper factory, on the other in a bar and disco district called "Drink Town." In between are the entrances to several Buddhist Temples, cut into the metal and neon mall as with a torch. One courtyard has a nylon tent pitched and there are old wooden floats standing here and there. We wonder if it possible that the procession starts in the arteries of this mall, but surely the hotel would have told us that. We locate a small walk-up noodle shop where no one else is eating, but the owner is busy making his own pasta. The tempura turns out to be delicious, the noodles fresh and flavorful enough to please a connoisseur.

To get in the festive spirit, we survey the clothing sale at a department store. This collection is particularly bizarre; the labels and decorative English prose are second only to the haiku and koans we contemplated in Kanazawa. There's a brand of pants with the unpromising title of "Second Rate." Then we encounter a child's shirt emblazoned with lively advice:

Act Golf
Take It Easy
Light Something
and Yourself

A T-shirt with two cats side by side catches our eye. Beneath the cats is penned a kinky and suggestive lyric:

Assignment Record
Association of Shebears
and Unsexed Humans Modesty

On the same rack we uncover another hard-hitting message to wear: "Slap-Bang Boy / G.W. Extreme Globe."

Most amazing is a child's line labeled boldly and brightly PEE CLUB. The logo is a pudgy kitty cat with a golf club, singing the club motto: "OK! LET'S PEE."

Invigorated by our reading, we retire in the festive mood. Outside, across the street, a small shrine is lighted up and a crowd is assembling something, we can't see what. There's an old Volkswagen van parked near the shrine, the first we've seen in Japan. We lie down together, act golf, take it easy, light something and ourselves.

XVII.

Yatsushiro:
Drinking with Horses

In the morning the hotel clerks insist on booking us a taxi to the festival, but from our eleventh-story window I can see men in samurai garb leading a white horse out of the shopping arcade. I suspect that the long procession is being staged right under our noses. The men are conducting the white horse to our hotel entrance where a table is set up to ply the marchers with treats and sake.

Inside the arcade wave after wave of celebrants are grouping, readying a dozen portable shrines and floats that will be wheeled through the streets. The floats, led by rows of children, are pulled by men. Sedan chairs are hoisted up by runners; inside these elaborate boxes children sit in samurai costumes. Old men in full warrior regalia, orange and gold, are mounting their steeds. We've stumbled into the right place.

The procession is led by two young armored soldiers, their black helmets flanked by golden horns. Within this troop is a Shinto priest in white robes escorting a tree draped in curling white ribbons. The old portable shrines that follow are magnificently decorated. Some are in the shape of pagodas, the eaves draped in red velvet, the walls carved in relief and painted, tassels dangling like Christmas ornaments. All are topped with symbolic statuary—royal ladies, bonsai palm trees, geishas, fabulous birds, mythological animals. Before we join the flow from the arcade, we meet the owners of the Volkswagen van—a young couple from Israel who have been driving and camping across Japan for two months, hopping from festival to festival.

The centerpiece of the festival is an enormous creature known as *game*, half turtle, half serpent. *Game* is red and black, trimmed in gold. A dozen people support the beast beneath his draped shell; it's operated like the lion in a Chinese lion dance. *Game*'s origins are ultimately

Chinese, perhaps by way of Korea. In the Yatsushiro festival, dating from 1635, *game* is the chief god incarnate, the *Myoken Bosatsu* who has returned from his voyages to China and India. His long serpent's neck twists and contracts, and along the route he stops at storefronts and offices, rearing up, then bowing to the earth. It is *game* who brings prosperity to the town; and as *game* passes us, a marcher plucks a few strands of hair from its coarse red tail and hands them to Margaret. She's to fold the hair into her wallet. This charm will make her rich.

The children in the parade distribute pieces of candy, while others, young women dressed in blue and white open jackets, matching shorts, golden sashes and split-toed boots that stretch up the leg like long socks, are ladling drafts of new sake from wooden boxes. They invite us to take a swig, and when I down a ladle, they flash the V-sign.

Out in the streets, the procession leaders call out the beat with shouts or whistles. At every intersection men with long crooked poles raise the electric wires so the floats can pass under. The horses are outfitted in banners and headdresses, tassels and shawls, their ankles taped, their hooves shod in straw sandals to match those on their handlers' feet. Like *game*, they are frequently wheeled up the steps of businesses along the way where the merchants come out to receive their blessings, exchanging donations on a platter for tree branches. A group of preschoolers mount stick horses and trot along the two-mile route in formation.

At the train station, the crowds form a large circle. Each float, each marching unit, all the neighborhood groups arrive and make an inner circle for review. A wall of bleachers is filled at one end of the station. As we learn later, the price of a ticket for the morning festivities is not cheap: ten thousand yen. It is in this arena that the horses undergo their trials. Led by the bridle, they are urged to complete a circuit at a breakneck gallop. The best handlers leave the ground with every step. They seem to fly weightless along side; clutching the horse's neck, they become one with the mane. The horses are urged on by the crowds until they become exhausted. Stomping, rearing, their sides heave, about to burst. All along the route they have been fed on sake. Now they reel and foam as men pound the ground with bamboo sticks.

A white steed is the last to run this gamut, but the last to appear is *game*. The great serpent-turtle storms into the circle and captures its center, rearing out of control and scaring the small children clinging to their grandparents on the sidelines. The men surrounding the beast fight to tame it, until at last *game* is subdued. When *game* bows down, the whole town sighs.

Game is now spun around like a top, recapitulating its journey around Asia and across the sea, coming to rest pointed north. This monster is the guardian of the north, the direction from which barbaric evils have come since before China put up its Great Wall. A white tiger guards the west, a dragon the east, a sparrow the south, and at Yatsushiro *game* is now restored to his post.

The festival is a long wild blur; it takes the whole of a town to mount it every year, molding each neighborhood into a single unit with a single purpose. That purpose is prosperity; the blessing, money; but underneath is a ritual of darkness and light. An alien beast crosses the sea to devour the populace and swallow its fortune. To bring this beast to its knees, to convert it to guardianship over the threat of darkness, the city unites, the warriors serve, the drunken horse is ridden to submission within the compass of the village.

✸   ✸   ✸

In the swamp of festival-goers, we are picked out by a young woman from Taiwan, Huang Ei June. She has been studying Japanese in Yatsushiro and is set to return to the Republic of China in a few days. June fills us in on the details of the Myoken festival, points out the expensive seats on the bleachers behind us, and identifies the smokestack of a pulp mill that rises over the eaves of the train station. Hashiguchi Setsuko, in whose house June is boarding, invites us to lunch. Setsuko and June grab a taxi as the crowd breaks up. We are driven through Yatsushiro into its suburbs.

Setsuko's home contains an American living room, complete with piano and sofa. She telephones her husband, a vice-principal, to bring home some *nori maki*, then disappears into the kitchen to prepare our meal. Setsuko's a hurricane, nervous but excited by her visitors. We comb through picture albums on the coffee table with June providing the commentary. When Setsuko's husband arrives, he gives us a long, difficult dissertation on *game,* with June translating as best she can. He wants to know the order in which three big-nosed masks were paraded today. The color of the mask that leads this little procession forecasts next year's weather. If the first *sauta hiko* mask is red it indicates a year of good sunny weather; if it is black, the winds are on their way; if blue, expect rain. The forecast is kept secret until the festival.

For lunch, we step behind the sofa through sliding screens into a matted room and squat down on pillows at a low table. This is a meal we will not soon forget. Setsuko has prepared an enormous chicken salad, heaped in a glass bowl, the lettuce fresh, the chicken chunks lean. We can't eat enough. We stuff ourselves with seconds and thirds. Through the doorway to the kitchen we can see a formal dining table, Danish modern-style, on a parquet floor. This is a house of screens and mats, sofas and upright chairs, chopsticks and pink finger towels, lace tablecloths and bottles of beer, one room West, the next room East. Setsuko wears a white blouse and black skirt with high heels; her husband, black suit and tie. Their home is at the edge of rice fields diced into neat plots.

After lunch, Setsuko ushers us to Lord Matsui Naoyuki's teahouse and garden; it was here that Emperor Hirohito drank tea on a visit, and no one seems to have forgotten that event. The teahouse is closed today, but Setsuko has friends there, and we are guided through the grounds by lovely people who struggle to come up with the English word that will explain the significance of the iris by a large river-fed pond. The Lord of Yatsushiro built his teahouse on the shores of this pond in 1688 as a gift to his mother, a Buddhist nun. He built it at a time when Japan had closed its doors and entered a long self-contained journey into unified feudalism. The pond survives. The iris are sewn to its edges like lace.

As we part from Setsuko, we learn for the first time that she has only an hour to make it to the airport, from where she is scheduled to embark on a ten-day tour of Europe—England and France, Germany and Switzerland. June holds open the taxi door. "I love travel abroad," Setsuko says. "I'm excited. Europe is my first trip." Europe is a continent beyond the flowery dreams of those first lords and ladies of old Yatsushiro, but it may now be bridged in a single day, even setting out from a tiny city in southern Japan.

That evening from our hotel room I watch a festival float being dismantled plank by plank by a team at the shrine across the street. As it collapses, the people shed their samurai gowns and change to blue jeans and T-shirts. Every piece is numbered and packed in its crate, then stored in the neighborhood temple. The storage boxes are stacked in dark cupboards behind the altar. I watch as the float comes down like an elaborate wooden umbrella, fitted together without a single nail. The god who rode in it today vanishes without a trace, not even a waft of smoke—a particle of space discharged from its magnet of carved and enameled wood.

XVIII.

Ibusuki:
Jungle Bath Fever

The early train from Yatsushiro hugs Japan's final western shore. The farther south we're hauled, the more we like what we see. Even Minamata is steeped in this uncontaminated wash of morning; it appears to be an innocent, drowsy port, resplendent with orange groves netted against flocks of birds. The old volcanoes have deposited rocks that here tumble into the sea; the fisherman cast their nets from large boulders. The threat of typhoons is past this year; the winter skies are a tropical blue; the sun on the forests is warm. Farms and straw roofs have replaced the cement and tile of the cities to the north. We are a century's remove from Kumamoto, Nagasaki, Fukuoka.

We cut a long southeast arc across the bottom of Kyushu and change trains at Kagoshima. I catch a glimpse of Kagoshima's volcano expelling an immense cloud of ash, a sight difficult to believe, and I've no time to place it in perspective. It looks like the world is blowing to pieces.

The final spur of track runs south from Kagoshima down Kinko Bay. There's a considerable oil refinery in these waters, the largest I've seen in Japan. This is the same bay St. Francis Xavier sailed up in 1549 to inaugurate the Christian Century in Japan; it's now clogged with freighters and tankers, vast floating cathedrals of commerce. The mountain range that parallels the shore has added a new spire since Xavier was by: a metallic rocket on a launching pad, monument to Kyushu's burgeoning space program.

We disembark at Ibusuki, plush with palms and spa waters. Next door to the station is an establishment with our name on it, so to speak: the Question Hotel. I consider booking a room there, just to see if they also have the answers. Instead, we procure a local map and hop the bus for the Ibusuki Kanko Hotel, a big beach resort that caters to Japanese honeymooners and claims to be the largest resort hotel facing the Pacific. It's a copy of Hawaii, a light-hearted copy, as a Japanese pension is a copy of a Swiss chalet: a copy in fun. The main building is a luxurious monstrosity of long corridors and wide basements tapering into an underground bowling alley, a stroll hotel in which it's easy to lose one's way. Some sections are twenty years old; others, thirty. There's a Japanese side and a Western side, story after story, all with balconies, all facing the sea. There are immense theater-restaurants and stadium-sized bathing complexes too. All chambers connect to the lobby, an empty crossroads when we walk in. We receive a room on the seventh floor, Western side.

The Kanko's grounds are also sprawling. Wide paths loop through forests of palm, eucalyptus, and Japanese oak; through gardens of camellia, cherry trees, bougainvillea, hibiscus, hydrangea and azalea; past courts for tennis and croquet; through open fields of spongy grass, groomed by hand to the tolerance of golf greens, the women in bonnets on their knees with spades and black scissors. We take a long solitary walk; there's no one else in the park in November, save a few workers. The circular swimming pool has been drained. The art gallery is closed. It contains original oils by Matisse and Gauguin—a strange residence for nineteenth-century European masterpieces. Sea eagles spin overhead and roost in the high branches of the oaks that surround an artificial waterfall and pond.

The longer we walk, the more gritty we feel. There's an invisible dust painting our skin. When I rub my face I feel fine particles of glass drag across my cheeks—the debris of Kagoshima's volcano thirty miles up Kinko Bay, drifting south. We can see a light gray sprinkling on the path. Our footprints line up behind us, then are erased by the suggestion of a breeze, the blast of a rocket, a puff in a ship's languid sail.

❋   ❋   ❋

The big restaurant at the Ibusuki Kanko Hotel is called The Jungle Park—a permanent canvas tent pitched over palm trees that seats fifteen hundred for table-side barbecues. We are surprised to find it nearly full for the first of its two seatings tonight, since the hotel was deserted; but the guests have arrived in group packages and have spent the day elsewhere, sightseeing, while we poked through the catacombs.

A troupe from Hawaii dances on stage. They hula. They eat fire. They cajole guests into joining them on stage. The gas-fired braziers at each table fill the big top with smoke.

To reach the Jungle Park restaurant, we had to hike across the lobby, through a corridor, down a set of stairs, and into an arcade of shop counters selling souvenirs. Departing, we must retrace our steps. Every dinner guest receives a lottery ticket, and by following the signs ("Rottery") back into the shopping arcade, we end up in a line where the prizes are distributed: cologne, tiny spa towels, liquor. We are lucky; we receive towels.

We return to our room as a tour group arrives on our floor. Luggage is deposited at doorways; tourists follow with their keys. The walls are so thin that from inside our room we can hear every movement and reconstruct the opera of this tour group in detail: suitcases flopped on beds; hasty showers; changes of clothes; doors opening and closing; elevators delivering passengers to dinner. The couple next door will be skipping dinner, however; they barely took time to drop their suitcases. They're in bed, making love with the volume turned up; they scream and sigh and plead like actors in an overdone X-rated sound track. They couldn't wait any longer, whoever they are. It is the first time we've heard sex in Japanese.

Tonight I have promised myself a Jungle Bath. *Junguro-Furo*. Margaret expresses no interest in *junguro-furo*; she prefers her own batho-tubo. I change into a *yukata*, then attempt for the first time to cover it with a second robe—a kimono that is two feet too long. I can't understand whom it would fit. I gather it up at my waist and secure the folds with a wide sash, but I'm dubious it will hold. I have not mastered the art of gift wrapping, and my kimono is slipping down over my ankles.

I stride gingerly to the elevators; at the bottom, the doors open on a lobby crammed with dozens of Japanese tour groups, everyone milling around in robes. The men wear blue robes; the women wear orange—a gigantic public slumber party. I wade through the throng, eyes on my belly, my kimono reefed in precariously. I make it to the shopping arcade, determined to reach the men's side of the Jungle Bath without exposing myself.

The Jungle Bath protocol is the same as it was at the hotel bath in Noto. There's a modern locker room, a precinct of showers and basins, and a marble stairway down to the baths—the fifty-nine pools of varied size, shape, temperature, color, and substance, landscaped with tropical plants and Las Vegas-style plaster statuary. I set out through the jungle and plunk in the first pool that appears. I should sample as many dips as possible before shriveling up, but my mind and heart are elsewhere. I'm thoroughly bored. My sole concern is struggling back into that seven-foot-long robe and sash for the walk, the very dainty walk past all the shop clerks, receptionists, and Japanese guests to my room. We're the only Westerners in the entire resort and the only guests not in a group. We stick out dreadfully, especially in kimonos and thongs.

Junguro-Furo is a jungle without insects, without predators, paved and well-groomed; an Amazon-in-a-Bubble for weary travelers from distant cities; a cement Lake District flushed with twelve tons of hot spring water a day. And the only way to get there and back is via the shopping arcade. Returning from dinner or bath, few guests can run this gauntlet without acquiring a shopping bag.

At sunset, we step out on our balcony. The artificial waterfall is filling the manmade pond. The swimming pool is as smooth as a scooped out crater. A ferry, its lights just peeping on, is setting out to cross the channel. No sight of schooner or spaceship; not even a barge tonight. Just birds. Birds fill the bay sky without crowding it, entering and leaving without a smudge. An eagle soars over the hotel balconies. Caravans of cranes are driven like disintegrating wedges through a sky of ash. This Japanese rendition of Hawaii, cheesy as an Atlantic City casino, happens to be stationed on the flyway to Siberia.

✳   ✳   ✳

"Their hot springs are of this sort," Jorge Alvares reported after his journey to southern Kyushu in 1546. "At the place where I stayed, I saw a stream entering the sea at a very rocky part where there was but little sand; in the morning at low tide lukewarm water may be found by digging a few inches into the ground. Both winter and summer, many of the poor men scoop out caves in which they lie and wash themselves for several hours, either at sunrise or at sunset when the tide is low and the stream flows into the sea. Most of the women of that place get into the water at sunrise, or even earlier, and quickly douche their heads three times, even though it may be snowing."

It is not snowing when Margaret agrees to follow in this tradition. I have convinced her that to be buried alive in the volcanically-heated beach sands of Ibusuki constitutes the ultimate spa experience. After all, Ibusuki bills itself as the possessor of the only natural hot steam beach sand sauna—*sunamushi*—in the world, no doubt a sweet prevarication launched by its chamber of commerce, but one that any true traveler should be willing to swallow at least once.

Pedaling our rented bicycles along the promenade, past fish hanging out to sun cure on bamboo poles, we have no trouble finding the spot where billows of steam rake a half-mile section of black sands. Margaret checks into the adjacent public bathhouse where for 510 yen she's issued a towel, a ticket, and a *yukata* she has to keep closed with her fist. The clerk of the baths reminds her twice that she must remove her underwear; and twice Margaret asks if this is the widest robe available.

I accompany Margaret to the beach. Two barefoot lady attendants, dressed in black sweat pants, white bonnets, and long cotton coats tied at the waist with aprons, take up their square shovels at her approach, scoop out a furrow, and direct Margaret to lie in it. Wrapping her hair in the spa towel, Margaret scrunches in bravely. The attendants bury her up to her neck and impale a small beach umbrella beside her head.

"I wouldn't have done this naked," Margaret announces, looking less than comfortable.

I sample the sands with my fingertips. The grains are warm and moist. "How hot it it?" I ask.

"Hot and getting hotter," she answers. "How long am I supposed to lie here?"

I glance seaward at a clock hung from a rope tied to a driftwood pole. "According to the historical record, several hours at least. And remember to douche your head three times when you finish."

Margaret lasts a full fifteen minutes. The two attendants sit down, put their feet up, and scan the ranks of bathers. There is a Chinese woman from Taiwan, part of a tour group, and an elderly Japanese gentleman, there when we arrive and there when we leave. Two young Japanese girls show up just before Margaret comes to a rolling boil. Other heads pop up here and there in neat rows next to their umbrellas. The beach looks like an outdoor dormitory, everyone bedded down.

When Margaret finally throws off the hot blanket of sands, she spreads her arms as wide as the wings of a crane. "Not one more minute," she declares. "I feel like one of Edgar Allan Poe's catatonic damsels in a heated crypt." Brushing herself off, she heads to the showers, grains of sand grinding into her creases with each stride. "You're beautiful," I call; and, in fact, a hot beach sand bath is supposed to beautify the skin. The warm saline solution, heavy with sodium chloride, is also touted as a comfort, if not an outright cure, for neuralgia and rheumatism. At the very least, it's a novel method to produce sweat.

The tubes and channels that heat this strip of beach at Ibusuki lace the entire Satsuma Peninsula, popping up as hot springs, spreading out in creases beneath the tropical mask of Kyushu, running under the floor of the sea, knotting like fire roots in the deep vents of volcanoes.

At Ibusuki Station there is a monument to the volcano and spa trade: a man and a woman in life-size bronze, their toddler between them, all rounded and naked except for a hand towel, striding forward, rather heroically, from an island platform surrounded by steaming water. We buy train tickets north back up Kinko Bay, leaving the town in off-season to its fishermen and those who plant the heads of tourists in a garden by the sea.

Across the street, we have our final look at the Question Hotel, enigmatic as ever, set in featureless blocks of concrete. One day I'll be sorry I didn't ask when I had the chance.

XIX.

Chiran:
Garden-Variety Samurai

C hiran is a sweet little samurai town preserved for tourists on a hill north of Ibusuki, nineteen miles inland from the city of Kagoshima. One lane of Chiran is lined with the garden estates of retainers of the Shimazu Lords who ruled the whole Satsuma region of southern Kyushu. The samurai's descendants still occupy these houses, and seven owners keep their gates open for visitors to enter their private gardens, some of the most exquisite of Shogunate Japan. This makes Chiran a fine place to catch one's breath, to imagine that the days of refined isolation and feudal order still exist in the Orient, uncomplicated and unbesmudged by a disorienting modernism. Of course, one must suspend disbelief completely, ignoring the main street of Chiran where the buses unload, where the telephone and electrical cables are buried in concrete sidewalks, where 7-Elevens and Circle Ks serve the descendants of warriors.

Samurai lane is bordered by a winding wall of fitted mossy stones, favored by white cats and bedecked with podocarpe hedges trimmed to evoke a mountain ridge. The oldest of Chiran's gardens was laid out by the Mori family in 1741. A traditional villa and stone warehouse, its roof lashed down by ropes for quick release in the event of a fire, are of the same era. The Mori garden is a fantasy of shaped rocks and a pool; boulders and plants taper up a steep hillside. Above this garden, two centuries ago, stood the castle of Chiran, one of the one-hundred-thirteen outer castles in the system of fortified villages that encircled old Kagoshima, the great castle town of southwestern Kyushu.

While the Shimazu rulers of this region could call upon these gardeners to take up arms, most of a samurai's life was spent in more domestic arts, particularly in landscaping, the dry landscaping in which white sands represent water and blue boulders tumble down to suggest cascades and waterfalls. The Chiran gardens are compact, at once an intensification of nature and a suspension of tension.

The inspiration came from the rear gardens of temples in Kyoto, which representatives from Chiran saw when traveling as attendants to their Kagoshima lords. Since they came home to build gardens for houses rather than for temples, the samurai added several homey touches. They located the toilet beside the front gate, facing the street, both for the convenience of visitors and for purposes of intelligence gathering. Ensconced within his clandestine listening post, a samurai master could collect gossip from the streets undetected. They also located long stone basins near the gate; when these gentle literati of the hedge returned from a campaign, they could immediately rinse the blood from their swords before retiring to the garden.

Samurai were banned from farming in Japan, but those in Chiran bent the edict from Edo to earn their livings as gentlemen tea farmers. These tea plantations flourish today, engulfing the town. The small close-cropped bushes are laid out in evenly-spaced rows. At the edge of Chiran, surrounded also by tea plants, is a more modern relic, the Chiran Tokko Peace Museum, the final resting place of "articles left by the departed" from World War Two, including a fighter plane. Based here were Chiran's modern samurai, the kamikaze pilots who delivered themselves with their planes into the fatal armor of American carriers at sea—pilots reduced in history to the effectiveness of gnats by the final atomic typhoon.

XX.

Kagoshima:
Net of Fire

The same day we catch the bus from Chiran to Kagoshima. The first half-hour is a pleasant drop toward Kinko Bay; the next hour is stop-and-go through an increasingly dense strip of car lots—more Volkswagens for sale than anywhere else we've been in Japan—and stores, some with mysterious names printed in English, such as the "Thankyou Home." The bus terminal is in the heart of downtown Kagoshima at the Yamatagaya Department Store. Inside, American and European clothing fills every rack.

Outside, we come across the cutest car in Japan, one they don't export to America. This is the sort of car no one could take seriously: four wheels, yes; two doors, yes; but room inside for only one. I mean one. There's not an inch left over, not space enough for a sack of groceries. It looks like a solo commuter car for the Jetsons. Its name, stamped in English, is the Abbey Carrot. In America we could fill our driveways with Abbey Carrots, one for every member of the family.

We enter Tenmonkan Dori, the covered shopping arcade—every city center has one; it must be the Japanese answer to the American Mall. After a cheap bowl of noodles for dinner, we discover a cosmetics shop patrolled by an elegant cat and stop to express our admiration. The proprietress tells us she owns sixteen cats; she invites us to pet a few. They are exactly like cats anywhere who are well-fed: indifferent, unimpressed, unassailable. There's not a Western face the whole length and breadth of the arcade, but we tally a McDonald's, a Kentucky-Fried Chicken, a Baskin-Robbin's, even a Tiffany's. The only obvious bit of feudal Japan here is a busy fortune-teller working the entrance to a neon-sculpted pachinko hall. We buy ice cream bars at the Haagen-Dazs outlet, seated among stylishly dressed teenagers and students on dates, not a samurai in the place.

You can move a long way in a day in Japan: entire centuries, whole hemispheres.

* * *

It keeps erupting without a break day and night, minute by minute, this volcano in Kinko Bay, Mt. Sakurajima. Remnant of the largest volcano on earth, its ash cloud unfurls in the sky like an upside down waterfall.

We watch the eruption for hours. Whenever we look east from downtown Kagoshima, we can see cone in the sea. It seems inches away—in fact is three miles east, a five-minute ferry ride from the Kagoshima's harbor. Ferries steam back and forth around the clock. This city of a half million is always in a shadow, even at noon.

When the winds shift to the west, umbrellas open, the streets slicken, and Kagoshima is dusted with a storm of ash. From our hotel room atop the Shiroyama ridge we possess the whole strange vista: a modern city, a clear bay, a volcano within walking distance rising from the sea like Atlantis on fire. The first day Mt. Sakurajima is terrifying. It is terrifying to think of living with a mountain in continuous eruption, but the locals tell us that the ash clouds are a good sign. Whenever Sakurajima puts a cap on its emissions, the pressure inside builds up; then the people, some of whom live on its flanks, begin to remember earlier catastrophes, of the sort that killed many just last year at Mt. Unzen.

After a day or two, however, it's true: we assume the indifference of any citizen of Kagoshima. We take almost no notice of the volcano and the ribbons of ash always in the sky. It is like living on a fault line that never stops quivering or on a coast where it drizzles. We rapidly forget, even when the signs are visible, that nature is everywhere and its laws are distinctly inhuman.

We explore Kagoshima by streetcar and on foot. Kagoshima fancies itself the Naples of Japan, and Naples is its first sister city. Other official relatives include Perth, Miami, and Changsha, China. Kagoshima has virtually nothing in common with its sisters, especially with dismal Changsha, which isn't tropical or a seaport. Then again, Kagoshima isn't really Italian, despite its Naples Street, its Napoli Dori Avenue, and its plethora of Italian restaurants dominated by take-out pizza joints. There's take-out pizza every few blocks with names in English, like "Kitchen," easily identified by the motorcycles blocking the sidewalks out front. The cycles are equipped with what look like book presses on the rear, mechanisms for the delivery of pizzas hot in the box. All evening these delivery bikes zoom up and bank down the twisting streets, the wide avenues with their film rental outlets named "Video Happy," beauty salons labeled "Make & Hair," and business hotels called "Washington," where our George never dreamed of sleeping.

Three miles from the center of town, Mt. Sakurajima keeps pumping out ash in its sleep, just as it did when the first Westerner, Jorge Alvares, sailed into Kagoshima four hundred years ago and wrote, "There are many volcanic islands which throw up smoke all year round, and sometimes fire as well." In the morning, under Mediterranean blue skies, Sakurajima is still at it, scrolling rock burnt to the thinness of paper in the shape of a dragon—the Oriental Vesuvius, its dead sister.

❄   ❄   ❄

"The life of a flower is brief but its sufferings are many," wrote one of Japan's greatest modern writers, Hayashi Fumiko (1903-1951). This line, which sums up her life (she wrote too beautifully and tragically to sell many copies, and lived but forty-seven years), is inscribed at a shrine in the shadow of the volcano, next to her small statue.

We have taken the five-minute ferry to Mt. Sakurajima—the first car ferry in Japan. A sinuous chain of dolphins erupted in our wake. The waters of Kinko Bay are clear to a depth of thirty feet. Beneath is the floor of a vast caldera, the southern anchor of Japan. We have changed to a local bus and rounded the southern shore of the mountain. We get off at Furusato Hot Springs, where Hayashi Fumiko's mother was born. The memorial to the poet is straight up from the roadside; above her figure is the smoking peak of Mt. Sakurajima. For the first time we are standing on the volcano in the bay. We can feel a light dusting of ash on the soles of our shoes.

No one else has stopped here this morning. The park is vacant, save for a vendor maintaining the concessions beside the memorial. Returning to the road, we attempt to find the famous seaside hot springs, which proves to be through the lobby of one of the resort hotels. The spa is closed for cleaning, we're told, but we are permitted to climb down to the shore. Furusato is an outdoor hot spring scooped out of the bubbly hollows of the steep seacliffs. Workers on high perches are hosing it out. We've never seen a more stunning bath. Everything is here: the sea where dolphins swim up for a closer look; a Shinto shrine chiseled into a cavernous wall of a natural onsen; a volcano erupting above. But we've come at the wrong hour. We return to the ferry landing and join an afternoon bus tour.

This volcano was an island until 1914, when it unleashed a massive lava flow that filled in a channel a quarter-mile long to a depth of 235 feet, thereby connecting itself to Kyushu on the east. But Sakurajima still feels every bit an island and looks like one from Kagoshima. The standard bus tour makes a clockwise thirty-mile circuit. We are the only Westerners aboard; the young woman up front in a guide's uniform provides a Japanese narrative and sings a few ditties over the loudspeaker. It's the usual bus tour.

Lava eruptions, dating back to 708 AD., have paved many wide avenues from peak to sea. Winsome and fantastical monoliths of lava rock gild the margins of the highway. Sakurajima is in the habit of plastering itself nearly every day in lunar gray dust, and the villages that creep up its flanks have to wash themselves off morning and night. There are eight thousand residents on the volcano. The children sometimes must wear yellow hard hats to school. Umbrellas are common. When the mountain is cranky, it spews out stray rocks, and houses are equipped with backyard volcano shelters, bus stops with concrete shelters. Even cemeteries are helmeted in corrugated tin.

This is the last place on earth to choose to live a normal, quiet life, which is precisely what people choose to do here. There's a tiny island in the bay, Moejima, which was created during a minor eruption in 1979; and as soon as it appeared, forty fearless people took up permanent residence there. We all know that nothing is permanent, so there is something to be said for living on a volcano; it's fearfully honest. It makes for a thoroughly existential existence, one in which death is ever present and, indeed, quite certain. During the 1914 eruption, Sakurajima could not be seen from Kagoshima for seven days. In this eclipse by dust, eight villages dissolved in tongues of lava. There's a torii gate on the mountain that was once ten feet tall; since 1914, it has been buried up to its neck.

In the first half hour of our tour, we pass three street sweepers mopping up a fresh layer of ash. The villages are coated, too, but we see laundry hanging out to dry. It's like living where it snows all year in the sunshine. The bus corkscrews up to observation points near enough the caldera that we can almost singe our fingers. Sakurajima is the most active of Japan's many active volcanoes, and its most stunning, rising 3,688 feet from the water in a cluster of cones, barren and wrinkled like the hide of an elephant. The volcano's flanks are famous for two extreme crops: for the world's largest radish, averaging thirty pounds a bulb, and for the earth's tiniest tangerine, the sweet Satsuma mandarin, an inch across. We see both growing, both for sale. We buy some seeds.

There's always the chance to shop on a Japanese tour. Every time we empty out for a stroll over lava fields, the fruit vendors, souvenir hawkers, and portrait photographers are on us. Cameras snip-snap like snare drums. Like nearly every peculiar or particularly picturesque sight in modern Japan connected by rail or road, this volcano peninsula, this Garden of Gulliver, is inundated with stands and pottery showrooms bunkered at every vista. You can choose to stay in your seat at each stop, of course, but even our tour bus is a shop. The bench seat in the rear has been replaced by a display case; riders may purchase keepsakes there without even venturing out the door—refrigerated radishes, vials of certified Mt. Sakurajima ash, everything from teapots to lava rocks.

*   *   *

One day it dawns on me that all the strands I have been seeking in my search for Japan are exposed in one place, in Kagoshima, and that I only need to draw their ends together and haul up my catch to land the Japan that disappears; but I'm fearful that the prize will slither through my net, no matter how fine or tightly drawn.

I make my first cast in a garden, Iso Tei-en, constructed on the grounds of a villa in 1660 by the nineteenth Shimazu lord. The Shimazu clan, founded in 1185 AD, ruled all of Satsuma—the Kagoshima region—for thirty generations, nearly seven hundred years. The Shimazu rank among Japan's most interesting rulers. They welcomed the first Christians to Japan, maintained trade with China and the West during years when the rest of the nation was self-enclosed, built the first Western-style factories, and led the Meiji Restoration that undid the Japan of samurai and shogun.

Iso Garden, although it came late in their long reign, is the Shimazu's most beautiful legacy. The three-hundred-year-old main villa, Senganen, stands solemnly, face-to-face with its borrowed scene, Mt. Sakurajima. A collection of large stone lanterns is strung along the volcanic shore, where a modern highway also runs. Early winter chrysanthemums add walls of color, unusual in grand Japanese gardens. There are mums of every scale, from the massive to the minuscule, and of every style, from trim to shaggy: yellow chrysanthemums, and white, crimson and double-colored flowers. They flow from pots, from rickshaws and palanquins, and from the porches and sliding screens of samurai houses and Satsuma pavilions. Margaret is particularly intrigued by the trained mums which begin as one or two stems and then sweep up into intricate formations with dozens of blooms. The more advanced specimens of the disciplined blossoms are housed in arcades, where manikins in samurai dress are decorated in mums.

Deeper inside Iso Garden is its old *kyokusui*, a winding stream where lords and ladies entertained themselves at poetry parties, spreading out on the banks of flat stones to compose verses in Chinese. The rules of the game required players to finish a verse before the next cup of sake set adrift upstream floated past their station. This winding stream is a page out of Tang Dynasty China, when villa gardens and poetic joustings became the essence of Oriental refinement. But this is also modern Japan, and on the hilltop above the garden, connected to it by aerial cable car, is Isoyama Recreation Ground, an amusement park overlooking stately garden, volcano, city, and bay, and featuring a race track for noisy go-carts, an amusement copied from ever-popular 1950s America.

Iso is the last great garden we will visit on our two rounds of Japan. I consider the severe sprawling stroll garden at Kanazawa and the compact sand garden in a Kyoto temple, the picture garden at Kumamoto, and now this flowery villa garden in Kagoshima. The Japanese art of landscaping is firmly connected to Golden China, and there is no more visible manifestation of how Japan copies, perfects, and elaborates the foreign surfaces that strike its fancy. Japan preserves its copies long after most of the originals have disappeared. I am wondering what Japan might freeze of America for future centuries, if anything. Is our popular culture aesthetically challenging enough for the Japanese? Will go-cart tracks and Disneylands be polished and displayed in Japan for the delight of twenty-fifth-century visitors?

Perhaps it is not the drive to preserve the past that keeps these glorious copies and reductions of nature, these Japanese gardens, in existence; but rather, a delight in rendering the fleet floating world, the manifest beauty of an inner Japan. These gardens are an expression of the passage of time, the invisible force that propels the flowering of an ultimately fatal design in which we are entrapped, the web of life, sublime but tragic.

Next door to Iso Garden is Shoko Shuseikan, a stone factory complex established in 1852 by the 28th lord, Shimazu Nariakira. This is the cusp of a change of worlds in Japan, where the Oriental surfaces dissolve like glass chips in a kaleidoscope and are resolved into new arrangements, new beauty. The main factory building, dating from 1865, has been converted to a museum with rather dull exhibits from the Shimazu family closets. Lord Nariakira, it appears, was a bit of a Ben Franklin. His factory turned out everything from cannons to land mines, farming equipment to cut glass. His blast furnaces, smelters, and twelve-hundred factory workers created Japan's first Western-style sailing ship. He also constructed Japan's first modern cotton mill, sending nineteen young men to England to purchase the equipment. British engineers arrived in Kagoshima to assist in production, which began in 1867, and their house remains near the factory, although we find it empty and unrestored.

The black hulk of the original cotton spinning machine remains in the museum factory, a squat metal beetle the size of a rhinoceros that signifies a feudal, insular Japan crossing the border of industrial statehood. Nariakira was among Japan's first modern industrialists, but he was also fascinated by Western art, literature, and especially photography. He had a camera, and the photographs of the Shimazu clan in Western dress on the factory walls date back to 1857.

Nariakira came to power in the most old-fashioned way. His father refused to make him the clan leader, preferring to spend his days with his concubine and naming one of her children the new daiymo. The family factions fought it out; exiles and suicides ensued; but in the end Nariakira and his followers triumphed. They supported the modernization of Japan. As resistance to the West crumbled, they constructed a new order, and Japan began to reshape itself in another foreign image. Shimazu Nariakira was exactly the sort of tinkerer who welcomed the fantastic toys of the West and made something of them in nineteenth-century Japan. In Kagoshima, feudal garden and modern factory exist side by side.

We walk away along the waterfront a mile to a memorial marking the landfall of the first Christian missionary to Japan, St. Francis Xavier. His Portuguese ship docked at Kagoshima on August 15, 1549, six years after a similar vessel, the first ever from the West, drifted onto the nearby isle of Tanegashima and introduced firearms to Japan.

Xavier's guide was a native Japanese, Anjiro, who, wanted for murder, fled on an earlier Portuguese ship and met the great Jesuit in Goa, India. Once baptized, Anjiro led Xavier on a voyage to Japan where for ten months they were guests of the Shimazu lords; at

Japan's first six hundred converts to Christianity were secured. For several more years, Xavier set about introducing Christianity to Japan, where it gained a modest foothold it would never entirely relinguish, despite imperial bans, sustained witch hunts, and group crucifixions.

The monument to Xavier's landing in Japan, modest but haunting, surprises us. Erected in 1949, it consists of a curving wall on which are cast reliefs of Japanese martyrs to the faith; to one side is a separate marble pillar on which, four feet above the ground, is pinned a life-size bronze statue of St. Francis Xavier, his cape and robes flowing, his arms outstretched, the palms turned upward and rising, his bare head tilted back to the sky. He floats in space like a man magically freed from crucifixion—both martyred and transcendent. In the background are the palm trees and heated cone of Mt. Sakurajima that Xavier must have seen as he sailed up Kinko bay, ashen banners of an unknown kingdom unfurling in the winds.

Gardens, factories, Christians—it's quite a snarled catch for a single morning. We pause for a lunch of lavish Satsuma fare in a downtown restaurant, Kumasotei. Not a word of English is spoken by the geisha-clad waitresses who serve us the courses in a matted room. Surrounded by businessmen at the other five tables, no female diner in sight but Margaret, we partake of *katsuo no tataki*, the raw bonito slices from Kinko Bay; of *satsuma-jiro*, a miso soup; of *tonkotsu*, pork ribs boiled three hours to the tenderness of a pork roast; of *sake-zushi*, vegetables and sushi seasoned in *jizake* wine; of *shochu*, the local sweet potato wine; of *torisashi*, the raw chicken neither of us can quite touch to our lips; and of my Kyushu favorite, *kibinago*, the tiny, raw blue-silver sardines arranged in a circle to evoke a chrysanthemum. This is a Japanese meal to remember southern Japan by: each dish its simple self, served on its own graceful plate—cuisine done up much the way nature is in a Japanese garden: succulence for the eye, to be devoured and erased by the inner organs.

After lunch, we stroll uptown to Reimeikan Museum, a collection of thirty-five thousand artifacts of the region all set in the highest of high-tech displays, built on the ruins of the Tsurumaru Castle in the centennial year of the Meiji Restoration. I buy a ticket; Margaret, who eschews most museums, relaxes in the marble and glass lobby. The crafts, the farm implements, the samurai costumes and armor, the displays of trade and Christianity, the portraits of leading local players in the modernization of Japan, are laid out in a chronological hierarchy three floors high. Forecasts for the future are projected onto five screens. The displays, while not terribly interesting to Westerners, are superbly displayed. I emerge longing oddly enough for China, stimulated perhaps by a trivial display of a game adopted from China, *nanko*, played with two sticks. It's a drinker's game. Your companion conceals the sticks in his hand and you guess the number it represents. The loser must drink. It is a game played in every worker's restaurant in China today where beer is served by the bowl or plastic cup, except that on the mainland it is played with fingers, the elegant sticks having vanished long ago.

Outside the museum are the empty walls of the great Satsuma castle, built in 1602. We decide to walk back to our hotel atop the Shiroyama hill through a large park, forever consecrated to the memory of Japan's last great samurai rebel, Saigo Takamori. He was Shimazu Nariakira's most famous vassal, a poor samurai who rose through the ranks to become a chief leader of the Meiji Restoration and its most famous hero. After this triumph in 1868 and the overthrow of the Tokugawa Shogunate, Saigo returned to Kagoshima with his loyal Satsuma soldiers, founded a school for samurai, and in 1877 reversed himself, leading the Satsuma Rebellion to restore samurai society. He meant to overthrow the very Meiji Restoration he had fought to bring about. Thirty thousand samurai, fearful of the elimination of their class, joined Saigo as he stormed the government military center in Kumamoto. Failing there, the rebels were hounded south to Kagoshima. The army of Japan stormed Tsurumaru Castle; the rebellion was undone. This last honorable stand against the modern forces of the outside world made Saigo a Japanese hero. His plump figure and crew-cut crown are immortalized in statues throughout Kagoshima, and throughout Japan; the most famous stands in Tokyo's Ueno Park.

Saigo, of course, did not surrender; he would not have become a Japanese hero had he done so. Fleeing up the steep cliffs of Shiroyama, he held out in a cave, and there he ended life in the traditional manner, as did 2,023 of his loyal samurai. While we in the West know samurai as soldiers, in Japan they viewed themselves as sustainers of the highest national values. "The people of other classes deal with visible things. while the samurai deal with invisible, colorless, and intangible things," reads a seventeenth-century samurai's instruction manual. "But if there were no samurai, righteousness would disappear from human society, the sense of shame would be lost, and wrong and injustice would prevail."

This strand of the samurai way ate away at Japan's greatest twentieth-century novelist, Mishima Yukio. He felt that selfishness and greed ruled modern Japan; while life was affluent, it was a wealth and luxury without meaning, without a soul. "We have seen post-war Japan stumble into a spiritual vacuum, preoccupied only with its economic prosperity, unmindful of its national foundations," Mishima declared. On the eve of his dramatic disembowelment, he wrote, "We will die to return Japan to her true form." On November 25, 1970, he and a few of his dedicated new samurai, members of Mishima's own private army, stormed Japan's Self-Defense Forces headquarters and called for a general revolt. Unheeded, Mishima then took dagger to belly and proffered his head to a companion's sword. "Right now we will show you that there is a value higher than reverence for life," he wrote to explain this moment. "It is neither freedom nor democracy. It is Japan. Japan, the country whose history and traditions we love." Mishima's rebellion struck those in the West as bizarre, completely outside any human context; but Saigo and countless others with similar reservations about Japan's new course had expressed their protest in the same way.

Most modern Japanese find Saigo heroic, but Mishima ridiculous, a theatrical throwback to an era they have crossed off. For an outsider, traveling through modern Japan where the Oriental past has eroded into a few temples, where the traditions in arts and ceremonies have been preserved largely to sustain the tourist trade, it is tempting to call for a wholesale leveling of Western architecture, Western values, above all, Western pop culture in all its blemishing manifestations; but such nostalgia, such idealism, is nonsense. The world has changed, Japan with it. To Mishima, what disappeared was not a matted room or a suit of samurai armor, but the soul of Japan. Perhaps so; I can't tell. But in the surfaces I have been studying, I sense the same hand at work in this century as was at work on Chinese culture a thousand years ago, the same spirit-hand.

By the time we troop to the top of Shiroyama, my net is empty, just as I feared. Musing on difficult issues, drawing tenuous connections between Christians and samurai, gardens and museums, everything escapes, everything takes on its own competing visibility.

Our hotel, the Shiroyama Kanko, has Kagoshima's most commanding view, particularly of bay and volcano. Inside is a deluxe

Western complex of rooms, restaurants, and high-priced shops. In the basement is an exquisite Chinese restaurant with private dining rooms built over watery pools, fed by an artificial waterfall. Outside, connected by an elaborate walkway, is a bakery, and beyond it the Holt Garden House Italian Restaurant with a sliding-glass domed roof, a large tree in its midst, and outdoor seating with a view of Mt. Sakurajima. The hotel's last grand jewel is a tall narrow chapel built of marble, trimmed in blue tile and stained glass, its facade decorated with three golden balls and a cross on its steeple. We peek inside. There are software-controlled baptismal fonts, television monitors, and remote VCR cameras. This is a chapel for weddings. A young woman who works behind the front desk, who spent her less-than-happy high school years in Los Angeles, tells us that this chapel is extremely popular with young couples getting hitched. Its sole reason for existence is to serve couples dressed in full Western wedding regalia who wish to walk through the ceremony they've seen in foreign films and American soap operas. Many of these weddings entail a change of clothing and religious setting so that a Shinto service can be held immediately after the Christian version. East meets West. But poor St. Xavier; despite the years of mission and all the cruel martyrdoms, despite centuries of underground faith in Kyushu, Japan is no Christian nation. Christianity is a prominent piece of the new surface, to be sure: a chunk of the exotic that is in high demand, rented by the hour. For most Japanese, however, Western religion is little more than that, another masquerade, another pretty rite, explored as one explores another culture or a distant resort. What if Moslems ruled the world as Christians do now? Would the wedding chapels become mock mosques?

We order pasta and take our plates outside for a view of the volcano. It is still a considerable, frightening object. I am half-tempted to take up residence there. The unpretentious villages are untrammeled by tourists, native or foreign. To wake up every morning in such an impermanent place, to hear the mountain speak, to feel it tremble: it is a place for minds that keep their desires spare, their beliefs unanchored.

The fresh pasta, we notice, is shaped like its Italian models, but tastes thoroughly Japanese. *Soba*-like. *Udon*esque.

Walking back to our room as the sunset pinkens the dusty plume of Sakurajima, we are stepping on the graves of the last samurai, but the ghosts have fled. The railing is fitted with lamps to light us to bed, and fitted as well with synchronized stereo speakers that emit sugary pop tunes from America—elevator music for a volcano.

Tomorrow I will climb another volcano, Japan's most venerable, and cast this torn net into the crater where Japan was born.

✳   ✳   ✳

"Every morning make up your mind how to die."

So advises an eighteenth-century handbook for samurai. I couldn't agree more.

"Every evening freshen your mind in the thought of death," it continues. "And do this without ceasing. Thus your mind will be prepared. When your mind is set always on death, your way through life will always be straight and simple. . . ."

This is the precise course I have set to reach Mt. Takachiho in Kirishima National Park, an hour north of Mt. Sakurajima by train. I go alone in the morning, food packed, timetable and map in hand. I go as if this is my final journey in Japan. And no place could be more final. This is the beginning of Japan, at least in myth.

Takachiho-no-Mine is the volcanic peak where Niniji-no-Mikoto, grandson of the Sun Goddess, Amaterasu Omikami, first touched earth on a mission to rule the world. He descended to the peak bearing three symbols of the Sun Goddess: sword, mirror, and jewel. The sword of heaven he cast down to earth like a bolt of lightning, implanting it deep in the crater rim. His feet on the ground, Niniji immediately went shopping for a wife and found one, Konohanasakuya-hime, whose name means tree-flower princess. At the same time, he was offered her ugly sister as a consort, but Niniji rejected her. Shamed, the father set a curse upon the offspring of Niniji, that their lives would be as brief as flowers upon a tree. Thus was the race of mortals born on the slopes of Mt. Takachiho.

Niniji's grandson, Jimmu, became Japan's first emperor; his reign was established as 660-585 BC by the Yamato Clan which first united Japan and wished to give divine and ancient validity to its imperial line. It is a line that stretches unbroken over two thousand years, down to the present emperor of Japan. This was imperial myth-making on a Chinese scale, a fabrication designed to reinforce legitimacy, and it worked. If there was a Jimmu, he probably ruled the Kyoto region not in 667 BC, as fixed in the clan chronicles, but a thousand years later, when Japan's connections with Korea and China are documented by artifacts. The Yamato Court set down its official version of the origins of Japan in the eighth century. In this creation myth, two gods, one male, one female, stirred the primordial mud with the sword of heaven, the droplets from its tip forming the islands of Japan. They mated and begat still more islands and gods. Fire, too, was born of this union, and the female goddess was destroyed. Her mate cleansed himself in a river in which were born the three great *kami*: Susano'o, god of the oceans; Tsukuyomi, goddess of the dark; and Amaterasu, goddess of light. These three supreme *kami* engaged in a bitter rivalry that sent a distraught Sun Goddess to a cave, depriving the world of light. Light was restored only when a sexual dance was performed and Amaterasu was lured out. Seeing her reflection in a mirror, she was transfixed, seized, bound, and dragged from eclipse.

When eventually the *kami* were reconciled, Niniji the grandson descended to rule and populate the earth. The Shinto shrines of Japan trace their origins back to the various lower *kami* who walked the earth in the age of the gods. To this day, Japan's emperor performs national rites that harken back to myth, including a ritual in which he mates with the earth to insure large harvests. Buddhism, too, was incorporated in this genesis: Buddha mirrored Amaterasu at top, and the identifications continued on down the line, zipped together so that the two religious orders merged seamlessly.

Shinto and Buddhism also reflected each other in mountain worship. Koyasan was one of the first Buddhist mountain monasteries to draw upon the Shinto worship of mountains as divine, a practice that has even older roots in China. In the old tradition, the pilgrimage to the mountaintop was a return to the womb; the backpack represented the uterus.

The first Kirishima Shrine, dedicated to Niniji, was built on top of Mt. Takachiho in the sixth century; it now occupies holy ground at the foot of the volcanic range. I take a local bus from the train station to the shrine's entrance, pass under the largest torii gate in Western Japan, seventy-three feet tall, and pay homage at the temple of Niniji. Rebuilt many times and destroyed by lava, this version of the shrine was erected below the mountain in 1715 by the twenty-first Satsuma lord, Shimazu Toshitaka. Here are modern portraits of Niniji and the eight lesser gods who accompanied him on the first mission to earth. Here too is the stone of Japan referred to in the National Anthem as an emblem of the people working as a unit.

I withdraw to the tourist office and learn that there is no bus to Mt. Takachiho for hours. I spend the price of a fine dinner for a fifteen-minute cab ride up the foothills into the home of the gods, a range of twenty-three volcanic peaks. This is a shameful way for the rugged hiker, his thoughts on death, to reach the remote trailhead of his pilgrimage, but I do not have days to make the journey. I have arrived too late in the year for the festival of the fire god, celebrating the coming down of Niniji, held in November, and too early for the mass climb on New Year's Eve by torch and flashlight to the summit. This time of year, the mile-and-a-half ascent to the five-thousand-foot peak is virtually deserted.

I strike out alone though lush forests over a path of irregular lava stones that rises and falls before narrowing into rock and gravel at a wide clearing. A barren cone of red pumice, Mt. Takachiho, rises before me. Unmarked ridges are the only trail. I head straight up the slippery flank, quickly losing my breath, pausing every hundred paces to regain it.

The terrain could not be more purely the product of eruption and fire, a cascade of cinders. I am reminded of an interview given by the first woman researcher in residence at the Japanese outpost in Antarctica. Asked to name her greatest concern, she responded that there was no shopping: all she could bring back as gifts were rocks.

Ankles crumbling, I finally reach Takachiho's caldera. The peak is five hundred feet above this crater, but I doubt I can go on. Against the blue sky I can see the summit and on it the sword of heaven like a bare twig. Next to Niniji's Excalibur is a souvenir stand.

A solitary Japanese hiker descends from Takachiho to the caldera, and as he passes, we both speak the peak's name, nothing more. He heads west along a chain of peaks that leads to the sea separating Japan from Asia. I can see the sister peaks he will visit: Mt. Nakadake and Mt. Shinmoedake—the youngest of the volcanic clan and the most active, sending up a billow of white smoke—then Mt. Shishikodake and Mt. Karakunidake. Beyond are the hot springs of the Ebino tablelands. To the south, I have a splendid view of Mt. Sakurajima erupting over Kinko Bay.

The sad truth is I now lack the strength to make a final assault, to scale one more cone and stand beside the sword of heaven. I sit down on the rim of the caldera. Perhaps I have come far enough. More would be too much for one who has outspent his youth. Here, after all, is the basin of fire nearest to heaven, the old onsen of the gods. The empty crater is three hundred feet deep, twice that across. It seems a purer form than the peak above. There is no sword replica in a rock, no concession stand, just a hole in the mountain, a concave mirror that focuses the rays of heaven to a single invisible point.

I concentrate on the advice a Zen master, Harada-roshi, once gave to an American businessman, Philip Kapleau, in his quest for enlightenment: "Put your mind in your belly and focus on nothing but Mu." But Mu is also a word meaning nothing. My thoughts sink into my belly. My belly is empty, empty as this crater of heaven hollowed out by the force of creation. My thoughts ignite and burn, but then I feel the whack of the master's stick at my back, smashing the inner wind that erupts from my throat, that disappears in the wind. In this moment of violence, I melt into the crater, filling it with empty space, filling it full like a cup of air. I become the mind of winter, the snow man, not thinking of "any misery in the sound of the wind, / In the sound of a few leaves, / Which is the sound of the land / Full of the same wind / That is blowing in the same bare place. . . ." I am in the crater of the world's birth. I am nothing that is not there. I am the nothing that is.

※　※　※

When I come to my senses, I remember what I saw in reality when I looked into the crater of Japan. It was graffiti. The caldera floor was littered with rocks arranged to spell out the names of hikers who had dared to enter it, initials in English, words in Japanese characters. It is a crater defaced by scribbles. My brief scrape with satori is already erased; the womb is empty. I am still part of the pathetic race that inhabits the earth, mortal and insignificant, a mere scrawl on the mirror of the soul.

Descending a spine of the mountain, I encounter a group of Japanese tourists inching up another, each member attired in the latest Gore-Tex ensemble of windbreaker, mountain pack, gaiters, and expensive boots, etched in the latest neon colors. The group leader holds the company flag. They will probably make it all the way to the souvenir stand at the peak of Japan's genesis.

Riding the train back down to Kagoshima, I notice two competing pachinko parlors a block apart. The first is named NEW YORK and is capped with a large replica of the Statue of Liberty in white plaster; the second is named KING KONG and is presided over by the dark hulking statue of that cinematic gorilla. No refined GINZA geisha, no cute GODZILLA of atomic dreams, but imported icons, stations on the road to the West.

Back to China, forward to America. . . . It is too early to tell if the West will assume the bulk of history that once filled Japan with the Orient, but it is clear that the China version of Japan belongs to the past. Centuries from now, when America has disappeared to the extent that Tang Dynasty China has today, will one be able to revisit it in Japan, mummified and perfected, enshrined as ancient Changan is now in modern Kyoto? Strange tours await the sightseers of the future. In the present, one world is dying and another is being born.

And I am done with the mountains of Japan. Indeed, I should be done with Japan. As the old handbook for samurai cautions: "When you leave a festive place, depart while you still want to stay. When you feel you are satisfied and ready to leave, you have already had too much. Enough is too much." But there is more ahead and much more to learn. The circle we begin must be completed.

So, the morning after Mt. Takachiho, we wait for the train. Every day in Japan begins on a new groove in the wooden cyclotron. Sluggish at the start, we accelerate at each station as the velocity reaches that of the photon, the successive intersections of vista and impression compressed with the force of multiplied gravity until, by dusk, we are so numb and dense we cease to move at all.

The winds have shifted, bearing the ash cloud west over Kagoshima at last, and at the train station we can see the streets fill with minute particles. In the waiting room, the TV monitors are switched on to the morning aerobics show; passengers are seated, smoking cigarettes and reading newspapers. Outside, pedestrians in black and tan raincoats raise their orange umbrellas. The yellow snowplows creep along the avenue, lowering their blades. The curbs automatically ignite their hidden sprinklers, scouring the streets. We head for the eastern shore of Kyushu in a volcanic storm, the warm air snowing ash.

Behind us is the rounded crater of Japan's birth, at Kagoshima; and farther back, the flat crater of Japan's death, the one at Nagasaki; products of the first and second suns; one fashioned by the indifferent sword of nature, the other by the indifferent sciences of man. In this century, the gods have truly changed guard, descending to earth a second time, again in Japan, to fire a new race in their image.

XXI.

Miyazaki:
Net of Stone

T rains are our second home in Japan, our rolling residence. We know the train cars intimately—the sleek Shinkansen cars of Honshu, the main island, but also the serviceable and spartan old cars of Kyushu with their toasty velvet benches and electric heaters under the seats. The same sorts of passengers always come and go. Students in uniform crowd on, then thin out as we pull farther into the southeast hinterlands between Kagoshima and Miyazaki. A businessman stands in the aisle, turns his back to us, and without a care in the world, proceeds to scratch his rear for the longest time; a most satisfying scratch, it appears, dispatching every last tickle.

The Nichinan coast, stretching sixty miles south of Miyazaki, is a vacation destination in the summer, but a few couples are heading there even this winter. Across from us is a perfect example. The wife begins by unpacking a small case, sorting through its items on the seat, and repacking everything much as it was in a large handkerchief which she ties off in a perfect knot, elegant as a blossom. Then she's at her clothes, smoothing them down. Fiddling with her shoes, she swaps them for a pair with lower heels. Her husband fidgets, too, unfolding and consulting maps, recreasing brochures, and trimming errant facial hairs with a a tiny battery-operated shaver the size of a lighter. She applies make-up, a torturous task. She yanks at her scarf, adjusts and readjusts it; unrolls a bath towel, then folds it up. The mountain scenery floats by their unattended window. There's a lunch, too, that needs straightening. Finally she stands up and begins to peel down her skirt, a pink skirt of a thousand pleats, elastic at the waist. We stop staring as it lowers. I don't know how far the waist came down, but now she's hiked it back up and she's sitting down, legs crossed. We know she won't stay still for long. She asks her husband to haul down a suitcase from the luggage shelf. From it, she extracts a diary; in it, she records her morning's laborious notations.

The Japanese are world champion futzers. I'm not surprised when later I read (courtesy of the great translator, Donald Keene) that the Japanese keep diaries as no other race on earth do, that schoolchildren are often expected to keep a day-by-day account during summer months, that in the last war nearly every Japanese soldier kept a personal journal (issued by the Army) while American soldiers were forbidden to do so for security reasons (not that we are given to such meticulous literary jottings). The oldest surviving diary in Japan is the *Tosa Nikki*, a tenth-century account of a fifty-five-day journey; it is still read today. The detailed diary is another branch of futz-itis, one I seem to share with the Japanese when I'm on the road, recording whatnot. Vacation snapshots, for which the Japanese are also infamous around the world, is but the latest sprouting of this compulsion to capture and mount the commonplace, the otherwise ephemeral. More than an aid to memory or mere egotism is afoot here. I remember how my mother kept annotated scrapbooks of our family vacations to then distant points—Iowa, California—which I would consult during show-and-tell . . . scraps brought to order, meaning given to the "actual," as if we had been taught from earliest childhood that reality was something we could impose our own pattern upon through word and picture. The Japanese take this notion to its extreme. The group tour is appealing; it comes with a ready-made pattern, courtesy of the tour company, its plot and themes already concocted. The pachinko ball, however, is closer to reality, random within its inflexible tracks, except that in the actual world there is no jackpot, only a hole at the bottom into which pellets disappear one by one.

❊   ❊   ❊

We disembark at Miyazaki and visit the Information Center, run by Nakashima Ayako. She tells us that she lived in the city of New York three years on her own. Ayako's back home now working for what must be low wages, but everyone works who doesn't live at home. She leads an independent life in Miyazaki, probably an unusual one, not dressing in skirts and heels, but jeans and a knit sweater. She invites us to lunch, her spot, a rundown cafeteria where students go for a cheap meal. It's cheap, all right, and not very tasty, but it's good to see that not all of Japan eats at flashy, overpriced restaurants. This cafeteria reminds me of a workers' restaurant in China, down to its untidy bathroom.

When we get back to the Information Center, Ayako has to deal with an elderly American woman who seems to have arrived on her doorstep from nowhere seeking leads for a job. She wants to teach English in Miyazaki, a daring thought. Miyazaki seems far from anywhere, even Japan.

We catch a commuter train south a few stops to Aoshima along a coast strange for its rock formations, deserted in the winter rain. For the first time in our circuit of Kyushu the rains are falling steadily; the green landscape fades to gray. We unpack our umbrellas. At Aoshima Station we walk south along the busy coast highway to our abode, the Minshuku Take, *take* meaning bamboo, but we don't see any bamboo, just the outskirts of a deserted beach town, trucks, cars and buses whining by—a dark sea to the east, and on the other side of the highway, a two-story building of poured concrete with aluminum framed windows. This is where we come to rest, on the other side of the volcano, on the other side of the earth.

The Minshuku Take owners, the Take family, are warm hosts. We take to them at once. Their main floor is the dining room and kitchen; down the hall are the baths and a few rooms, presumably their living quarters. Upstairs are a half-dozen matted rooms for guests. Ours, on the backside, has a wide balcony beyond the shoji screen; has its own Eastern-style toilet, too, with blue plastic toilet shoes. In the upper hall is a small Sanyo Coin Laundry Washer, where for 100 yen a load we cleanse a week's worth of attire. The machine starts, then stops for a fulsome ten-minute agitation—more a bounce and slosh—after which it empties the spent water onto the floor and begins the first rinse. A common cold water sink is located on the wall next to the washer.

We're the only guests this time of year. After a fine dinner, we dress in *yukatas* and sit on the floor of our room, the laundry stretched on a line we rig overhead. The rain stiffens after dark and we do nothing much, refusing to feed the TV with coins. The Take's eleven-year-old daughter has played for us on the piano, we've signed the guestbook and posed for Polaroid snapshots with the family. Our portrait will join those of other foreigners on the wall or on the piano top. We are shown an album of postcards and letters from former guests, one of whom is from our own town in Oregon.

After an American breakfast the next morning, umbrellas up, we walk to the tiny island for which Aoshima is known across Japan. There are vendors lined up near the shore. We take the wide causeway to the island, nestled in three thousand betel-nut palms. There's nothing here but temple, forest, and a long rocky beach where we search aimlessly for tiny shells. The rocks are laid down in segment after segment like a series of steps that never rise but imperceptibly merge with the sea. Fittingly, this is the setting for the legend of two brothers—Umisachi, man of the sea, and Yamasachi, man of the mountain—who traded places for a day. These two were the sons of Niniji, the god who descended to Mt. Takachiho; their circular island is an Eden of palms at the center of a lava washboard sculpted by the sea; but the resort town of Aoshima, bordered by dozens of blocky cement hotels, is an emblem of this late century, when myth traded the staff of pilgrimage for the air-conditioned tour bus.

Before noon, we lower our umbrellas and catch the inter-city bus that runs down the Nichinan coast. The long ragged plates of beach rock resemble black waves of suspended lava, the mats of the gods who once bedded down on Kyushu. Along the way we see plenty of summer stops for the busloads, including a hillside planted in one-hundred-thousand cacti, advertising itself as a taste of old Mexico. The beaches, vacant in winter, look inviting, but when we step off the bus after an hour, we find them littered.

We've come to visit Udo Shrine, lodged in a sea cave among odd, mud-smooth sea castles, and we find it on foot some distance from town. As late as the beginning of this century, Udo was remote, requiring a long trek without benefit of highway or bus. Today, there are only a few tourists about and some Shinto priests. A walkway lined with red rails winds down to the sea, to the cave of the Udo Shrine, where the newly married couples still pay playful visits.

Inside the cave, beyond a bright orange torii gate, there is a temple, its roof crumpled under a flat roof of stone. To one side are counters set up by the monks and nuns to dispense amulets, incense, and souvenirs. For centuries, couples have come to Udo to pray for easy childbirth and rich breast milk, and there is something uterine in the long slit of this cave—its very ceiling pocked, yet sanded smooth, like some inner room of the body—and something mammarian in the rounded boulders congregating in the breakers outside. By legend, these rocks are the breasts of an ancient Princess of the Sea, Toyotamahime.

The nearest of these Neptunian monoliths is shaped like a turtle. On its back is a small crater, a few feet wide and deep, encirlced by a braided rope. Into this small pool visitors pitch coins from the edge of the cliff, difficult as ring toss at the county fair. The prize is the granting of a wish.

The god in residence at Udo Cave and Shrine is no less than the father of Jimmu, the legendary first emperor of Japan. The shrine traces its founding back to the tenth emperor, who reigned over two thousand years ago. In the eighth century and again in the tenth, Udo became Buddhist, but over the last few centuries it has reverted to Shinto. The water that drips from the cave ceiling is said to benefit nursing mothers who drink it. We see no tourists licking the walls, but milk candies are a staple of the Shinto concessions inside the cave.

It is to the entrance of this cave that the Princess of the Sea pressed her nipples to suckle the son of one of Aoshima's legendary brothers, Yamasachi, the man of the mountain. Yamasachi, in turn, was the son of Niniji, the first god on earth. In Udo cave the sea princess gave birth to Jimmu—Japan's first emperor. Thus the genesis of Japan dovetails, finding its visible markers in volcanoes and sea caves, its spirits enshrined in temples, the race of mortals beginning where mountain and sea merge.

Many have likened the sea stones of this coast to a washboard, but I see them as strands of a petrified net, filaments of mountain lava cast into the sea by the eruption of a god descending into mortal form. In the Japanese myth of creation, the natural and the divine are in exact correspondence; genesis is written in the shoreline of Kyushu's southeast coast. The stone nets cast down from Mt. Takachiho here reached the sea, clouds of fire cooled and molded into earth.

✳   ✳   ✳

The next day's breakfast waits for us under wraps. The cloths lift like lacy clouds from glasses and plates of fresh fruit, juice, coffee, eggs and toast, which we tackle with chopsticks. After a round of snapshots, we set out through the drizzle for Aoshima Station where we learn that the train to Miyazaki has been canceled due to flooded tracks; we wait an hour for the next.

At Miyazaki we have time to say farewell to Nakashima Ayako at the Information Center. She's too busy assisting new visitors to pay us much attention, so we are surprised when she catches up with us just as we board the train north. She's breathless. She comes aboard and gives us several small gifts, disembarking only as we pull away. We wave farewell. The mist congeals into rain, a fierce rain, as we follow the train timetable to Beppu, clicking off each stop on a journey of many hours. The rain is solid enough now to leak through the passenger car ceiling and soak the luggage overhead, but the heaters under the seat keep us toasty.

This would have been another long train ride through the provinces had the lady in the seat across the aisle not attempted to kidnap us. We notice her fussing over a bento box of salmon as we leave Miyazaki and are startled when she leans across and starts barking a jumble of phrases in English. She's nearly shouting. We sort through the language with her, tell her our names, where we've been, where we're bound.

At each stop our kidnapper steps up the volume and gains momentum. She's fifty-seven. She's been to Miyazaki, we believe, for her weekly blood test. She acts out what has happened to her at the clinic, a pantomime in which an enormous syringe is plunged ruthlessly and repeatedly into her left arm. She calls me "darling," a label she also uses when she describes her husband. She wants us to stop at her town on the way and attend a "dinner party," and she's not about to take no for an answer.

No is our answer. We try to explain our schedule. She retreats, as if she understands, but a few minutes later she's on to us with another strategem. From her home (where a teacher from California may or may not be staying, we're not sure) she will drive us in her car—"whoosh!"—to Beppu, where she knows a cook at Beppu's biggest spa hotel. "Whoosh, darling, whoosh! Dinner party. America is wonderful." After every stop she springs to her feet, gesticulating with abandon.

We think of a half-dozen ways to decline her invitation, insisting that our schedule is too tight to permit her kind detour. She's momentarily pacified.

At one point, she tries to give us a one-thousand-yen note, we're not sure why; perhaps it's to defray the final portion of our train ticket. Everyone aboard is transfixed by her gyrations; sets of eyes bob up and down over the backs of seats. Now she's spitting salmon bits and yanking on an imaginary steering wheel again. She wants to trade earrings with Margaret, but hers are of pearl. We turn down everything and try to defuse her by exchanging name cards. She writes down her address and, three stops north of Nobeoka, she gives in and disembarks, waving in large circles from the platform as we leave her there, her dinner party invitation and drive to Beppu untaken.

Just south of Beppu an industrial park on the sea parts the rain with smoke. Weakened by the siege of a human geyser, we collapse.

XXII.

Beppu:
Sex with Santa

It was a mistake to press on. Any true traveler would have accepted a dinner party with a wild woman, no matter the schedule. We have become too rigid in our motion, unable to bend, and we must hereafter follow every chance encounter to its end. Otherwise, we might as well read a guidebook and stay home. I am thinking these sensible thoughts because we have just been shown the worst room we've paid for in all of Japan, the one our budget guide praised to the heavens. The matron behind the counter has forced us to pay in advance and held us to a rate higher than the one posted on her very door; she's even locked up our money in the safe.

This room is more dismal than a week of rain and wet luggage; from ragged carpet scraps to torn bedspreads, nothing has been aired since the guidebook writer passed through what must have been a decade earlier. We debate for ten minutes. We know we must request a refund, something not easily done in polite Japanese society. We do it anyway; we're Americans. Fortunately, the stern owner has turned over the desk to the hired help; we check out with barely an apology.

I flip again through the guidebook. There's a listing for a business hotel nearby, the Green Hotel. Down the main street we turn in at a sign that we think says Green Hotel, walk up a flight, and confront a young woman at the desk. We ask her if this is the Green Hotel; she nods, a polite way of saying she probably doesn't understand our question. We don't care. We check the rates. They have a small double room for less than we were to pay at the stripped-down, seedy inn a block away. The Green Hotel, if this is the Green Hotel, has a bigger double, she points out, but we insist on the small one. The clerk starts to giggle. She disappears into the back, and we hear more giggles, but she returns with a key. We take the elevator to the fifth floor and find a clean room the size of a closet with its own modern bath. No question; it's a deal. There's a locked balcony at the end of the hall with a view onto the main street. There's a large pachinko parlor across the street where a fortune teller under an umbrella plies his trade.

It doesn't feel like our kind of town, too commercial, one of Japan's biggest spa vacation spots, but it is off season in Beppu and we decide to take it on. We unpack completely, set up our packs to dry in the bathtub, and trot back to the train station in search of a late dinner. Gliding from window to window, we compare the plastic food models and their prices. Before we decide, we are spotted by another Western couple, travelers from Australia who are in Beppu to do a book on the Japanese economic miracle, but with every other chapter on the sex trade. They latch on to us like saviors, complaining about the "Japanese mentality" which they see as aggressive, even sinister. Their local thesis is that Beppu is underpinned at every seam and snarl with houses of prostitution posing as hotels and hot springs. Even the public baths are suspect. Before we can all sit down for dinner, we latch onto yet another couple, a retired pair from England who are touring Japan because their son is teaching English in Osaka. The Australians come on as the Japanese experts; the rest of us sit back and keep them at arm's length, because as knowledgeable as they seem about things Japanese they are clearly lonely and desperate for Western company and find things in Kyushu a bit frightening.

We have a six-way dinner at one of the station restaurants and spend an hour exchanging traveler's tales. The Australians are prying their way through the seamier layers of Japan, turning up evidence of a pitiless nation that's all business and conquest, a nasty Japan that's out to exploit the world, beginning with the Gold Coast of Australia. The Britishers are touring a more seemly Japan of exquisite customs, sights, and mysteries; they are on the opposite side of the wheel. We'd like to talk to them at length, especially about their son's experience living in Japan, but the Australians spotted us first and our chief concern is to disentangle ourselves from their clutches, especially when we learn that they are ensconced in the best inn in Beppu, a first-rate find, they say. It is the very place where we demanded our money back, of course, but as their ears are open only to its praises, we have no trouble pawning off our copy of the guidebook. We're through with it, we say, but it has your name on it.

Walking back alone, we pause at a bakery to buy pastries for breakfast at the Green Hotel. The rain has let up. We feel remarkably like ourselves again, unencumbered. It's strange to have dinner with so many foreigners. Tomorrow is entirely free, that's the main thing. I would like every day to be that way: wide open, unimagined.

❋   ❋   ❋

Beneath the island of Kyushu there must lie an ocean of lava, judging from the sheer volume of volcanoes and hot springs that crack its surface. Beppu is particularly fissured, the supreme hot springs resort of western Japan, punctured by three thousand boiling caldrons of every conceivable color and ejecta from mud to mineral water. Of these "hells," eight form the standard tourist route, for which a single ticket provides admission. Dutiful tourists, we buy our tickets and make the rounds. We begin high in the hills above the city where thatched huts hatch out effervescent nodules of sulphur on their bare green clay floors, Beppu's famous hot spring crystals that you can add to your bath at home. From here we have a view of urban sprawl in the shape of a fan folded out to the sea and inundated with large plumes of hot steam. Margaret remarks that it's all down hill from here, and as usual I do not take her meaning literally.

These are hot springs not for bathing, but for viewing, a sort of Yellowstone Park paved over by a port city that attracts a million sight-seers a year. The old inns, public baths, and cobbled streets that ca-tered to the onsen crowd a century ago are crammed in between the new high-rise hotels and apartments, but we see plenty of white-haired bathers out for a stroll in *yukata* robes clutching plastic bags of snacks and Marlboro cigarettes, clomping along on tall wooden getas to their next carbonic immersion, their next sauna on a bamboo drain board, or, as it turns out, their next hot sand bath of just the sort Margaret tried in Ibusuki where we were assured they were the only true such baths in the world.

There's a hell for every taste here, and each has its own hokey theme. The paths within each walled hell force you through the sou-venir stands. At the first stop, Sea Hell (*Umi Jigoku*), we pause for lunch. The proprietor turns out to be a commercial photographer; he intercepts the school groups at the entrance and clicks their portraits. At the center of the garden is a big green pond of bubbling water laced with iron sulphate where eggs are boiled in a basket suspended from a bamboo pole. The pool is four hundred feet deep, heated to two hundred degrees F, the product of a thousand-year-old eruption on the Beppu hillside.

We march on, our ticket punched at each gate. In Mountain Hell (*Yama Jigoku*), a cascade of foul-smelling mud pools warms a dismal zoo (described in the brochure as "a sanitarium for animals utilizing the hot spring's heat"). A sad zoo indeed—a series of wire cages in which we count one lonely elephant, two elderly lions, two unenthusiastic chimps, and two hippos in a steam bath. The hot springs can't get much tackier. At Oven Hell (*Kamado Jigoku*), the steam simmers in the rocks, incubating chickens. At White Pool Hell (*Shiraike Jigoku*) an underlayer of white mud gives the waters a milky sheen. At Golden Dragon Hell (*Kinryu Jigoku*) there's another green pool presided over by the statue of a painted dragon, garish as an amusement arcade, a carnival link between heaven and earth.

There's more. At Devil's Mountain Hell (*Oniyama Jigoku*), a hundred crocodiles lounge listlessly in the ooze; in Monk's Hell (*Bozu Jigoku*), mud pots bubble; and at Blood Pool Hell (*Chinoike Jigoku*), iron oxide turns the lake red, its waters converted to a dye or bottled as a cure for skin diseases. Last on our route, the showstopper, is Tornado Hell (*Tatsumaki Jigoku*), where we wait in a tropical amphitheater for a geyser. This tiny Old Faithful erupts every twenty-five minutes, a sixty-foot pop of heated rain.

The Eight Hells of Beppu pivot on a point occupied by the Ashiya Restaurant, which is attached to a Sex Museum. A large metal signboard at the entrance is decorated with sculptures in relief, a brass Kama Sutra of men and topless Rubenesque women embracing. The label is stamped in English: "The Sculpture of India." Inside are automatons that cavort at the touch of a button and plenty of carved phalluses, so many that a friend of mine calls this establishment the Penis Museum. At 1500 yen a head, neither of us are up for a tour. It would be cheaper to spend an hour at one of the love hotels with facades of castles and dungeons that line the freeway: the Hotel P-Cosmo, perhaps, or the Hotel With, or even the Hotel Milk. At any rate, this tawdry tour of Beppu's natural eruptions has put neither of us in a romantic mood.

We ride the city bus back to the train station. While I avail myself of the public rest room, Margaret waits outside and is accosted by a little old man with an orange toothpick on a string. He's wearing a baseball cap and a kimono.

"Where you from?" he demands.

Margaret tells him. "You speak English," she says.

"My son went to university in America."

"Where? What city."

"I . . . America."

"You what? Could you say that again?"

"I respect America," he says, but he says it with such terrible vengeance that Margaret is quite relieved to see me emerge from the men's room. The man with the orange toothpick on a string melts into the crowd.

We trek down main street to the Green Hotel. At every intersection we wait for the light to change, signaled from a corner speaker by a digital rendition of "Coming Through the Rye" that sounds like a piercing birdcall. We've run across these lyrical signals elsewhere in Japan, all playing Western ditties for the benefit of the blind or color-blind, but Beppu has more than its share of these repetitive devices, cranking on and off every thirty seconds. If I hear "Coming Through the Rye" one more time, I think I'll climb the offending light pole and throttle the speaker with my bare hands.

*   *   *

I switch on the Japanese equivalent of "Good Morning America" as the studio cameras pan the nude form of a young model, scanning the image from top to bottom, missing no topographical feature. Boys will certainly be boys in Japan, even on network TV, where upon the flimsiest excuse pornography (fixated on cute underage schoolgirls, for the most part) titillates the national airwaves.

This morning is rather an extreme example. The homey "Today Show"-style panel, including one apple-pie mom, are passing around copies of a book and a newspaper ad that has just made front page news in Japan. The cameras enable us to read over their shoulders, to examine for ourselves the contours of this wholesome Japanese Madonna.

The two male hosts swap book and ad, supplying TV viewers with nonstop commentary. Eventually they turn on their female co-host for her opinion. She joins in with that ever-present but not over-done smile, the high-pitched voice, and for once I truly miss having a translator at my side. I can only speculate as to her response—certainly not the response the nude ad and book of portraits would prompt if shown on Paula Zahn's watch or under Joan Lunden's kindly gaze.

The excuse to wake up the nation with a display of full-frontal nudity came about when a feminist organization in Tokyo complained about a full-page advertisement featuring pop idol Rie Miyazawa in the buff. The ad ran on the pages of a respectable national newspaper,

Yomiuri Shimbun, and the following day in a second big paper, *Asahi Shimbun*. Kodosuru Onnatachi No Kai (that is, the Active Women's Association) accused the papers of violating "readers' confidence" and of encouraging "the commercialization of sex." The man in charge of the *Yomiuri Shimbun*'s Advertisement Examining Committee saw no problem. "I don't think readers felt repulsed by the ad," he declared. That seems to miss the point, but the feminists of Japan are hardly militant in their rhetoric. "We didn't say that a nude in itself is bad or that the advertisement is obscene," they emphasized. "It's just inappropriate for a major daily with a national circulation."

The advertisement, by the way, is for a book of nude photographs of the popular young singer shot against the spectacular naked scenery of a desert. The book's title is *Santa Fe*. And for ten minutes TV watchers all over Japan are conducted on a microscopic tour of the Southwestern United States, at least those tiny background portions of it framed between legs, spilling over nipples, or bunched on either side of the buttocks of Rie Miyazawa.

We pack up and descend to the lobby to check out. The girl at the counter takes our money into the back room and an older gentleman returns with her. He addresses us in English, thanking us for staying in his hotel. It is a sweet farewell. Satisfied that we understand his English, he retires in victory.

Across from the Takiwa Department Store, we purchase express bus tickets to Fukuoka. It's high time to complete the Kyushu circle; we're spent. All travels are circular, of course; the hidden arc of completion always takes one home. An extended journey in a foreign land is bearable only because we know we will return home, that there is something to which to return; otherwise, the traveler and the travels become forever one, aimless, without anchor, featureless and homeless as the sea.

A scaffolding has been erected over the main entrance to the Tokiwa Department Store and seated on it is a two-story inflated Santa Claus, crouching forward, arms dangling and swaying like the pinchers of a merry crab. In red plastic suit and cap, trimmed in white, sporting a big nose and stalactite beard, this Santa is jolly and bright, but intimidating. Shoppers must pass under his bouncing gloved fingers and through his bowed legs to enter the store; the little children are scared. One father lifts his daughter high to touch this monster of a distant, inflated holiday. Here is our last look at Beppu before we board the air-conditioned express: Santa squatting on a portal to commerce, the glass walls of the department store tower decked with twinkling lights, a red and white banner proclaiming as we pull out of sight ***MERRY CHRISTMAS***MERRY CHRISTMAS***MERRY CHRISTMAS***OPEN UNTIL 9 EVERY NIGHT***

POSTLUDE
Closing the Book

We complete our oval at Fukuoka, the city where we started. It has become a city so like any other in Japan that we have difficulty separating it from Nagoya, Toyama, even Tokyo. We dine in a noodle shop named "Gourmet City," one of a hundred little restaurants in the labyrinth of shopping aisles that branch through the main subway station. No windows open to the street; everything in the mall is kept inside, even the neon light. The waitresses are thrilled to see us; they are taking English language classes at a junior college.

The next morning we descend into the Tenjin underground shopping arcade. Its motif is vaguely Victorian, with London phone booths and mock gaslights at the intersections. The information girls are uniformed in nineteenth-century British finery. The goods are mostly Western, terribly expensive, and the crowds so thick we can browse on only one side of the aisle with each pass.

Above ground, it's a short hike to Nakasu Island, originally a sandbank in the middle of the Naka River, now a nightlife quarter of theaters, cabarets, discos, and some three thousand bars. We could be in any bar district in Japan. In daylight, the dives are uninviting fronts where the barkers—older women, mostly—pace and clear their throats; inside, we assume, are strippers and sex acts, the walls coated in plush velvet. Down one narrow block we ford across a throng of office workers milling outside what looks like a funeral parlor, decked with wheels of flowers. It turns out to be a pachinko parlor; the crowd is waiting to storm it for some lunch hour leisure. A man in a suit and tie is sweeping up cigarette butts in the midst of the puffing crowd. Along the river's edge, the street vendors set up their pushcarts, wooden trailers that unfold into stand-up or sit-down noodle and tempura stops.

Across the cement-banked Naka river rises the pink and white tower of the Hotel With; next door is the With Annex. "With what" we do not know.

Every few blocks, there's the gate to a temple, but this is a city sculpted by the blades of a vast machine able to mold and erect block after block of granite, glass, and poured concrete in a pattern at once uniform and ugly.

Recalling our first visit to Fukuoka—the start of the circle—we wonder what has become of the homeless man with bicycle sitting on a park bench by the playground. Is he still singing aloud from an open book?

✳ ✳ ✳

We link our two circles of Japan by air. The plane to Tokyo's Narita Airport is teeming with schoolchildren returning from field trips to Kyushu. The sun is setting on the China Sea; it will be dark when we land on the eastern shore.

I am convinced now that the next century belongs to America, not to Japan. Japan is too narrow and deep, deep in itself; it mimics but can not absorb the larger world. In America there is still sufficiently wide space for the future, for the ungainly and compound. That's where it will be worked out, where everything crosses, in America, for good or ill. America's vastness is a mirror of sorts, too, a desert mirror—blank, flat, unfocused, but able to receive the electricity of the world.

In reality, of course, America is neither so open nor so flexible as I would have it, and Japan is not so closed or self-absorbed. The shape of the next century seems today to depend foremost on both nations, but nothing is written in stone except the past.

Our plane descends on Tokyo. It could be Los Angeles, Shanghai, Cairo, London, Mexico City. From here, the earth looks unrounded, its mountains flattened, rivers paved, marshes drained. All I can see is strip after strip of lights, like a brain pan on fire. It's difficult to believe there's a human element in it. Perhaps Japan is the future, all moving into a single city.

✳ ✳ ✳

It's our final night in Japan. We'll connect to America in the morning. But by the time we locate the information center in Narita Airport, the only hotel within walking distance is booked. All we require is a simple place to sleep overnight, nothing fancy, nothing expensive, and there are plenty of budget ryokans in Narita town; so we descend into the airport basement and catch the ten-minute train.

When we arrive in town, however, the local visitor's desk has been shut down for thirty minutes. Dipping into the remnants of our last reliable guidebook, we try the recommended spot, Hotel Tsukuba, which is more than we want to pay for a place that looks from the lobby every bit as dubious as the inn we rejected in Beppu—but we've run out of options. Tsukuba wants about a hundred dollars for two. The woman behind the check-in counter isn't about to make small talk or discuss whether or not there's any sort of cheaper room for the night. We start to fill in the guest card. Margaret asks to see the room first. The clerk scowls, picks up the incomplete check-in card, and says, "No. All full."

We're outraged and reply, "That's ridiculous." The clerk remains impassive. "All full." Welcome to the big city, mean and expensive. We limp into the night.

The station is surrounded by neon-signed buildings. Large deluxe hotels are visible. We cross the street and peek into the gilded lobby of the Hotel Let's Narita. Spacious, glittering, and, as we know from the hotel listing we snatched at the airport, extremely expensive. "We may end up back at the airport," Margaret says, but we've heard that the airport closes down at midnight.

We can't sleep on the streets of Narita. There's nowhere to lie down, it's dark, and there's a criminal atmosphere, a hurly-burly we encountered nowhere in Kyushu. We're babes here, provincials. No place looks inviting for dinner. Besides, we may need every penny we have left just to spend the night under a roof. We don't know Narita town at all. Tokyo is two hours away, and to get there and back would cost us more than a night at the Hotel Let's.

We buy rolls and ice cream bars at a 7-Eleven. As we bolt our convenience dinner down, we meet up with another stranded couple beside a pay phone. He's a young Australian, a language teacher; she's one of his Japanese students. They're on the tail end of a lovers' holiday. We exchange matching tales of woe: they too can't find a room at the inn. We team up and call every hotel on our list, but all attempts are futile. Narita's full up. We're famished, worn out, and nothing looks the least promising. It's coming down to a question of how long we hold out before paying top dollar. Even then there's no guarantee. All these exorbitant hotels could well be full this very minute.

A Japanese man comes to our aid. He's an air-traffic controller at Narita just off work. He makes a few calls on our behalf, but even a distant ryokan is full. Hotels fill up nearly every night, he reports. It's late, and we try to persuade him to go home; don't worry, we'll find something. He nods, but he sticks with us. I realize we have become his responsibility. He won't leave us stranded in the streets of his town. His name is Shindo Tatsumi. He's never been to America, but he's talked to hundreds of American pilots and, I suspect, to scores of passengers like us in Narita.

Shindo finally finds us a place to stay: it's his own house. He'd be only too glad to put up the four of us. But when we learn he has five children and when we think of what his house in Narita must be like, certainly not the seven-bedroom model, we know we can't accept. It's a standoff; he must conduct us to safety; we can't impose on his hospitality.

In fact, it is our duty to get Shindo home to his wife and kids; to his dinner. We describe the Hotel Let's lobby to the romantic Australian and Japanese couple; they agree it's worth springing for; they haven't had a decent hotel since they left Osaka together. She calls the Hotel Let's; they still have some rooms for two at 17,490 yen, their cheapest. Shindo isn't convinced. He walks us to the hotel to make sure. Only when we sign the guest register does he leave us.

Let's what? Our room, in an the annex down an endless hall of scratched doors, is a modern Western hotel room that wouldn't be acceptable in an American motel at a third the price. The green rug is stained. There's but one *yukata* in the closet; no slippers. The bedspread is not just torn; it's riddled with holes the size of quarters.

We burrow in at midnight; we rise at dawn and check out. The hotel desk wants to charge us at a rate a thousand yen higher, saying there must have been some mistake. Yes, we say, your mistake. We haven't been treated this rottenly in all of Japan; it takes us back to a few brutal nights battling with hotels in Shanghai. The duty manager is telling us we must pay the higher rate and we are pissed a very blue blue.

We hold our ground; we will pay what we agreed to pay last night, not a *go-en* more, not a farthing. The manager cannot lose face. He cannot budge. He disappears into his office. A young woman clerk appears next; we pay our original bill without a word. So it's settled; everyone still has face.

We have hours to kill before our plane, and nothing to do but expose our flesh to more of nasty Narita. Were it not for the kindness of an air-traffic controller on his way home, we would have spent our last night in Japan in extreme bitterness.

* * *

As it turns out, Narita is charming in the daylight. The avenue that runs past the nasty ryokan of the night before now winds through tourist shops and restaurants to a superb temple, Narita-san Shinsho-ji. We have not one thing better to do than shop and eat.

A hawking grandmother yanks us into Kiku-ya, the Chrysanthemum Cafe, where we have a superb lunch of curry and yakitori. No torn or burnt tablecloths here, but a dark wooden interior from an earlier century. We shop the street that runs to the temple in high Japanese style, filling our plastic bags with bargain souvenirs—inexpensive glass plates, ceramic tea cups, wooden beckoning cats, calendars, rice bowls, and green tea gum.

Everything is rounded and full. The sun relaxes; the sky is blue around it. Our two circles of Japan collapse into one. Every city is laid upon every other, and every street ends in a temple.

The Narita temple is in perfect repair, no expense spared, splendid in its imitation of imitations. This one dates from 940 AD, when the Priest Kanjo built a Buddhist temple dedicated to Fudo Myo-o, the god of fire. The original sect was Shingnon, established by Kobo Daishi, and I remember the cold night and day we spent atop Koyasan, a lifetime ago, perhaps our finest day in Japan.

We discover a Buddhist service under way in the main temple. The temple is named Hondo and was built of concrete in the 1960s in such a way as to perfectly simulate the wooden construction of the ancients. We pause a few minutes as monks and worshippers chant and bow.

There's a stately pagoda, a high carved gate, and as we descend to leave the complex, a tall wooden prayer wheel in its own pavilion. An old woman in a kimono with a wide golden sash has led her family inside and is pushing the massive column clockwise. We go inside. The prayer wheel is an octagon mounted on a stone base with a massive red wooden porch, its floor beams extended at chest height so that worshippers can lean forward and turn its contents, the thousands of sutras piled inside. It's a Buddhist merry-go-round.

I toss a few coins in the box and take a turn. Every cycle is the equivalent of a hundred thousand chants. I'm on the opposite side of the wheel. I can't see the old woman but I know she is there, turning the same wheel as she walks ahead of me or behind.

There's no lateral progression here. I have no prayer of my own, no wish. My mind is empty. The wheel turns as I walk with surprising ease, given its tonnage; it makes no sound save a ghostly whisper, the laugh of hidden gears. Ahead of me, behind me, an old Japanese woman walks the circuit, her shoulder against the wheel, until there's no circle left and no center.

Words in brushed ink unscroll from the cylinder top, spinning outward like a cyclone without weight, without light, pinioning the earth to the sky.

❋ ❋ ❋

While perusing a stately book concerned with Shisendo, a mountain retreat in northern Kyoto built by poet Jozan Ishikawa in 1641, I chanced upon a few lines of commentary that sent me in search of a disappearing Japan.

Jozan, "the first true Chinese-style literatus in Japanese history," had withdrawn from worldly life into a prolonged retreat in nature, where he perfected the inseparable arts of classical Chinese poetry and calligraphy. Remarking on Jozan's imitation of an ancient Chinese calligraphic style in which Jozan composed a poem, Stephen Addiss writes: "Jozan's simulation of an effect rather than recreation of a process reflects his position in one culture trying to follow the ideals of another."

This is exactly how it is with Japan. First, it simulated the high culture of China; now, it imitates the genius of America.

Japan did not recreate a Golden China or a technological America from within; it has not recapitulated the processes that led to the flowering of these cultures. All that is true. But as Mr. Addiss goes on to write: "When someone copies a result instead of recreating the impetus that led to the result, something new emerges which must be judged on its own terms."

So it is that Japan alters what it copies, reflecting less the source of the original than the hand of the copyist. In Japan, that hand is driven to perfect the exterior world, to bring the underlying order and beauty to the surface. Japan is America and it is ancient China, but it is an America and a China the way Japan would have made them.

❋ ❋ ❋

Jozan's retreat still exists in Kyoto. It is known as Shisendo, the "Hall of the Poetry Immortals." I did not visit Jozan's "hall," but J.

Thomas Rimer has, many times. His conclusions about Shisendo parallel those I would draw about Japan:

> I have tried to learn something about the Shisendo and the man who built it. I have read what there is to know, but it is not enough. There is still a gap, a kind of pause in our modern understanding. Indeed, it has occurred to me that with our own cultural preferences for certain kinds of knowledge we may seek to know the wrong things about Jozan; or if not wrong, at least irrelevant things.

In Japan, I sense that gap. No doubt I have sought to know many of the wrong things about Japan. Perhaps it all comes down to the poem Jozan wrote as the inscription for his tomb:

> The old man is eighty—his years are running out.
> He gets his coffin ready, a hollow clay jar.
> Alone I stand in the midst of this limitless universe;
> my body will decompose inside a little hill.

Japan adopted certain foreign models because their vocabularies suited it so well; but thereby Japan also sought to escape its hollow clay jar, the heart of its self.

❋　　❋　　❋

The *sozu* is a bamboo tube on a pivot. Filled with water from one end, the *sozu* tips to the other, the water spills out, splashing on a stone—a clear pitched sound.

Originally installed on mountain fields to frighten away deer and wild boars, the *sozu* may have first been domesticated—brought into the Japanese garden—by Jozan to intensify the silence of retreat, to remind him of remote hillsides.

I set out to write about Japan in a prose to startle deer, to channel water, to strike stones on a mountain, but failed; I failed as I failed to reach the peaks of Japan. The best I can hope for is expressed by Jozan:

> Of ten poems I write, eight or nine are clumsy—
> I go by feeling and don't seek perfect form.

The only way I can speak of Japan is to express what disappears. "Gardens that a traveler cannot see are private gardens," Suzuki

Hiroyuki writes. "And precisely because they are private, they have such a strong allure."

I came to Japan hoping to force my way into its private gardens; that is the way to destroy. Gardens are what they are only so long as they remain unseen. This is the art of seeing through the mirror, and I am just beginning to master it. As Suzuki writes:

> Private gardens lie hidden away in the recesses of homes on Kyoto's busiest, most bustling streets. The existence of these invisible gardens lends the city a stillness, an indescribable depth. Visitors from afar walk the city's streets aware of these countless unseen gardens, and their invisible presence lends the city a rare charm.

✳ ✳ ✳

In Jozan's "Recording My Feelings," there is a final convergence of China and Japan. I would have done well to study it first:

> Years ago I went into retirement
> and built this place beside the mountain.
> Among the trees there is no worldly noise;
> beneath the eaves, the tranquil flow of a stream.
> Once I sought the benefit of books;
> now I'm more at home playing with sand.
> And after all, what isn't a child's game?
> Confucius and Lao Tzu—each is a cupful of earth.

Exile, mortality, oblivion—those should be my spare themes, too, no matter how wildly out of fashion. Why else have I come to Japan? To write like a child again.

Sources

Our travels in Japan would have been more difficult without the kind assistance of Ms. Akemi Fujimoto of Japan National Tourist Organization, Morris Simoncelli of Japan Airlines, and Tom Chapman of *Winds* Magazine.

In Japan we were further assisted by those who befriended us along the way, among them Suzuki Yumi, I.L.G. Hesmondhalgh, Iwasawa Hideo, Tanino Toshikazu, Shimizu Kentaro, Suzuki Noriko, Itsuo and Elizabeth Kiritani, Watanabe Miwa, Yumi Corrigan, Huang Ei June, Hashiguchi Setsuko, Shimpuku Osamu, Takada Kozo, Matsuo Tomoko, Nishiyama Chisayo, Maekawa Tomoko, Watanabe Satsuki, Nakashima Ayako, Shindo Tatsumi, and Wai Po and Rebecca Loui.

For invaluable information about Japan, as well as quotations in the text, we drew upon *They Came to Japan* (Berkeley: University of California Press, 1965), edited by Michael Cooper, S.J.; Percival Lowell's *Noto: An Unexplored Corner of Japan* (Boston: Houghton, Mifflin, 1891); Isabella Bird's *Unbeaten Tracks in Japan* (1880; rpt. London: Virago Press, 1984); Kenichi Yoshida's *Japan Is A Circle* (New York: Kodansha, 1976); Donald Keene's translation of Kenko's *Essays in Idleness: The Tsurezuregusa of Kenko* (New York: Columbia University Press, 1967); Noboyuki Yuasa's translation of Matsuo Basho's *The Narrow Road to the Deep North and Other Travel Sketches* (London: Penguin, 1966); J. Thomas Rimer, Jonathan Chaves, Stephen Addiss, and Hiroyuki Suzuki's *Shisendo: Hall of the Poetry Immortals* (New York: Weatherhill, 1991); *Through Japanese Eyes* (New York: Praeger, 1974), edited by Richard H. Minear; Donald Keene's *Travelers of a Hundred Ages* (New York: Holt, 1989); James L. McClain's *Kanazawa: A Seventeenth-Century Japanese Castle Town* (New Haven: Yale University Press, 1982); Katherine Plummer's *The Shogun's Reluctant Ambassadors: Japanese Sea Drifters in the North Pacific* (Portland, Oregon: The Oregon Historical Society, 1991); Lonely Planet Publication's *Japan: A Travel Survival Kit*; Beth Reiber's Frommer's Dollarwise Guide to Japan & Hong Kong; June Kinoshita and Nicholas Palevsky's *Gateway to Japan* (Tokyo: Kodansha, 1990); Leila Philip's *The Road Through Miyama* (New York: Vintage, 1991); Juan Williams's "West Meets East," *The Washington Post Magazine* (5 January 1992), pp. 12-19, 24-28; David Mura's *Turning Japanese: Memoirs of a Sansei* (New York: Atlantic Monthly Press, 1991); and Norma Field's *In the Realm of a Dying Emperor* (New York: Pantheon, 1991).

The writing would have been of less merit without the assistance of a Fellowship in Creative Non-Fiction from the National Endowment for the Arts.